Fast and Scalable Cloud Data Management

Felix Gessert • Wolfram Wingerath • Norbert Ritter

Fast and Scalable Cloud Data Management

 Springer

Felix Gessert
Baqend GmbH
Hamburg, Germany

Wolfram Wingerath
Baqend GmbH
Hamburg, Germany

Norbert Ritter
Department of Informatics
University of Hamburg
Hamburg, Germany

ISBN 978-3-030-43508-0   ISBN 978-3-030-43506-6   (eBook)
https://doi.org/10.1007/978-3-030-43506-6

This Springer imprint is published by the registered company Springer Nature Switzerland AG.
The registered company address is: Gewerbestrasse 11, 6330 Cham, Switzerland

Preface

Our research for this book goes back a long way. It all started as early as 2010 with a bachelor's thesis on how to make use of the purely expiration-based caching mechanisms of the web in a database application with rigorous consistency requirements. Strong encouragement by fellow researchers and growing developer interest eventually made us realize that the task of providing low latency for users in globally distributed applications does not only pose an interesting research challenge but also an actual real-world problem that was still mostly unsolved.

This revelation eventually led to the creation of Baqend, a Backend-as-a-Service platform designed for developing fast web applications. We built Baqend on knowledge gathered in many bachelor's and master's and a number of PhD theses. Technically, Baqend is rooted in our research systems, Orestes for web caching with tunable consistency, its extension Quaestor for query result caching, and InvaliDB for scalable push-based real-time queries for end-users. We are telling you all this for a reason: Because given its origin, this book does not only condense our knowledge after years of research done in a practical context but it also encapsulates our view on the concepts and systems that are currently out there. While we try to provide a balanced overview of the current state of affairs in data management and web technology, we are clearly opinionated with regard to certain best practices and architectural patterns. We would like to consider this a positive trait of this book— and we hope you agree;-)

Hamburg, Germany
Hamburg, Germany
Hamburg, Germany
December 2019

Felix Gessert
Wolfram Wingerath
Norbert Ritter

Contents

About the Authors

Felix Gessert is the CEO and co-founder of the Backend-as-a-Service company Baqend.[1] During his PhD studies at the University of Hamburg, he developed the core technology behind Baqend's web performance service. He is passionate about making the web faster by turning research results into real-world applications. He frequently talks at conferences about exciting technology trends in data management and web performance. As a Junior Fellow of the German Informatics Society (GI), he is working on new ideas to facilitate the research transfer of academic computer science innovation into practice.

Wolfram "Wolle" Wingerath is the leading data engineer at Baqend[1] where he is responsible for data analytics and all things related to real-time query processing. During his PhD studies at the University of Hamburg, he conceived the scalable design behind Baqend's real-time query engine and thereby also developed a strong background in real-time databases and related technology such as scalable stream processing, NoSQL database systems, cloud computing, and Big Data analytics. Eager to connect with others and share his experiences, he regularly speaks at developer and research conferences.

Norbert Ritter is a full professor of computer science at the University of Hamburg, where he heads the Databases and Information Systems (DBIS) group. He received his PhD from the University of Kaiserslautern in 1997. His research interests include distributed and federated database systems, transaction processing, caching, cloud data management, information integration, and autonomous database systems. He has been teaching NoSQL topics in various courses for several years. Seeing the many open challenges for NoSQL systems, he, Wolle, and Felix have been organizing the annual Scalable Cloud Data Management Workshop[2] to promote research in this area.

---

[1] Baqend: https://www.baqend.com/.
[2] Scalable Cloud Data Management Workshop: https://scdm.cloud.

Chapter 1
Introduction

Today, web performance is governed by round-trip latencies between end devices and cloud services. Depending on their location, users therefore often experience latency as loading delays when browsing through websites and interacting with content from apps. Since latency is responsible for page load times, it strongly affects user satisfaction and central business metrics such as customer retention rates or the time spent on a site. Users expect websites to load quickly and respond immediately. However, client devices are always separated from cloud backends by a physical network. The latency for data to travel between devices and cloud servers therefore dominates the perceived performance of many applications today.

A wealth of studies [Eve16] shows that many business metrics as well as basic user behavior heavily depend on web performance. At the same time, websites and workloads continuously become more complex while the amount of processed and stored data increases. Additionally, more and more users access websites and services from unreliable mobile networks and different geographical locations. Performance therefore constitutes one of the central challenges of web technology.

Cloud computing has emerged as a means to simplify operations and deployment as well as improve the performance of application backends. The rise of cloud computing enables applications to leverage storage and compute resources from a large shared pool of infrastructure. The volume and velocity at which data is generated and delivered have led to the creation of NoSQL databases that provide scalability, availability, and performance for data-driven workloads. Combining these two technology trends as **cloud data management**, scalable database systems are now frequently deployed and managed through cloud infrastructures. While cloud data management supports various scalability requirements that have been impossible with deployments on-premises [LS13, Zha+14], it introduces a performance problem: high latency between application users and cloud services is an inherent characteristic of the distributed nature of cloud computing and the web.

In this book, we present a comprehensive discussion of current latency reduction techniques in cloud data management. Throughout the book, we therefore explore

© Springer Nature Switzerland AG 2020
F. Gessert et al., *Fast and Scalable Cloud Data Management*,
https://doi.org/10.1007/978-3-030-43506-6_1

the different ways to improve application performance in the frontend (e.g. through optimizing the critical rendering path), at the network level (using protocol optimizations), and within the backend (via caching, replication, and other measures). In doing so, we aim to facilitate an understanding of the related trade-offs between performance, scalability, and data freshness.

1.1 Modern Data Management and the Web

Across the application stack, slow page load times have three sources, as illustrated in Fig. 1.1. When a web page is requested, the first source of loading time is the **backend**. It consists of application servers and database systems that assemble the page. The latency of individual OLTP queries and the processing time for rendering HTML further slow down the delivery of the site [TS07]. The **frontend**, i.e. the page displayed and executed in the browser, is another source of delay. Parsing of HTML, CSS, and JavaScript as well as the execution of JavaScript that can block other parts of the rendering pipeline all contribute to the overall waiting time. As of 2018, loading an average website requires more than 100 HTTP requests [Arc] that need to be transferred over the **network**. This requires numerous round-trip times that are bounded by physical network latency. This source of delay typically has the most significant impact on page load time in practice [Gri13].

Any performance problem in web applications can be allocated to these three drivers of latency. When a website is requested by a client, it is generated by the

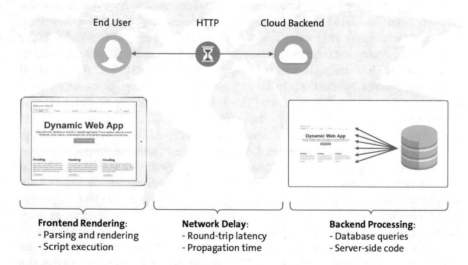

Fig. 1.1 The three primary sources of latency and performance problems of web applications: frontend rendering, network delay, and backend processing

backend, thus causing processing time. The website's HTML is transferred to the browser and all included resources (e.g., scripts, images, stylesheets, data, queries) are requested individually causing additional network latency. Rendering and script execution in the client also contribute to overall latency.

1.2   Latency vs. Throughput

Network bandwidth, client resources, computing power, and database technology have improved significantly in recent years [McK16]. Nonetheless, latency is still restricted by physical network round-trip times as shown in Fig. 1.2. When network bandwidth increases, page load time does not improve significantly above 5 MBit/s for typical websites. If latency can be reduced, however, there is a proportional decrease in overall page load time. These results illustrate that cloud-based applications can only be accelerated through latency reduction. Since latency is incurred at the frontend, network, and backend levels, it can only be minimized with an **end-to-end system design**.

The increasing adoption of cloud computing has led to a growing significance of latency for overall performance. Both users and different application components are now frequently separated by wide-area networks. **Database-as-a-Service** (DBaaS) and **Backend-as-a-Service** (BaaS) models allow storing data in the cloud to substantially simplify application development [Cur+11a]. However, their distributed nature makes network latency critical [Coo13]. When clients (e.g., browsers or mobile devices) and application servers request data from a remote DBaaS or BaaS, the application is blocked until results are received from the cloud data center. As web applications usually rely on numerous queries for every screen, latency can quickly become the central performance bottleneck.

Fueled by the availability of DBaaS and BaaS systems with powerful REST/HTTP APIs for developing websites and mobile apps, the **single-page application architecture** gained popularity. In this two-tier architecture, clients directly consume data from cloud services without intermediate web and application servers as in three-tier architectures. Single-page applications allow more flexible frontends and facilitate a more agile development process. In single-page applications, data is not aggregated and pre-rendered in the application server, but assembled in the client through many individual requests. Consequently, the number of latency-critical data requests tends to be even higher in two-tier applications than in typical three-tier stacks [Wag17].

1.3   Challenges in Modern Data Management

The latency problem has been tackled mainly by **replication** [DeC+07, Cha+08, Hba, Qia+13, Coo+08, Sov+11, Llo+13, Llo+11] and **caching** techniques [Lab+09,

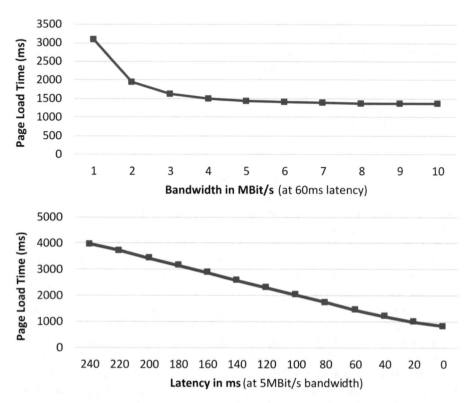

Fig. 1.2 The dependency of page load time on bandwidth (data rate) and latency. For typical websites, increased bandwidth has a diminishing return above 5 MBit/s, whereas any decrease in latency leads to a proportional decrease in page load time. The data points were collected by Belshe [Bel10] who used the 25 most accessed websites

PB03, Dar+96, Alt+03, LGZ04, Luo+02, Bor+03] to distribute the database system and its data. However, the majority of work on replication and caching is limited by a lack of generality: Most solutions are tied to specific types of data or applications (e.g., static web content), trade read latency against higher write latency, or do not bound data staleness. Furthermore, latency and performance improvements for database systems do not solve the **end-to-end performance problem**. The core problem is that state-of-the-art database systems are not designed to be directly accessed by browsers and mobile devices as they lack the necessary abstractions for access control and business logic. Therefore, servers still need to aggregate data for clients and thus increase latency [Feh+14]. The goal of this book is to provide an overview over the spectrum of techniques for low latency in all architectural layers, ranging from the frontend over the network to the backend.

Improving the performance of mostly static data has a long history [GHa+96]. However, latency and consistency are particularly challenging for **dynamic data** that in contrast to static data can change unpredictably at any point in time

[WGW+20]. A typical website consists of some mostly static files such as scripts, stylesheets, images, and fonts. Web APIs, JSON data, and HTML files, on the other hand, are dynamic and therefore commonly considered uncacheable [Lab+09]. Dynamic data can have various forms depending on the type of the application and the underlying storage [Kle17]. Hence, the latency problem is equally relevant for both standard file- and record-based access via a primary key or an identifier (e.g., a URL) as well as query results that offer a dynamic view of the data based on query predicates. As an example, consider an e-commerce website. For the website to load fast, files that make up the application frontend have to be delivered with low latency, e.g., the HTML page for displaying the shop's landing page. Next, data from the database systems also needs to be delivered fast, e.g., the state of the shopping cart or product detail information. And lastly, the performance of queries like retrieving recommended products, filtering the product catalog or displaying search results also heavily depends on latency.

Latency is not only problematic for end users, but it also has a detrimental effect on **transaction processing** [Bak+11, Shu+13, DAEA10, PD10, Kra+13, DFR15a, Kal+08, Zha+15b, Dra+15]. Many applications require the strong guarantees of transactions to preserve application invariants and correct semantics. However, both lock-based and optimistic concurrency control protocols have an abort probability that depends on the overall transaction duration [BN09, Tho98]. If individual operations are subject to high latency, the overall transaction duration is prolonged and consequently, the probability of a deadlock or conflict exhibits a superlinear increase [WV02]. In environments with high latency, the performance of transaction processing is thus determined by latency. This is for example the case if an end user is involved in the transaction (e.g., during the checkout in reservation system) or if the server runs the transaction against a remote DBaaS. To increase the effectiveness of transactions, low latency is therefore required, too.

Besides the problem of high network latencies, the applicability of database systems in cloud environments is considerably restricted by the lack of **elastic horizontal scalability** mechanisms and missing abstraction of storage and data models [DAEA13, Stö+15]. In today's cloud data management, most DBaaS systems offer their functionalities through REST APIs. Yet today, there has been no systematic effort on deriving a unified REST interface that takes into account the different data models, schemas, consistency concepts, transactions, access-control mechanisms, and query languages to expose cloud data stores through a common interface without restricting their functionality or scalability.

The complete ecosystem of data management is currently undergoing heavy changes. The unprecedented scale at which data is consumed and generated today has shown a large demand for scalable data management and given rise to non-relational, distributed **NoSQL database systems** [DeC+07, Cha+08, Hba, LM10, CD13, SF12, ZS17]. Two central problems triggered this process:

- vast amounts of user-generated content in modern applications and the resulting request loads and data volumes

- the desire of the developer community to employ problem-specific data models for storage and querying

To address these needs, various data stores have been developed by both industry and research, arguing that the era of one-size-fits-all database systems is over [Sto+07]. Therefore, these systems are frequently combined to leverage each system in its respective sweet spot. **Polyglot persistence** is the concept of using different database systems within a single application domain, addressing different functional and non-functional needs with each system [SF12]. Complex applications need polyglot persistence to deal with a wide range of data management requirements. The overhead of and the necessary know-how for managing multiple database systems prevent many applications from employing efficient polyglot persistence architectures. Instead, developers are often forced to implement one-size-fits-all solutions that do not scale well and cannot be operated efficiently. Even with state-of-the-art DBaaS systems, applications still have to choose one specific database technology [HIM02, Cur+11a].

The rise of polyglot persistence [SF12] introduces two specific problems. First, it imposes the constraint that any performance and latency optimization must not be limited to only a single database system. Second, the heterogeneity and sheer amount of these systems make it increasingly difficult to select the most appropriate system for a given application. Current research and industry initiatives focus on solving specific problems by introducing new database systems or new approaches within the scope of specific, existing data stores. However, the problem of selecting the most suitable systems and orchestrating their interaction is yet unsolved as is the problem of offering low latency for a polyglot application architecture.

In this book, we address each of the aforementioned challenges by providing a detailed view on the current technology for achieving and maintaining high performance in cloud-based application stacks. We aim to clarify today's challenges, discuss available solutions, and indicate problems that are yet unsolved. Reading this book will help you choose the right technology for building fast applications—throughout the entire software stack.

1.4   Outline of the Book

In Chap. 2, we start with a 10,000 feet view of web-based application stacks today and make the case that low latency for end-users can only be achieved when optimizing the backend, the frontend, and the network in between. To paint the big picture of where latency arises in globally distributed applications, we contrast client-rendered two-tier with server-rendered three-tier application stacks and provide a quick overview over current cloud service and deployment models.

Next in Chap. 3, we address the relevance of the HTTP infrastructure and REST communication paradigm as the prevalent mechanisms for global data access in many Web and mobile applications. After a technical primer on the lower-level protocols involved in information exchange over HTTP, we summarize caching mechanisms defined in the HTTP specification for achieving low latency and scalability. We subsequently turn to performance considerations for application developers. To this end, we first describe the rendering process in modern web applications and then establish the context between the critical rendering path, client caching and storage, and application performance.

Chapter 4 then focuses on technology for scalable data management as the primary challenge for achieving low latency. We first explore the design space of (NoSQL) data management systems along different axes, especially data models (key-value, document, wide-column) and different notions of consistency (CAP/-PACELC, weak/eventual/strong consistency). In greater detail, we consider the relationship between latency, consistency, and availability in order to expound the conception that they cannot be considered separately during system design: Optimizing system performance with respect to one of these properties often leads to degraded performance with respect to the others.

In Chap. 5, we drill further down into caching technology as a means to compensate physical distance between servers and clients, categorizing the topic along three different dimensions. First, we distinguish the different locations at which caching takes place, namely the client, the server, or intermediate parties such as reverse proxies. Second, we distinguish the granularity of the cached entities such as files, records, or pages. Third, we distinguish expiration- and invalidation-based caching as competing strategies for keeping caches up-to-date. To underpin the importance of caching for performance in modern data management, we put an emphasis on approaches for caching database query results in this chapter and also shed light on the relationship between (geo-)replication and caching.

We start Chap. 6 with a brief recap of the ACID principle as the gold standard for transactional guarantees and of the different concurrency control schemes, such as pessimistic lock-based, multi-version, and forward-oriented and backward-oriented optimistic approaches. After a brief illustration of the impact of transactions on latency, we discuss the wealth of systems in research and practice that offer relaxed guarantees in favor of accelerated data access. We then consider different approaches for transactions in distributed architectures such as entity group or multi-shard transactions. Finally, we contrast client- and middleware-coordinated transactions and discuss the benefits and limitations of purely deterministic transactions.

In Chap. 7, we consider the different challenges related to polyglot persistence architectures. We discuss cloud-hosted data management services (DBaaS/BaaS) as an alternative to on-premise solutions and the different challenges of operating systems in federated deployments, such as multi-tenancy and virtualization, privacy and encryption, as well as resource management and scalability. We briefly dive into the area of database performance benchmarking with respect to both traditional measures such as latency or throughput, but also consistency properties which and ways to quantify them. The chapter closes with a brief consideration of REST APIs, multi-model databases, and Backend-as-a-Service offerings available today.

The gist of the book is condensed into Chap. 8 where we present the NoSQL Toolbox as a concept for mapping functional and non-functional application requirements to the concrete technologies used for implementing them. The toolbox acknowledges four major building blocks for data management systems which are dissected one by one: sharding, replication, storage management, and query processing. The chapter closes with succinct case studies to exemplify how the capabilities of real data management systems translate to a toolbox classification.

Finally in Chap. 9, we present the NoSQL Decision Tree as the prime take away of this book: It provides a simple way to steer application architects towards a set of potentially useful data management systems, provided only few input parameters on the application requirements. The remainder of the book covers aspects of data management that are not covered extensively here, specifically stream management and push-based real-time database systems, business analytics, and machine learning.

References

[Alt+03] Mehmet Altinel et al. "Cache Tables: Paving the Way for an Adaptive Database Cache". In: *VLDB*. 2003, pp. 718–729. URL: http://www.vldb.org/conf/2003/papers/S22P01.pdf.

[Arc] *HTTP Archive*. http://httparchive.org/trends.php. Accessed: 2018-07-14. 2018.

[Bak+11] J. Baker et al. "Megastore: Providing scalable, highly available storage for interactive services". In: *Proc. of CIDR*. Vol. 11. 2011, pp. 223–234.

[Bel10] Mike Belshe. *More Bandwidth Doesnât Matter (much)*. Tech. rep. Google Inc., 2010.

[BN09] Philip A. Bernstein and Eric Newcomer. *Principles of Transaction Processing*. Morgan Kaufmann, 2009. ISBN: 1-55860-415-4.

[Bor+03] Christof Bornhövd et al. "DBCache: Middle-tier Database Caching for Highly Scalable e-Business Architectures". In: *Proceedings of the 2003 ACM SIGMOD International Conference on Management of Data, San Diego, California, USA, June 9–12, 2003*. Ed. by Alon Y. Halevy, Zachary G. Ives, and AnHai Doan. ACM, 2003, p. 662. DOI: 10.1145/872757.872849.

[CD13] Kristina Chodorow and Michael Dirolf. *MongoDB - The Definitive Guide*. O'Reilly, 2013. ISBN: 978-1-449-38156-1. URL: http://www.oreilly.de/catalog/9781449381561/index.html.

[Cha+08] Fay Chang et al. "Bigtable: A distributed storage system for structured data". In: *ACM Transactions on Computer Systems (TOCS)* 26.2 (2008), p. 4.

[Coo+08] B. F. Cooper et al. "PNUTS: Yahoo!'s hosted data serving platform". In: *PVLDB* 1.2 (2008), pp. 1277–1288. URL: http://dl.acm.org/citation.cfm?id=1454167 (visited on 09/12/2012).

[Coo13] Brian F. Cooper. "Spanner: Google's globally-distributed database". In: *6th Annual International Systems and Storage Conference, SYSTOR '13, Haifa, Israel - June 30 - July 02, 2013*. Ed. by Ronen I. Kat, Mary Baker, and Sivan Toledo. ACM, 2013, p. 9. DOI: 10.1145/2485732.2485756.

[Cur+11a] Carlo Curino et al. "Relational Cloud: A Database-as-a-Service for the Cloud". In: *Proc. of CIDR*. 2011. URL: http://dspace.mit.edu/handle/1721.1/62241 (visited on 04/15/2014).

[DAEA10] Sudipto Das, Divyakant Agrawal, and Amr El Abbadi. "G-store: a scalable data store for transactional multi key access in the cloud". In: *Proceedings of the 1st ACM symposium on Cloud computing*. ACM. 2010, pp. 163–174.

[DAEA13] Sudipto Das, Divyakant Agrawal, and Amr El Abbadi. "ElasTraS: An elastic, scalable, and self-managing transactional database for the cloud". en. In: *ACM Transactions on Database Systems* 38.1 (Apr. 2013), pp. 1–45. ISSN: 03625915. DOI: 10.1145/2445583.2445588. URL: http://dl.acm.org/citation.cfm?doid=2445583. 2445588 (visited on 11/25/2016).

[Dar+96] Shaul Dar et al. "Semantic Data Caching and Replacement". In: *VLDB'96, Proceedings of 22th International Conference on Very Large Data Bases, September 3–6, 1996, Mumbai (Bombay), India*. Ed. by T. M. Vijayaraman et al. Morgan Kaufmann, 1996, pp. 330–341. URL: http://www.vldb.org/conf/1996/P330.PDF.

[DeC+07] G. DeCandia et al. "Dynamo: amazon's highly available key-value store". In: *ACM SOSP*. Vol. 14. 17. ACM. 2007, pp. 205–220. URL: http://dl.acm.org/citation.cfm?id= 1294281 (visited on 09/12/2012).

[DFR15a] A. Dey, A. Fekete, and U. Röhm. "Scalable distributed transactions across heterogeneous stores". In: *2015 IEEE 31st International Conference on Data Engineering*. 2015, pp. 125–136. DOI: 10.1109/ICDE.2015.7113278.

[Dra+15] Aleksandar DragojeviÄ et al. "No compromises: distributed transactions with consistency, availability, and performance". en. In: *Proceedings of the 25th Symposium on Operating Systems Principles*. ACM. ACM Press, 2015, pp. 54–70. ISBN: 978-1-4503-3834-9. DOI: 10.1145/2815400.2815425. URL: http://dl.acm.org/citation.cfm? doid=2815400.2815425 (visited on 11/25/2016).

[Eve16] Tammy Everts. *Time Is Money: The Business Value of Web Performance*. O'Reilly Media, 2016. URL: https://www.amazon.com/Time-Money-Business-Value-Performance-ebook/dp/B01GGQKXPS%3FSubscriptionId %3D0JYN1NVW651KCA56C102%26tag%3Dtechkie-20%26linkCode%3Dxm2 %26camp%3D2025%26creative%3D165953%26creativeASIN%3DB01GGQKXPS.

[Feh+14] Christoph Fehling et al. *Cloud Computing Patterns - Fundamentals to Design, Build, and Manage Cloud Applications*. Springer, 2014. ISBN: 978-3-7091-1567-1. DOI: 10.1007/978-3-7091-1568-8.

[GHa+96] Jim Gray, Pat Hell and, et al. "The dangers of replication and a solution". In: *SIGMOD Rec*. 25.2 (June 1996), pp. 173–182.

[Gri13] Ilya Grigorik. *High performance browser networking*. English. [S.l.]: O'Reilly Media, 2013. ISBN: 1-4493-4476-3 978-1-4493-4476-4. URL: https://books.google.de/books? id=tf-AAAAQBAJ.

[Hba] *HBase*. http://hbase.apache.org/. (Accessed on 05/25/2017). 2017. URL: http://hbase. apache.org/ (visited on 07/16/2014).

[HIM02] H. Hacigumus, B. Iyer, and S. Mehrotra. "Providing database as a service". In: *Data Engineering, 2002. Proceedings. 18th International Conference on*. 2002, pp. 29–38. URL: http://ieeexplore.ieee.org/xpls/abs_all.jsp?arnumber=994695 (visited on 10/16/2012).

[Kal+08] R. Kallman et al. "H-store: a high-performance, distributed main memory transaction processing system". In: *Proceedings of the VLDB Endowment* 1.2 (2008), pp. 1496–1499.

[Kle17] Martin Kleppmann. *Designing Data-Intensive Applications*. English. 1 edition. O'Reilly Media, Jan. 2017. ISBN: 978-1-4493-7332-0.

[Kra+13] Tim Kraska et al. "MDCC: Multi-data center consistency". In: *EuroSys*. ACM, 2013, pp. 113–126. URL: http://dl.acm.org/citation.cfm?id=2465363 (visited on 04/15/2014).

[Lab+09] Alexandros Labrinidis et al. "Caching and Materialization for Web Databases". In: *Foundations and Trends in Databases* 2.3 (2009), pp. 169–266. DOI: 10.1561/1900000005.

[LGZ04] Per-Åke Larson, Jonathan Goldstein, and Jingren Zhou. "MTCache: Transparent Mid-Tier Database Caching in SQL Server". In: *Proceedings of the 20th International Conference on Data Engineering, ICDE 2004, 30 March - 2 April 2004, Boston, MA, USA*. Ed. by Z. Meral Özsoyoglu and Stanley B. Zdonik. IEEE Computer Society, 2004, pp. 177–188. DOI: 10.1109/ICDE.2004.1319994.

[Llo+11] Wyatt Lloyd et al. "Don't settle for eventual: scalable causal consistency for wide-area storage with COPS". In: *Proceedings of the Twenty-Third ACM Symposium on Operating Systems Principles*. ACM, 2011, pp. 401–416. URL: http://dl.acm.org/citation.cfm?id=2043593 (visited on 01/03/2015).

[Llo+13] Wyatt Lloyd et al. "Stronger semantics for low-latency geo-replicated storage". In: *Presented as part of the 10th USENIX Symposium on Networked Systems Design and Implementation (NSDI 13)*. 2013, pp. 313–328.

[LM10] Avinash Lakshman and Prashant Malik. "Cassandra: a decentralized structured storage system". In: *ACM SIGOPS Operating Systems Review* 44.2 (2010), pp. 35–40. URL: http://dl.acm.org/citation.cfm?id=1773922 (visited on 04/15/2014).

[LS13] Wolfgang Lehner and Kai-Uwe Sattler. *Web-Scale Data Management for the Cloud*. Englisch. Auflage: 2013. New York: Springer, Apr. 2013. ISBN: 978-1-4614-6855-4.

[Luo+02] Qiong Luo et al. "Middle-tier database caching for e-business". In: *Proceedings of the 2002 ACM SIGMOD International Conference on Management of Data, Madison, Wisconsin, June 3–6, 2002*. Ed. by Michael J. Franklin, Bongki Moon, and Anastassia Ailamaki. ACM, 2002, pp. 600–611. DOI: 10.1145/564691.564763.

[McK16] Martin McKeay. *Akamaiâs State of the Internet Report Q4 2016*. Tech. rep. Akamai, 2016.

[PB03] Stefan Podlipnig and László Böszörményi. "A survey of Web cache replacement strategies". In: *ACM Comput. Surv.* 35.4 (2003), pp. 374–398. DOI: 10.1145/954339.954341.

[PD10] Daniel Peng and Frank Dabek. "Large-scale Incremental Processing Using Distributed Transactions and Notifications." In: *OSDI*. Vol. 10. 2010, pp. 1–15. URL: https://www.usenix.org/legacy/events/osdi10/tech/full_papers/Peng.pdf?origin=publication_detail (visited on 01/03/2015).

[Qia+13] Lin Qiao et al. "On brewing fresh espresso: LinkedIn's distributed data serving platform". In: *Proceedings of the 2013 international conference on Management of data*. ACM, 2013, pp. 1135–1146. URL: http://dl.acm.org/citation.cfm?id=2465298 (visited on 09/28/2014).

[SF12] Pramod J. Sadalage and Martin Fowler. *NoSQL distilled: a brief guide to the emerging world of polyglot persistence*. Pearson Education, 2012.

[Shu+13] Jeff Shute et al. "F1: A distributed SQL database that scales". In: *Proceedings of the VLDB Endowment* 6.11 (2013). 00004, pp. 1068–1079.

[Sov+11] Yair Sovran et al. "Transactional storage for geo-replicated systems". In: *Proceedings of the Twenty-Third ACM Symposium on Operating Systems Principles*. ACM, 2011, pp. 385–400.

[Sto+07] M. Stonebraker et al. "The end of an architectural era:(it's time for a complete rewrite)". In: *Proceedings of the 33rd international conference on Very large data bases*. 2007, pp. 1150–1160. URL: http://dl.acm.org/citation.cfm?id=1325981 (visited on 07/05/2012).

[Stö+15] Uta Störl et al. "Schemaless NoSQL Data Stores - Object-NoSQL Mappers to the Rescue?" In: *Datenbanksysteme für Business, Technologie und Web (BTW), 16. Fachtagung des GI-Fachbereichs "Datenbanken und Informationssysteme" (DBIS), 4.-6.3.2015 in Hamburg, Germany. Proceedings*. Ed. by Thomas Seidl et al. Vol. 241. LNI. GI, 2015, pp. 579–599. URL: http://subs.emis.de/LNI/Proceedings/Proceedings241/article13.html (visited on 03/10/2015).

[Tho98] A. Thomasian. "Concurrency control: methods, performance, and analysis". In: *ACM Computing Surveys (CSUR)* 30.1 (1998). 00119, pp. 70–119. URL: http://dl.acm.org/citation.cfm?id=274443 (visited on 10/18/2012).

[TS07] Andrew S. Tanenbaum and Maarten van Steen. *Distributed systems - principles and paradigms, 2nd Edition*. Pearson Education, 2007. ISBN: 978-0-13-239227-3.

[Wag17] Jeremy Wagner. *Web Performance in Action: Building Faster Web Pages*. Manning Publications, 2017. ISBN: 1617293776. URL: https://www.amazon.com/Web-Performance-Action-Building-Faster/dp/1617293776?SubscriptionId=

0JYN1NVW651KCA56C102&tag=techkie-20&linkCode=xm2&camp=2025& creative=165953&creativeASIN=1617293776.

[WGW+20] WolframWingerath, Felix Gessert, ErikWitt, et al. "Speed Kit: A Polyglot & GDPR-Compliant Approach For Caching Personalized Content". In: *36th IEEE International Conference on Data Engineering, ICDE 2020, Dallas, Texas, April 20–24, 2020*. 2020.

[WV02] G. Weikum and G. Vossen. *Transactional information systems*. Series in Data Management Systems. Morgan Kaufmann Pub, 2002. ISBN: 9781558605084. URL: http://books.google.de/books?hl=de&lr=&id=wV5Ran71zNoC&oi=fnd&pg=PP2& dq=transactional+information+systems&ots=PgJAaN7R5X&sig=Iya4r9DiFhmb_ wWgOI5QMuxm6zU (visited on 06/28/2012).

[Zha+14] Liang Zhao et al. *Cloud Data Management*. Englisch. Auflage: 2014. Springer, 2014.

[Zha+15b] Irene Zhang et al. "Building consistent transactions with inconsistent replication". In: *Proceedings of the 25th Symposium on Operating Systems Principles, SOSP 2015, Monterey, CA, USA, October 4–7, 2015*. Ed. by Ethan L. Miller and Steven Hand. ACM, 2015, pp. 263–278. DOI: 10.1145/2815400.2815404.

[ZS17] Albert Y. Zomaya and Sherif Sakr, eds. *Handbook of Big Data Technologies*. Springer, 2017. ISBN: 978-3-319-49339-8. DOI: 10.1007/978-3-319-49340-4.

Chapter 2
Latency in Cloud-Based Applications

The continuous shift towards cloud computing has established two primary architectures: two-tier and three-tier applications. Both architectures are susceptible to
latency at different levels. The concrete realization can build upon different cloud
models, in particular, Database/Backend-as-a-Service, Platform-as-a-Service, and
Infrastructure-as-a-Service [YBDS08].

Modern web applications need to fulfill several non-functional requirements:

- **High availability** guarantees that applications remain operational despite failure
  conditions such as network partitions, server failures, connectivity issues and
  human error.
- **Elastic scalability** enables applications to handle any growth and decrease in
  load (e.g., user requests and data volume), by automatically allocating or freeing
  storage and computing resources in a distributed cluster.
- **Fast page loads** and response times are essential to maximize user satisfaction,
  traffic, and revenue.
- An **engaging user experience** significantly helps to make users productive and
  efficient.
- A **fast time-to-market** is the result of the appropriate development, testing, and
  deployment abstractions to quickly release an application to production.[1]

In this chapter, we discuss the three- and two-tier architectures in the context of
the above requirements, before examining the technical foundations of the backend,
network, and frontend in the following chapters.

---

[1] Despite all recent advances in programming languages, tooling, cloud platforms, and frameworks,
studies indicate that over 30% of all web projects are delivered late or over-budget, while 21% fail
to meet their defined requirements [Kri15].

© Springer Nature Switzerland AG 2020
F. Gessert et al., *Fast and Scalable Cloud Data Management*,
https://doi.org/10.1007/978-3-030-43506-6_2

2.1   Three-Tier Architectures

The three-tier architecture is a well-known pattern for structuring client-server applications [TS07, Feh+14, HW03]. The idea is, to segregate application concerns into three different functional tiers (components). This has the advantage that tiers are loosely coupled, thus facilitating easier development. Furthermore, each tier can be scaled independently based on required resources. The canonical tiers are the **presentation tier**, the **business logic tier** and the **data tier**. In the literature, different definitions of three-tier architectures are used. Tanenbaum and van Steen [TS07] differentiate between web servers, application servers and database servers as three different tiers of a web application. Fehling et al. [Feh+14] argue that web and application servers are typically just one tier, whereas in a real three-tier application, the presentation tier is completely decoupled from the business logic tier, e.g., by message queues.

We will distinguish between the two-tier and three-tier architecture based on the location of the presentation tier. As shown in Fig. 2.1, the classic three-tier architecture includes the presentation layer as part of the backend application. This means that an application or web server executes the presentation and business logic while the data tier serves and stores data using one or more database systems. The client's browser is served the rendered representation, typically in the form of an HTML file and supporting stylesheets (CSS) and JavaScript files (JS). As the client does not execute any significant portion of the presentation and business logic, this architecture is also referred to as a *thin client* architecture. Any user interactions that require business logic (e.g., posting a comment on a social network) are forwarded to the server tiers, which are responsible for performing the desired task. This usually implies the server-rendering of a new HTML view representing a response to the invoked action. An advantage of separating the data tier and business logic tier is that business logic can be stateless and scales efficiently.

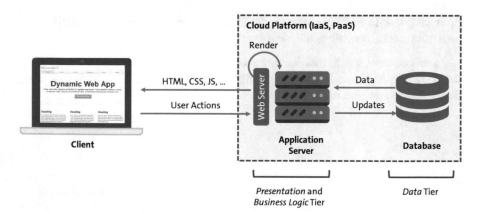

Fig. 2.1 The three-tier web application architecture

2.1.1 Request Flow

The high-level request flow in a server-rendered three-tier architecture is the following (cf. [Feh+14]):

1. The client requests the website over the HTTP protocol.
2. The web server accepts the request and calls the components for handling the corresponding URL. Usually, the web server is not requested directly, but a load balancer distributes requests over available web servers. The request can be directly executed in the web server (e.g., in PHP) or invoked over the network (e.g., through AJP) or using a queuing system (e.g., RabbitMQ) [Cha15].
3. In the application server, the business logic is executed.
4. Any data required to render the current view is queried from the database and updates are applied to reflect the application state.
5. The response is sent to the client as an HTML document. The web server directly answers subsequent requests for static resources like images and scripts.

2.1.2 Implementation

As a large part of the web uses three-tier architectures, a considerable amount of environments and frameworks for developing and hosting three-tier applications exist. In the context of cloud computing, three-tier architectures can be implemented on **Infrastructure-as-a-Service** (IaaS) and **Platform-as-a-Service** (PaaS) clouds [HDF13, MB16].

PaaS cloud providers such as Microsoft Azure [Azu], Google App Engine [App], and Heroku [Clob] offer managed operating systems, application servers, and middleware for running web applications in a scalable fashion. While the provider prescribes the runtime environment (e.g., supporting Python applications), the application logic can be freely defined. The PaaS abstracts from maintenance and provisioning of operating systems and servers to unburden the application from operational aspects such as scaling, system upgrades, and network configuration. It therefore provides a useful paradigm for the development of three-tier applications. For example, Microsoft Azure [Azu] has a built-in notion of the three tiers, as it distinguishes between web roles (the presentation tier), storage services (the data tier) and worker roles (the business logic tier). Web roles and worker roles are scaled independently and decoupled by storage abstractions such as queues, wide-column models, and file systems [Cal+11].

In the IaaS model, full control over virtual machines is left to the tenant. This implies that three-tier architectures can use the same technology stacks as applications in non-cloud environments (**on-premises**). For example, Amazon Web Services (AWS) [Amab] and Google Cloud Platform (GCP) [Gooa] provide the management infrastructure to provision individual virtual machines or containers that can run arbitrary software for each tier in the architectures. Typically, a web server (e.g., Apache, IIS, or Nginx [Ree08]), application server (e.g., Tomcat or Wildfly [Wil]) or reverse proxy (e.g., Varnish [Kam17]) is combined with a web application framework in a particular programming language running the business logic and parts of the presentation tier (e.g., Python with Django, Java with Spring MVC, or Ruby with Sinatra [The, Wal14]). The business logic tier in turn either employs a database system also hosted on the IaaS provider or connects to Database-as-a-Service offerings to persist and retrieve data.

The **microservice architecture** is a refinement of the three-tier architecture that decomposes the three tiers of the backend [New15, Nad+16]. The central idea of microservices is to decompose the application into functional units that are loosely coupled and interact with each other through REST APIs. Microservices thus offer a light-weight alternative to service-oriented architectures (SOA) and the WebService standards [Alo+04]. In contrast to three-tier applications, microservices do not share state through a data tier. Instead, each microservice is responsible for separately maintaining the data it requires to fulfill its specified functionality. One of the major reasons for the adoption of microservices is that they allow scaling the development of large distributed applications: each team can individually develop, deploy, and test microservices as long as the API contracts are kept intact. When combined with server-rendering, i.e., the generation of HTML views for each interaction in a web application, microservices still exhibit the same performance properties as three-tier architectures. Some aspects even increase in complexity, as each microservice is a point of failure and response times for answering a request through aggregation from multiple microservice responses are subject to latency stragglers.

2.1.3   Problems of Server-Rendered Architectures

The non-functional requirements introduced at the beginning of this chapter are particularly challenging to fulfill in three-tier and service architectures with a server-side presentation tier:

High Availability.   As all tiers depend upon the data tier for shared state, the underlying database systems have to be highly available. Any unavailability in the data tier will propagate to the other tiers, thus amplifying potential partial failures into application unavailability.

Elastic Scalability.   All tiers need to be independently and elastically scalable, which can induce severe architectural complexity. For instance, if requests passed from the presentation tier to the business logic tier exceed the capacities of the business logic tier, scaling rules have to be triggered without dropping requests. Alternatively, non-trivial backpressure (flow control) mechanisms [Kle17] have to be applied to throttle upstream throughput. In practice, tiers are often decoupled through message queues, which—similar to database systems—have inherent availability-consistency-performance trade-offs.

Fast Page Loads.   Server-rendering implies that the delivery of a response is blocked until the slowest service or query returns which hinders fast page loads. Even if each query and service produces a low average or median response time, the aggregate response times are governed by extreme value distributions that have a significantly higher expected value [WJW15, VM14]. While the request is blocked, the client cannot perform any work as the initial HTML document is the starting point for any further processing in the browser and for subsequent requests [WGW+20]. Of the potentially hundreds of requests [Arc], each is furthermore bounded by *network latency* that increases with the distance to the server-side application logic.

Engaging User Experience.   As each user interaction (e.g., navigation or submitting a form) produces a new HTML document, the indirection between the user's interactions and observed effects become noticeable. A well-studied result from psychology and usability engineering is that for the user to gain the impression of directly modifying objects in the user interface, response times have to be below 100 ms [Mil68, Nie94, Mye85]. Even if the delivery of static assets is fast, rendering an HTML document, applying updates to the database and performing relevant queries is usually infeasible if any significant network latency is involved. For users, this conveys the feeling of an unnatural, indirect interaction pattern [Nie94].

Fast Time-to-Market.   Besides the above performance problems, server-side rendering also induces problems for the software development process. All user interactions need to be executed on the server. In modern web applications, the user interface has to be engaging and responsive. Therefore, parts of the presentation logic are replicated between the server-side presentation tier and the JavaScript logic of the frontend. This duplicates functionality, increasing development complexity and hindering maintainability. Furthermore, by splitting the frontend from the server-side processing, unintended interdependencies arise: frontend developers or teams have to rely on the backend development to proceed, in order to work on the design and structure of the frontend. This hinders agile, iterative development methodologies such as Scrum [SB02] and Extreme Programming (XP) [Bec00] from being applied to frontend and backend teams separately. As applications shift towards more complex frontends, the coupling of frontend and backend development inevitably increases time-to-market.

2.2 Two-Tier Architectures

The two-tier architecture evolved [Feh+14] to tackle the problems of rigid three-tier architectures. By two-tier architectures, we will refer to applications that shift the majority of presentation logic into the client. Business logic can be shared or divided between client and server, whereas the data tier resides on the server, to reflect application state across users. The two-tier model is popular for native mobile applications, that are fundamentally based on the user interfaces components

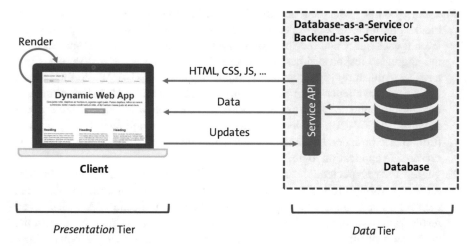

Fig. 2.2 The two-tier web application architecture

offered by the respective mobile operating system (iOS, Windows, Android) and packaged into an installable app bundle [Hil16]. Many web applications also follow this model and are referred to as **single-page applications (SPAs)**, due to their ability to perform user interactions without loading a new HTML page [MP14]. We will discuss the two-tier architecture in the context of web applications, but most aspects also apply to native mobile apps.

The two-tier architecture is illustrated in Fig. 2.2. Rendering in the client is performed through the browser's JavaScript runtime engine that consumes structured data directly from the server (e.g., product detail information), usually in the form of JSON[2] [Cro06]. The data tier is therefore responsible for directly serving database objects and queries to clients. The business logic tier is optional and split into unprotected parts directly executed in the client and parts that require confidentiality, security and stricter control and are therefore executed co-located with the data tier. Server-side business logic includes enforcing access control, validating inputs, and performing any protected business logic (e.g., placing an order in an e-commerce shop). Actions carried out by the client can be directly modeled as update operations on the database, with a potential validation and rewriting step enforced by the server.

---

[2]The JavaScript Object Notation (JSON) is a self-contained document format, consisting of objects (key-value pairs) and arrays (ordered lists), that can be arbitrarily nested. JSON has gained popularity due to its simpler structure compared to XML. It can be easily processed in JavaScript and thus became the widely-used format for document databases such as MongoDB [CD13], CouchDB [ALS10], Couchbase [Lak+16], and Espresso [Qia+13] to reduce the impedance mismatch [Mai90].

2.2.1 Request Flow

The request flow in two-tier web application architectures is slightly different from three-tier architectures:

1. With the initial request, the client retrieves the HTML document containing the single-page application logic.
2. The server or cloud service returns the HTML document and the accompanying JavaScript files. In contrast to server-rendered architectures, the frontend's structure is **data-independent** and therefore does not require any database queries or business logic.
3. The client evaluates the HTML and fetches any referenced files, in particular, the JavaScript containing the presentation logic.
4. Via JavaScript, the data required to display the current application view are fetched from the server via a REST/HTTP[3] API either in individual read operations or using a query language (e.g., MongoDB [CD13] or GraphQL [Gra]).
5. The frontend renders the data using the presentation logic of the JavaScript frontend, typically expressed through a template language.
6. User interactions are sent as individual requests and encode the exact operation performed. The response returns the data necessary to update the frontend accordingly.

2.2.2 Implementation

The technology choices for three-tier architectures also apply to the realization of two-tier architectures. IaaS and Paas offer low-level abstractions for building REST APIs consumed by single-page applications. Most web application frameworks have support for developing not only server-rendered HTML views, but also for structuring REST APIs. In the Java ecosystem, REST interfaces have been standardized [HS07]. In most other web languages such as (server-side) JavaScript (Node.js), Ruby, Python, and PHP, frameworks employ domain-specific languages or method annotations for minimizing the overhead of defining REST endpoints (e.g., in Ruby on Rails, Django, .NET WCF, Grails, Express, and the Play framework [WP11, The]). Static files of single-page applications are delivered from a web server, the web application framework, or a content delivery network. The REST APIs are consumed by the frontend that is technologically independent of the backend and only requires knowledge about the REST resources to implement client-server interactions. One notable exception is the idea of *isomorphic* (also

---

[3]Besides HTTP, real time-capable protocols like Web Sockets, Server-Sent Events (SSE), or WebRTC can be employed [Gri13].

called universal) JavaScript that applies the concept of sharing code (e.g., validation of user inputs) between a frontend and backend that are both implemented in JavaScript [HS16, Dep, Hoo, Par].

Database-as-a-Service (DBaaS) and Backend-as-a-Service (BaaS) models provide high-level abstractions for building and hosting two-tier applications. In the case of a DBaaS, the data tier is directly exposed to clients. As this is insufficient if protected business logic or access control are required, BaaS systems extend the data APIs with common building blocks for business logic in single-page applications. Typical BaaS APIs and functionalities consumed in two-tier applications are:

- Delivery of static files, in particular, the single-page application assets
- DBaaS APIs for access to structured data
- Login and registration of users
- Authorization on protected data
- Execution of server-side business logic and invocation of third-party services
- Sending of push notifications
- Logging and tracking of user data

In Sect. 4.5 we will discuss the characteristics of the DBaaS and BaaS models in detail.

As the frontend becomes more complex and handles the presentation logic and significant parts of the business logic, appropriate tooling and architectures gained relevance. Therefore, numerous JavaScript frameworks for developing and structuring single-page applications have been developed. A large part of these frameworks is based on the Model-View-Controller (MVC) pattern [KP+88] or variants thereof (e.g., Model-View-ViewModel [Gos05]). In client-side MVC architectures, the views generate the document visible to the end user, usually by defining a template language. The model contains the data displayed in the views, so that it embodies both application state and user interface state. A model is filled with data retrieved from the server's data APIs. Controllers handle the interaction between views and models (e.g., events from user inputs) and are responsible for client-server communication. The MVC pattern has been adopted by most widely-used JavaScript frameworks such as Angular [Ang], Ember [Emb], Vue [Vue], and Backbone [Bac]. Recently, component-based architectures have been proposed as an alternative to MVC frameworks through projects such as Facebook's React [Rea]. Components represent views, but also encompass event handling and user interface state.

In contrast to two-tier applications, any technological decisions made in the frontend are largely independent of the backend, as a REST API is the only point of coupling. Some frontend frameworks additionally offer server-side tooling to pre-render client views. This can improve the performance of the initial page load and is necessary for crawlers of search engines that do not evaluate JavaScript for indexing. In native mobile applications, the same principles as for single-page applications apply. A major architectural difference is that the frontend is compiled ahead-of-time so that its business and presentation logic can only be changed with an explicit update of the app. Furthermore, static files are usually not provided by the backend, but packaged into an installable app bundle, which shifts the problem of initial load times to both client-side performance and latency of the consumed server APIs.

2.2.3   Problems of Client-Rendered Architectures

Two-tier architectures can improve on several of the difficulties imposed by three-tier architectures, while other non-functional requirements remain challenging:

High Availability and Elastic Scalability.   The task of providing high availability with elastic scaling is shifted to the BaaS or DBaaS backend. As these systems employ a standard architecture shared between all applications built on them, availability and scalability can be tackled in a generic, application-independent fashion. As a DBaaS/BaaS is a managed service, it can furthermore eliminate availability and scalability problems introduced by operational errors such as flawed deployments, inappropriate autoscaling rules, or incompatible versions.

Fast Page Loads.   Navigation inside a single-page application is fast, as only the missing data required for the next view is fetched, instead of reloading the complete page. On the other hand, data requests become very latency-critical, as the initial page load depends on data being available for client-side rendering. In two-tier applications, the client can start its processing earlier as there is no initial HTML request blocked in the server by database queries and business logic.

Engaging User Experience.   Single-page applications are able to achieve a high degree of interactivity, as much of the business logic can be directly executed on the client. This allows applying updates immediately to remain under the critical threshold of 100 ms for interaction delays.

Fast Time-to-Market.   As the frontend and backend are loosely coupled through a REST API and based on different technology stacks, the development process is accelerated. The implementation of the frontend and backend can proceed independently, enabling individual development, testing and deployment cycles for a faster time-to-market.

In summary, many applications are moving towards client-rendered, two-tier architectures, to improve the user experience and development process. This shift reinforces the requirement for low latency, as data transferred from the server to the client is critical for fast navigation and initial page loads.

2.3   Latency and Round-Trip Time

Two primary factors influence network performance: latency and bandwidth [Gri13]. **Latency** refers to the time that passes from the moment a packet or signal is sent from a source to the moment it is received by the destination. **Bandwidth** refers to the throughput of data transfer for a network link. We will use the wide-spread term bandwidth (measured in Megabit per second; MBit/s) throughout this book, though the formal term **data rate** (or transmission rate) is more precise, as bandwidth in signal theory defines the difference between an upper and lower frequency [Cha15].

Network packets sent from one host to another host travel through several routers and are nested in different network protocols (e.g., Ethernet, IP, TCP, TLS, HTTP). There are different delays at each hop that add up to the end-to-end latency [KR10]:

Processing Delay (d_{proc}). The time for parsing the protocol header information, determining the destination of a packet and calculating checksums determines the processing delay. In modern networks, the processing delay is in the order of microseconds [Cha15].

Queuing Delay (d_{queue}). Before a packet is sent over a physical network link, it is added to a queue. Thus, the number of packets that arrived earlier defines for how long a packet will be queued before transmission over the link. If queues overflow, packets are dropped. This packet loss leads to increased latency as the network protocols have to detect the loss and resend the packet.[4]

Transmission Delay (d_{trans}). The transmission delay denotes the time for completely submitting a packet to the network link. Given the size of a packet S and the link's bandwidth, resp. transmission rate R, the transmission delay is S/R. For example, to transfer a packet with $S = 1500$ B over a Gigabit Ethernet with $R = 1$ Gb/s a transmission delay of $d_{trans} = 12$ µs is incurred.

Propagation Delay (d_{prop}). The physical medium of the network link, e.g., fiber optics or copper wires, defines how long it takes to transfer the signal encoding the packet to the next hop. Given the propagation speed of the medium in m/s and the distance between two hops, the propagation delay can be calculated.

If a packet has to pass through $N - 1$ routers between the sender and receiver, the end-to-end latency L is defined through the average processing, queuing, transmission and propagation delays [KR10]:

$$L = N \cdot (d_{proc} + d_{queue} + d_{trans} + d_{prop}) \tag{2.1}$$

Latency (also called *one-way latency*) is unidirectional, as it does not include the time for a packet to travel back. **Round-trip time** (RTT) on the other hand, measures the time from the source sending a request until receiving a response. RTT therefore includes the latency in each direction and the processing time d_{server} required for generating a response:

$$RTT = 2 \cdot L + d_{server} \tag{2.2}$$

---

[4]The large buffer sizes can also lead to a problem called *buffer bloat* in which queues are always operating at their maximum capacity. This is often caused by TCP congestion algorithms that increase throughput until package loss occurs. With large queues, many packets can be buffered and delayed before a packet loss occurs, which negatively impacts latency[APB09, Gri13].

In most cases, the propagation delay will play the key role in latency, as networking infrastructure has improved many aspects of queuing, transmission, and processing delay significantly. However, propagation delay depends on the constant speed of light and the geographic distance between two hosts. For example, the linear distance between Hamburg and San Francisco is 8879 km. Given an ideal network without any delays except the propagation at the speed of light (299,792,458 m/s), the minimum achievable latency is $L \approx 29.62$ ms and round-trip time $RTT \approx 59.23$ ms. Therefore, to reduce end-to-end latency, distances have to be shortened.

We will discuss the effects of network protocols such as HTTP and TLS on end-to-end latency in Chap. 3. Grigorik [Gri13] gives an in-depth overview of latency and network protocols specifically relevant for the web. Kurose and Ross [KR10] as well as Forouzan [For12] discuss the foundations of computer networking. Van Mieghem [VM14] provides a formal treatment of how networks can be modeled, analyzed and simulated stochastically.

2.4 Cloud Computing as a Source of Latency

Besides the two-tier and three-tier architecture, there are numerous other ways to structure applications [Feh+14]. Cloud computing is quickly becoming the major backbone of novel technologies across application fields such as web and mobile applications, Internet of Things (IoT), smart cities, virtual and augmented reality, gaming, streaming, data science, and Big Data analytics. Cloud computing delivers on the idea of **utility computing** introduced by John McCarthy in 1961 that suggests that computing should be a ubiquitous utility similar to electricity and telecommunications [AG17]. In the context of cloud computing, there are several sources of latency across all types of application architectures. In this section, we will summarize the architecture-independent latency bottlenecks that contribute to the overall performance of cloud-based applications.

In the literature, cloud computing has been defined in various different ways [LS13, YBDS08, MB16, Feh+14, Buy+09, MG09, TCB14]. Throughout this book, we will use the widely accepted NIST definition [MG09]. It distinguishes between five characteristics of cloud offerings and groups them into three service models and four deployment models. The nature of the service and deployment models motivates why latency is of utmost relevance in cloud computing.

2.4.1 Characteristics

The characteristics of cloud offerings explain how cloud computing is desirable for both customers and providers. Providers offer *on-demand self-service*, which means that consumers can provision services and resources in a fully automated process.

Broad network access enables the cloud services to be consumed by any client technology that has Internet access. Cloud providers apply *resource pooling* (multi-tenancy) to share storage, networking, and processing resources across tenants to leverage economies of scale for reduced costs. *Rapid elasticity* demands that resources can be freed and allocated with minimal delay, building the foundation for scalability. The provider exposes a *measured service* that is used for pay-per-use pricing models with fine-grained control, monitoring and reporting of resource usage to the consumer. In practice, the major reasons for companies to adopt cloud computing is the ability to replace capital expenditures (CAPEX) that would have been necessary to acquire hardware and software into operational expenditures (OPEX) incurred by the usage of pay-per-use cloud services. The major incentive for providers is the ability to exploit economies of scale and accommodate new business models.

2.4.2   Service Models

Based on increasing degree of abstraction, three high-level service models can be distinguished:

Infrastructure-as-a-Service (IaaS).   In an IaaS cloud, low-level resources such as computing (e.g., containers [Mer14] and virtual machines [Bar+03]), networking (e.g., subnets, load balancers, and firewalls [GJP11]) and storage (e.g., network-attached storage) can be provisioned. This allows deploying arbitrary applications in the cloud while leaving control of the infrastructure to the IaaS provider. In IaaS clouds, latency is particularly relevant for cross-node communication, potentially across different data centers (e.g., between an application server and a replicated database). Example offerings are Amazon Elastic Compute Cloud (EC2) [Amab], Softlayer [Sof], Joyent [Joy], and Google Compute Engine (GCE) [Gooa].

Platform-as-a-Service (PaaS).   Consumers of PaaS clouds run applications on a technology stack of services, programming languages, and application platforms defined by the provider including explicit support for developing, testing, deploying and hosting the application. In addition to the infrastructure, a PaaS provider also manages operating systems and networks. The role of latency in a PaaS is critical: as there is no control over native computing and storage resources, data management has to be consumed as a service either from the same provider or an external DBaaS. Examples of PaaS vendors are Microsoft Azure [Azu], Amazon Beanstalk [Aws], IBM Bluemix [Ibm], Google App Engine [App], and Heroku [Clob].

Software-as-a-Service (SaaS).   A SaaS provides a specific cloud-hosted application to users (e.g., email, word processors, spreadsheets, customer relationship management, games, virtual desktops). The provider completely abstracts from the cloud infrastructure and only allows customization and configuration of the application. Almost all SaaS offerings are consumed as web applications via HTTP, so that client-server latency is crucial for both initial loads and performance of interactions. Examples include Microsoft Office 365 [Off], Salesforce [Onl], and Slack [Sla].

Besides the above three models, other "XaaS" (Everything-as-a-Service) models have been proposed, for example, Storage-as-a-Service, Humans-as-a-Service, and Function-as-a-Service amongst many others [KLAR10, Din+13, TCB14, MB16, Has+15]. Database-as-a-Service (DBaaS) and Backend-as-a-Service (BaaS) as discussed in Sect. 4.5 cut across the three canonical levels of IaaS, PaaS, and SaaS and can be employed in each of the models.

2.4.3   Deployment Models

Deployment models describe different options for delivering and hosting cloud platforms.

Public Cloud.   A public cloud is operated by a business, academic, or government organization on its infrastructure and can be used by the general public. Commercial cloud offerings such as Amazon EC2, Google App Engine, and Salesforce fall in this category. In public clouds, latency to users and third-party services is critical for performance.

Private Cloud.   A private cloud provides exclusive use for one organization and is hosted on-premises of the consumer. This implies that the hardware resources are mostly static and in order to gain elasticity, public cloud resources may be added on demand, e.g., during load spikes (*cloud bursting* [Guo+12]). Besides commercial solutions such as VMWare vCloud [Cloc], various open-source platforms for private PaaS and IaaS clouds have been developed, including OpenStack [BWA13], Eucalyptus [Nur+09], and Cloud Foundry [Cloa]. As private clouds usually cannot exploit a globally distributed set of data centers, tackling wide-area latency to end users is a key challenge.

Hybrid Cloud.   In a hybrid cloud (also called multi-cloud deployment), two or more clouds are composed to combine their benefits. There are frameworks for addressing multiple clouds through a common API, e.g., jclouds [Apaa] and libCloud [Apab] as well as commercial providers for multi-cloud deployments, scaling and bursting such as RightScale [Rig], Scalr [Sca], and Skytap [Sky]. Any communication between different cloud platforms is highly latency-sensitive. When offloading critical components like data storage to a different cloud, incurred latency can be prohibitive and outweigh the advantages. On the other hand, if data management makes use of the broader geographic reach of multiple providers through caching or replication [WM13], latency can be reduced substantially as we will show in the next chapters.

The NIST definition [MG09] also defines a community cloud, as a cloud shared between organizations with common concerns. Though the model is not in common use, the same latency challenges apply: composed backends and remote users are subject to latency bottlenecks.

2.4.4 Latency in Cloud Architectures

In cloud-based applications, latency stems from various sources introduced by the composition of different service and deployment models. We group the latency into three categories:

1. Round-trip times *within a data center* network or LAN are usually in the order of single-digit milliseconds.
2. Latencies between two *co-located data centers* are in the order of 10 ms.
3. For hosts from two *different geographical locations*, latency often reaches 100 ms and more.

Figure 2.3 illustrates the typical latency contributions of several communication links within a distributed web application. In the example, the client is separated from the backend by a high-latency wide area network (WAN) link. The application's business logic is hosted on an IaaS platform and distributed across multiple servers interconnected via local networks. The data tier consists of a database service replicated across different availability zones. For a synchronously replicated database system, the latency between two data centers therefore defines the response time for database updates (for example in the Amazon RDS database service [Ver+17]).

Most complex applications integrate **heterogeneous services** for different functions of the application. For example, an external DBaaS might be consumed from the main application over a high-latency network, since it is shared between two different applications or provides a level of scalability that a database hosted on an IaaS could not provide. Parts of the application might also be developed with a service model that fits the requirements better, for example by offloading user authentication to microservices running on a PaaS. A BaaS could be integrated to handle standard functions such as push notifications. High latency also occurs if third-party services are integrated, for example, a social network in the frontend or a SaaS for payments in the backend. Overall, the more providers and services are involved in the application architecture, the higher the dependency on low latency for performance. As almost all interactions between services evolve around exchanging and loading data, the techniques proposed in this book apply to the latency problems in the example.

For further details on cloud models, please refer to Murugesan and Bojanova [MB16], who provide a detailed overview of cloud computing and its foundational concepts and technologies. Bahga and Madisetti [BM13] review the programming models and APIs of different cloud platforms.

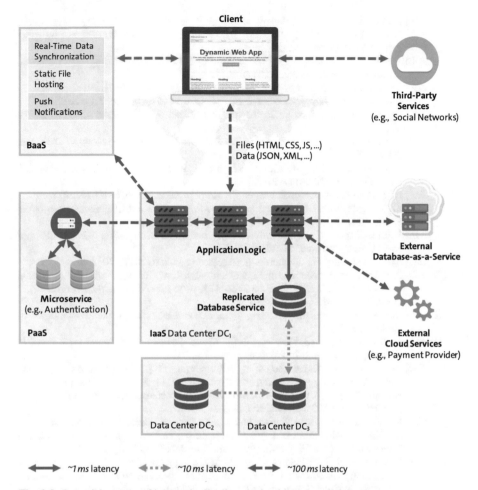

Fig. 2.3 Potential sources of latency in distributed, cloud-based applications

In the following chapters, we will provide detailed background on network performance and the state of the art in data management to highlight the different opportunities for tackling latency across the application stack.

References

[AG17] Nick Antonopoulos and Lee Gillam, eds. *Cloud Computing: Principles, Systems and Applications (Computer Communications and Networks)*. 2nd ed. 2017. Springer, July 2017. ISBN: 9783319546445. URL: http://amazon.com/o/ASIN/3319546449/.

[Alo+04] Gustavo Alonso et al. "Web services". In: *Web Services*. Springer, 2004, pp. 123–149.

[ALS10] J. Chris Anderson, Jan Lehnardt, and Noah Slater. *CouchDB - The Definitive Guide: Time to Relax*. O'Reilly, 2010. ISBN: 978-0-596-15589-6. URL: http://www.oreilly.de/catalog/9780596155896/index.html.

[Amab] *Amazon Web Services AWS â Server Hosting & Cloud Services*. https://aws.amazon.com/de/. (Accessed on 05/20/2017). 2017.

[Ang] *Angular Framework*. https://angulario/. (Accessed on 05/26/2017). 2017.

[Apaa] *Apache jclouds*. https://jclouds.apache.org/. (Accessed on 06/05/2017). 2017.

[Apab] *Apache Libcloud*. http://libcloud.apache.org/index.html. (Accessed on 06/05/2017). 2017.

[APB09] Mark Allman, Vern Paxson, and Ethan Blanton. *TCP congestion control*. Tech. rep. 2009.

[App] *App Engine (Google Cloud Platform)*. https://cloud.google.com/appengine/. (Accessed on 05/20/2017). 2017.

[Arc] *HTTP Archive*. http://httparchive.org/trends.php. Accessed: 2018-07-14. 2018.

[Aws] *AWS Elastic Beanstalk - PaaS Application Management*. https://aws.amazon.com/de/elasticbeanstalk/. (Accessed on 05/20/2017). 2017.

[Azu] *Microsoft Azure: Cloud Computing Platform & Services*. https://azure.microsoft.com/en-us/. (Accessed on 05/20/2017). 2017.

[Bac] *Backbone.js*. http://backbonejs.org/. (Accessed on 05/26/2017). 2017.

[Bar+03] P. Barham et al. "Xen and the art of virtualization". In: *ACM SIGOPS Operating Systems Review*. Vol. 37. 2003, pp. 164–177. URL: http://dl.acm.org/citation.cfm?id=945462%7C (visited on 10/09/2012).

[Bec00] Kent Beck. *Extreme programming explained: embrace change*. addison-wesley professional, 2000.

[BM13] Arshdeep Bahga and Vijay Madisetti. *Cloud Computing: A Hands-on Approach*. CreateSpace Independent Publishing Platform, 2013.

[Buy+09] R. Buyya et al. "Cloud computing and emerging IT platforms: Vision, hype, and reality for delivering computing as the 5th utility". In: *Future Generation computer systems* 25.6 (2009), pp. 599–616. URL: http://www.sciencedirect.com/science/article/pii/S0167739X08001957 (visited on 06/29/2012).

[BWA13] Meenakshi Bist, Manoj Wariya, and Amit Agarwal. "Comparing delta, open stack and Xen Cloud Platforms: A survey on open source IaaS". In: *Advance Computing Conference (IACC), 2013 IEEE 3rd International*. IEEE. 2013, pp. 96–100.

[Cal+11] Brad Calder et al. "Windows Azure Storage: a highly available cloud storage service with strong consistency". In: *Proceedings of the Twenty-Third ACM Symposium on Operating Systems Principles*. ACM. ACM, 2011, pp. 143–157. URL: http://dl.acm.org/citation.cfm?id=2043571 (visited on 04/16/2014).

[CD13] Kristina Chodorow and Michael Dirolf. *MongoDB - The Definitive Guide*. O'Reilly, 2013. ISBN: 978-1-449-38156-1. URL: http://www.oreilly.de/catalog/9781449381561/index.html.

[Cha15] Lee Chao. *Cloud Computing Networking: Theory, Practice, and Development*. Auerbach Publications, 2015. URL: https://www.amazon.com/Cloud-Computing-Networking-Practice-Development-ebook/dp/B015PNEOGC?SubscriptionId=0JYN1NVW651KCA56C102&tag=techkie-20&linkCode=xm2&camp=2025&creative=165953&creativeASIN=B015PNEOGC.

[Cloa] *Cloud Application Platform - Devops Platform | Cloud Foundry*. https://www.cloudfoundry.org/. (Accessed on 06/05/2017). 2017.

[Clob] *Cloud Application Platform | Heroku*. https://www.heroku.com/. (Accessed on 05/20/2017). 2017.

[Cloc] *vCloud Suite, vSphere-Based Private Cloud: VMware*. http://www.vmware.com/products/vcloud-suite.html. (Accessed on 06/05/2017). 2017.

[Cro06] Douglas Crockford. "JSON: Javascript object notation". In: *URL* http://www.json.org (2006).

[Dep] *Deployd: a toolkit for building realtime APIs*. https://github.com/deployd/deployd. (Accessed on 05/20/2017). 2017. URL: https://github.com/deployd/deployd (visited on 02/19/2017).

[Din+13] Hoang T Dinh et al. "A survey of mobile cloud computing: architecture, applications, and approaches". In: *Wireless communications and mobile computing* 13.18 (2013), pp. 1587–1611.

[Emb] *Ember.js Framework*. https://www.emberjs.com/. (Accessed on 05/26/2017). 2017.

[Feh+14] Christoph Fehling et al. *Cloud Computing Patterns - Fundamentals to Design, Build, and Manage Cloud Applications*. Springer, 2014. ISBN: 978-3-7091-1567-1. DOI: 10.1007/978-3-7091-1568-8.

[For12] A Behrouz Forouzan. *Data communications & networking*. Tata McGraw-Hill Education, 2012.

[GJP11] K. Gilly, C. Juiz, and R. Puigjaner. "An up-to-date survey in web load balancing". In: *World Wide Web* 14.2 (2011), pp. 105–131. URL: http://www.springerlink.com/index/P1080033328U8158.pdf (visited on 09/12/2012).

[Gooa] *Google Cloud Computing, Hosting Services & APIs – Google Cloud Platform*. https://cloud.google.com/. (Accessed on 05/20/2017). 2017.

[Gos05] John Gossmann. *Introduction to Model/View/ViewModel pattern for building WPF apps*. https://blogs.msdn.microsoft.com/johngossman/2005/10/08/introduction-to-modelviewviewmodel-pattern-for-building-wpf-apps/. (Accessed on 05/26/2017). Aug. 2005.

[Gra] *GraphQL*. https://facebook.github.io/graphql/. (Accessed on 05/25/2017). 2017.

[Gri13] Ilya Grigorik. *High performance browser networking*. English. [S.l.]: O'Reilly Media, 2013. ISBN: 1-4493-4476-3 978-1-4493-4476-4. URL: https://books.google.de/books?id=tf-AAAAQBAJ.

[Guo+12] Tian Guo et al. "Seagull: Intelligent Cloud Bursting for Enterprise Applications". In: *2012 USENIX Annual Technical Conference, Boston, MA, USA, June 13–15, 2012*. Ed. by Gernot Heiser and Wilson C. Hsieh. USENIX Association, 2012, pp. 361–366. URL: https://www.usenix.org/conference/atc12/technical-sessions/presentation/guo.

[Has+15] Ibrahim Abaker Targio Hashem et al. "The rise of "big data" on cloud computing: Review and open research issues". In: *Inf. Syst.* 47 (2015), pp. 98–115. DOI: 10.1016/j.is.2014.07.006.

[HDF13] Kai Hwang, Jack Dongarra, and Geoffrey C Fox. *Distributed and cloud computing: from parallel processing to the internet of things*. Morgan Kaufmann, 2013.

[Hil16] Tony Hillerson. *Seven Mobile Apps in Seven Weeks: Native Apps, Multiple Platforms*. Pragmatic Bookshelf, 2016. URL: https://www.amazon.com/Seven-Mobile-Apps-Weeks-Platforms-ebook/dp/B01L9W8AQS?SubscriptionId=0JYN1NVW651KCA56C102&tag=techkie-20&linkCode=xm2&camp=2025&creative=165953&creativeASIN=B01L9W8AQS.

[Hoo] *GitHub - hoodiehq/hoodie: A backend for Offline First applications*. https://github.com/hoodiehq/hoodie. (Accessed on 05/25/2017). 2017. URL: https://github.com/hoodiehq/hoodie (visited on 02/17/2017).

[HS07] Marc Hadley and P Sandoz. "JSR 311: Java api for RESTful web services". In: *Technical report, Java Community Process* (2007).

[HS16] Stephan Hochhaus and Manuel Schoebel. *Meteor in action*. Manning Publ., 2016.

[HW03] Gregor Hohpe and Bobby Woolf. "Enterprise Integration Pattern". In: *Addison-Wesley Signature Series* (2003).

[Ibm] *IBM Bluemix â Cloud-Infrastruktur, Plattformservices, Watson, & weitere PaaS-Lösungen*. https://www.ibm.com/cloud-computing/bluemix. (Accessed on 05/20/2017). 2017.

[Joy] *Joyent | Triton*. https://www.joyent.com/. (Accessed on 06/05/2017). 2017.

[Kam17] Poul-Henning Kamp. *Varnish HTTP Cache*. https://varnishcache.org/. (Accessed on 04/30/2017). 2017. URL: https://varnish-cache.org/ (visited on 01/26/2017).

[KLAR10] Heba Kurdi, Maozhen Li, and HS Al-Raweshidy. "Taxonomy of Grid Systems". In: *Handbook of research on P2P and grid systems for service-oriented computing: Models, Methodologies and Applications*. IGI Global, 2010, pp. 20–43.

[Kle17] Martin Kleppmann. *Designing Data-Intensive Applications*. English. 1 edition. O'Reilly Media, Jan. 2017. ISBN: 978-1-4493-7332-0.

[KP+88] Glenn E Krasner, Stephen T Pope, et al. "A description of the modelview- controller user interface paradigm in the smalltalk-80 system". In: *Journal of object oriented programming* 1.3 (1988), pp. 26–49.

[KR10] James F Kurose and Keith W Ross. *Computer networking: a top-down approach*. Vol. 5. Addison-Wesley Reading, 2010.

[Kri15] Michael Krigsman. *Research: 25 percent of web projects fail*. http://www.zdnet.com/article/research-25-percentof-web-projects-fail/. (Accessed on 04/30/2017). 2015. URL: http://www.zdnet.com/article/research-25-percent-of-web-projects-fail/.

[Lak+16] Sarath Lakshman et al. "Nitro: A Fast, Scalable In-Memory Storage Engine for NoSQL Global Secondary Index". In: *PVLDB* 9.13 (2016), pp. 1413–1424. URL: http://www.vldb.org/pvldb/vol9/p1413-lakshman.pdf.

[LS13] Wolfgang Lehner and Kai-Uwe Sattler. *Web-Scale Data Management for the Cloud*. Englisch. Auflage: 2013. New York: Springer, Apr. 2013. ISBN: 978-1-4614-6855-4.

[Mai90] David Maier. "Representing database programs as objects". In: *Advances in database programming languages*. ACM. 1990, pp. 377–386.

[MB16] San Murugesan and Irena Bojanova. *Encyclopedia of Cloud Computing*. John Wiley & Sons, 2016.

[Mer14] Dirk Merkel. "Docker: lightweight linux containers for consistent development and deployment". In: *Linux Journal* 2014.239 (2014), p. 2.

[MG09] Peter Mell and Tim Grance. "The NIST definition of cloud computing". In: *National Institute of Standards and Technology* 53.6 (2009), p. 50.

[Mil68] Robert B Miller. "Response time in man-computer conversational transactions". In: *Proceedings of the December 9–11, 1968, fall joint computer conference, part I*. ACM. 1968, pp. 267–277.

[MP14] M Mikowski and J Powell. *Single Page Applications*. 2014.

[Mye85] Brad A Myers. "The importance of percent-done progress indicators for computer-human interfaces". In: *ACM SIGCHI Bulletin*. Vol. 16. 4. ACM. 1985, pp. 11–17.

[Nad+16] Irakli Nadareishvili et al. *Microservice Architecture: Aligning Principles, Practices, and Culture*. "O'Reilly Media, Inc.", 2016.

[New15] Sam Newman. *Building microservices - designing fine-grained systems, 1st Edition*. O'Reilly, 2015. ISBN: 9781491950357. URL: http://www.worldcat.org/oclc/904463848.

[Nie94] Jakob Nielsen. *Usability engineering*. Elsevier, 1994.

[Nur+09] Daniel Nurmi et al. "The eucalyptus open-source cloud-computing system". In: *Proceedings of the 2009 9th IEEE/ACM International Symposium on Cluster Computing and the Grid*. IEEE Computer Society. 2009, pp. 124–131.

[Off] *Office 365 for Business*. https://products.office.com/enus/business/office. (Accessed on 06/05/2017). 2017.

[Onl] *Salesforce Online CRM*. https://www.salesforce.com/en. (Accessed on 06/05/2017). 2017.

[Par] *Parse Server*. http://parseplatform.github.io/docs/parse-server/guide/. (Accessed on 07/28/2017). 2017. URL: http://parseplatform.github.io/docs/parse-server/guide/ (visited on 02/19/2017).

[Qia+13] Lin Qiao et al. "On brewing fresh espresso: LinkedIn's distributed data serving platform". In: *Proceedings of the 2013 international conference on Management of data*. ACM, 2013, pp. 1135–1146. URL: http://dl.acm.org/citation.cfm?id=2465298 (visited on 09/28/2014).

[Rea] *React - A JavaScript library for building user interfaces*. https://facebook.github.io/react/. (Accessed on 05/26/2017). 2017.

[Ree08] Will Reese. "Nginx: the high-performance web server and reverse proxy". In: *Linux Journal* 2008.173 (2008), p. 2.

[Rig] *RightScale Cloud Management*. http://www.rightscale.com/. (Accessed on 06/05/2017). 2017.

[SB02] Ken Schwaber and Mike Beedle. *Agile software development with Scrum*. Vol. 1. Prentice Hall Upper Saddle River, 2002.

[Sca] *Scalr: Enterprise-Grade Cloud Management Platform*. https://www.scalr.com/. (Accessed on 06/05/2017). 2017.

[Sky] *Skytap*. https://www.skytap.com/. (Accessed on 06/05/2017). 2017.

[Sla] *Slack*. https://slack.com/. (Accessed on 06/05/2017). 2017.

[Sof] *SoftLayer | Cloud Servers, Storage, Big Data, & More IAAS Solutions*. http://www.softlayer.com/. (Accessed on 06/05/2017). 2017.

[TCB14] Adel Nadjaran Toosi, Rodrigo N Calheiros, and Rajkumar Buyya. "Interconnected cloud computing environments: Challenges, taxonomy, and survey". In: *ACM Computing Surveys (CSUR)* 47.1 (2014), p. 7.

[The] *Django Web Framework*. https://www.djangoproject.com/. (Accessed on 05/20/2017). 2017.

[TS07] Andrew S. Tanenbaum and Maarten van Steen. *Distributed systems - principles and paradigms, 2nd Edition*. Pearson Education, 2007. ISBN: 978-0-13-239227-3.

[Ver+17] Alexandre Verbitski et al. "Amazon Aurora: Design Considerations for High Throughput Cloud-Native Relational Databases". In: *Proceedings of the 2017 ACM International Conference on Management of Data, SIGMOD Conference 2017, Chicago, IL, USA, May 14–19, 2017*. Ed. by Semih Salihoglu et al. ACM, 2017, pp. 1041–1052. DOI: 10.1145/3035918.3056101.

[VM14] Piet Van Mieghem. *Performance analysis of complex networks and systems*. Cambridge University Press, 2014. URL: http://books.google.de/books?hl=de&lr=&id=lc3aWG0rL_MC&oi=fnd&pg=PR11&dq=mieghem+performance&ots=ohyJ3Qz2Lz&sig=1MOrNY0vHG-D4pDsf_DygD_3vDY (visited on 10/03/2014).

[Vue] *Vue.js*. https://vuejs.org/. (Accessed on 05/26/2017). 2017.

[Wal14] Craig Walls. *Spring in Action: Covers Spring 4*. Manning Publications, 2014. ISBN: 161729120X. URL: https://www.amazon.com/Spring-Action-Covers-4/dp/161729120X?SubscriptionId=0JYN1NVW651KCA56C102&tag=techkie-20&linkCode=xm2&camp=2025&creative=165953&creativeASIN=161729120X.

[WGW+20] Wolfram Wingerath, Felix Gessert, ErikWitt, et al. "Speed Kit: A Polyglot & GDPR-Compliant Approach For Caching Personalized Content". In: *36th IEEE International Conference on Data Engineering, ICDE 2020, Dallas, Texas, April 20–24, 2020*. 2020.

[Wil] *WildFly Homepage Âů WildFly*. http://wildfly.org/. (Accessed on 05/20/2017). 2017.

[WJW15] Da Wang, Gauri Joshi, and Gregory Wornell. "Using straggler replication to reduce latency in large-scale parallel computing". In: *ACM SIGMETRICS Performance Evaluation Review* 43.3 (2015), pp. 7–11.

[WM13] Zhe Wu and Harsha V. Madhyastha. "Understanding the latency benefits of multi-cloud webservice deployments". In: *Computer Communication Review* 43.2 (2013), pp. 13–20. DOI: 10.1145/2479957.2479960.

[WP11] Erik Wilde and Cesare Pautasso. *REST: from research to practice*. Springer Science & Business Media, 2011.

[YBDS08] Lamia Youseff, Maria Butrico, and Dilma Da Silva. "Toward a unified ontology of cloud computing". In: *Grid Computing Environments Workshop, 2008. GCE'08*. IEEE. 2008, pp. 1–10.

Chapter 3
HTTP for Globally Distributed Applications

For any distributed application, the network plays a significant role for performance. In the web, the central protocol is HTTP (Hypertext Transfer Protocol) [Fie+99] that determines how browsers communicate with web servers and that is used as the basis for REST APIs (*Representational State Transfer*). For cloud services across different deployment and service models, REST APIs are the default interface for providing access to storage and compute resources, as well as high-level services. Most DBaaS, BaaS, and NoSQL systems provide native REST APIs to achieve a high degree of interoperability and to allow access from heterogeneous environments. This chapter reviews relevant foundations of HTTP and networking with respect to performance and latency, as well as their role in cloud data management. In particular, we will highlight which challenges the standardized behavior of the web caching infrastructure imposes for data-centric services.

3.1 HTTP and the REST Architectural Style

The REST architectural style was proposed by Fielding as an a-posteriori explanation for the success of the web [Fie00]. REST is a set of constraints that—when imposed on a protocol design—yield the beneficial system properties of scalability and simplicity the designers of the HTTP standard developed for the web [Fie+99]. Most services in cloud computing environments are exposed as REST/HTTP[1] services, as they are simple to understand and consume in any programming language and environment [DFR15b]. Another advantage of HTTP is its support by mature and well-researched web infrastructure. REST and HTTP

---

[1]In principle, the REST architectural style is independent of its underlying protocol. However, as HTTP dominates in practical implementations, we will refer to REST as its combination with HTTP [WP11].

© Springer Nature Switzerland AG 2020
F. Gessert et al., *Fast and Scalable Cloud Data Management*,
https://doi.org/10.1007/978-3-030-43506-6_3

are not only the default for web and mobile applications but also an alternative to backend-side RPC-based (Remote Procedure Call) approaches (e.g., XML RPC or Java RMI [Dow98]), binary wire protocols (e.g., PostgreSQL protocol [Pos]) and web services (the SOAP and WS-* standards family [Alo+04]).

HTTP is an application-layer protocol on top of the Transmission Control Protocol (TCP) [Pos81] and lays the foundation of the web. With REST, the key abstractions of interactions are represented by HTTP *resources* identified by URLs. In a DBaaS API, these resources could for example be queries, transactions, objects, schemas, and settings. Clients interact with these resources through the *uniform interface* of the HTTP methods GET, PUT, POST, and DELETE. Any interface is thus represented as a set of resources that can be accessed through HTTP methods. Methods have different semantics: GET requests are called *safe*, as they are free of side-effects (nullipotent). PUT and DELETE requests are idempotent, while POST requests may have side-effects that are non-idempotent. The actual data (e.g., database objects) can take the form of any standard *content type* which can dynamically be negotiated between the client and server through HTTP (*content negotiation*). Many REST APIs have default representations in JSON, but other formats (e.g., XML, text, images) are possible, too. This extensibility of REST APIs allows services to present responses in a format that is appropriate for the respective use case [RAR13].

The integration and connection of resources is achieved through *hypermedia*, i.e., the mutual referencing of resources [Amu17]. These references are similar to links on web pages. A resource for a query result could for instance have references to the objects matching the query predicate. Hypermedia can render a REST interface self-descriptive. In that case, an initial URL to a root resource is sufficient to explore the complete interface by following references and interpreting self-describing standard media types. HTTP is a request-response protocol, which means that the client has to pose a request to receive a response. For the server to proactively push data, other protocols are required.

The *constraints* of REST describe common patterns to achieve scalability [Fie00]. In the context of cloud services, these constraints are:

Client-Server.   There is a clear distinction between a client (e.g., a browser or mobile device) and the server (e.g., a cloud service or web server) that communicate with each other using a client-initiated request-response pattern [Fie+99].

Statelessness.   If servers are stateless, requests can be load-balanced, and servers may be replicated for horizontal scalability.

Caching.   Using caching, responses can be reused for future requests by serving them from intermediate web caches.

Uniform Interface.   All interactions are performed using four basic HTTP methods to create, read, update, and delete (*CRUD*) resources.

Layered System.   Involving intermediaries (e.g., web caches, load balancers, firewalls, and proxies) in the communication path results in a layered system.

In practice, many REST APIs do not adhere to all constraints and are often referred to as web APIs, i.e., custom programming interfaces using HTTP as a transport protocol [RAR13]. For example, the Parse BaaS uses POST methods to perform idempotent operations and GET requests for operations with side-effects [Par]. As a consequence, such web APIs are potentially unscalable and may be treated incorrectly by intermediaries. Unlike web services, REST does not require interface descriptions and service discovery. However, the OpenAPI initiative is an attempt to standardize the description of REST APIs and allowing code generation for programming languages [Ope]. Richardson et al. [RAR13], Allamaraju [All10], Amundsen [Amu17], and Webber et al. [WPR10] provide a comprehensive treatment of REST and HTTP.

The challenge for data management is to devise a REST API that leverages HTTP for scalability through statelessness and caching and that is generic enough to be applicable to a broad spectrum of database systems. To this end, a resource structure for different functional capabilities is required (e.g., queries and transactions) as well as system-independent mechanisms for stateless request processing and caching of reads and queries.

3.2 Latency on the Web: TCP, TLS and Network Optimizations

For interoperability reasons, REST APIs are the predominant type of interface in cloud data management. HTTP on the other hand has to be used by any website. The performance and latency of HTTP communication are determined by the protocols that are involved during each HTTP request.

Figure 3.1 shows the latency components of a single HTTP request illustrated with exemplary delays:

1. First, the URL's domain (e.g., example.com) is resolved to an IP address using a UDP-based **DNS lookup**. To this end, the client contacts a configured DNS resolver. If the DNS entry is uncached, the resolver will contact a root DNS server that redirects to a DNS server responsible for the top-level domain (e.g., for .com). That name server will in turn redirect to the authoritative name server registered by the owner of the domain. This name server then returns one or

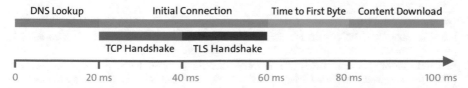

Fig. 3.1 Latency components across network protocols of an HTTP request against a TLS-secured URL

multiple IP addresses for the requested host name. Depending on the location of the (potentially geo-redundant) DNS servers and the state of their caches, a typical DNS query will return in 10–100 ms. Like in HTTP, DNS caching is based on TTLs with its associated staleness problems [TW11].

2. Next, a **TCP connection** between the client and the server is established using a three-way handshake. In the first round-trip, connection parameters are negotiated (SYN, SYN-ACK packets). In the second round-trip, the client can send the first portion of the payload. There is ongoing research on *TCP fast open* [Che+14], a mechanism to avoid one round-trip by sending data in the first SYN packet.

3. If the server supports and requires end-to-end encryption through HTTPS, respectively TLS (Transport Layer Security), a **TLS handshake** needs to be performed [Gri13]. This requires two additional round-trips during which the server's certificate is checked, session keys are exchanged, and a cipher suite for encryption and signatures is negotiated. TLS protocol extensions have been specified to allow data transmission during half-open TLS connections to reduce TLS overhead to one round-trip (*TLS false start*). Alternatively, clients can reuse previous session parameters negotiated with the same server, to abbreviate the handshake (*TLS session resumption*).[2]

4. When the connection is established, the client sends an HTTP request that consists of an HTTP method, a URL, the protocol version as well as HTTP headers encoding additional information like the desired content type and supported compression algorithms. The server processes the requests and either fully assembles the response or starts transmitting it, as soon as data is available (*chunked encoding*). The delay to the moment where the client receives the first response bytes is referred to as **time-to-first-byte** (TTFB).

5. Even though the connection is fully established, the response cannot necessarily be transmitted in a single round-trip, but requires multiple iterations for the **content download**. TCP employs a *slow-start algorithm* that continuously increases the transmission rate until the full aggregate capacity of all involved hops is saturated without packet loss and congestion [Mat+97]. Numerous congestion control algorithms have been proposed, most of which rely on packet loss as an indicator of network congestion [KHR02, WDM01]. For large responses, multiple round-trips are therefore required to transfer data over a newly opened connection, until TCP's congestion window is sufficiently sized.[3] Increasing the initial TCP congestion window from 4 to 10 segments is ongoing work

---

[2]Furthermore, the QUIC (*Quick UDP Internet Connections*) protocol has been proposed as UDP-based alternative to HTTP that has no connection handshake overhead [Gri13]. A new TLS protocol version with no additional handshakes has also been proposed [Res17].

[3]The relationship between latency and potential data rate is called the *bandwidth-delay product* [Gri13]. For a given round-trip latency (delay), the effective data rate (bandwidth) is computed as the maximum amount of data that can be transferred (product) divided by the delay. For example, if the current TCP congestion window is 16 KB and the latency 100 ms, the maximum data rate is 1.31 MBit/s.

[Chu+13] and allows for typically $10 \cdot 1500\,B = 15\,KB$ of data transmitted with a single round-trip, given the maximum transmission unit of $1500\,B$ of an Ethernet network.

In the best case and with all optimizations applied, an HTTP request over a new connection can hence be performed with one DNS round-trip and two server round-trips. DNS requests are aggressively cached, as IPs for DNS names are considered stable. The DNS overhead is therefore often minimal and can additionally be tackled by geo-replicated DNS servers that serve requests to nearby users (*DNS anycast*). To minimize the impact of TCP and TLS handshakes, clients keep connections open for reuse in future requests, which is an indispensable optimization, in particular for request-heavy websites.

The current protocol version 2 of HTTP [IET15] maintains the semantics of the original HTTP standard [KR01] but improves many networking inefficiencies. Some optimizations are inherent, while others require active support by clouds services:

- **Multiplexing** all requests over one TCP connection avoids the overhead of multiple connection handshakes and circumvents head-of-line blocking.[4]
- **Header Compression** applies compression to HTTP metadata to minimize the impact of repetitive patterns (e.g., always requesting JSON as a format).
- If a server implements **Server Push**, resources can be sent to the client proactively whenever the server assumes that they will be requested. This requires explicit support by cloud services, as the semantics and usage patterns define, which content should be pushed to reduce round-trips. However, inadequate use of pushed resources hurts performance, as the browser cache is rendered useless.
- By defining dependencies between resources, the server can actively **prioritize** important requests.

As of 2017, still less than 20% of websites and APIs employ HTTP/2 [Usa]. When all above protocols are in optimal use, the remaining latency bottleneck is the round-trip latency between API and browser clients and the server answering HTTP requests.

In **mobile networks**, the impact of HTTP request latency is even more severe. Additional latency is caused by the mobile network infrastructure. With the older 2G and 3G mobile network standards, latencies between 100 ms (HSPA) and 750 ms (GPRS) are common [Gri13, Ch. 7]. With modern 4G LTE-Advanced (*Long Term Evolution*) networks, the standards prescribe strict latency bounds for better user experience. As mobile devices share radio frequencies for data transmission, access has to be mediated and multiplexed. This process is performed by a radio resource controller (RRC) located in the radio towers of the LTE cells that together comprise the radio access network (RAN). At the physical level, several latency-critical steps are involved in a request by a mobile device connected via a 4G network:

---

[4]Head-of-line blocking occurs when a request is scheduled, but no open connection can be used, as responses have not yet been received.

1. When a mobile device sends or receives data and was previously idle, it nego-
   tiates physical transmission parameters with the RRC. The standard prescribes
   that this **control-plane latency** must not exceed 100 ms [DPS13].
2. Any packet transferred from the mobile device to the radio tower must have a
   user-plane latency of below 5 ms.
3. Next, the carrier transfers the packet from the radio tower to a packet gateway
   connected to the public Internet. This **core network latency** is not bounded.
4. Starting from the packet gateway, normal **Internet routing** with variable latency
   is performed.

Thus, in modern mobile networks, one-way latency will be at least 5–105 ms
higher than in conventional networks. The additional latency is incurred for
each HTTP request and each TCP/TLS connection handshake, making latency
particularly critical for mobile websites and apps.

In summary, to achieve low latency for REST and HTTP, many network
parameters have to be explicitly optimized at the level of protocol parameters,
operating systems, network stacks, and servers [Gri13]. In-depth engineering details
of TCP/IP, DNS, HTTP, TLS, and mobile networking are provided by Grigorik
[Gri13], Kurose and Ross [KR10], and Tanenbaum [TW11]. However, with all
techniques and best practices applied, physical latency from the client to the server
remains the main bottleneck, as well as the time-to-first-byte caused by processing
in the backend. Both latency contributions can be addressed through caching.

3.3 Web Caching for Scalability and Low Latency

HTTP allows resources to be declared cacheable. They are considered fresh
for a statically assigned lifetime called time-to-live (TTL). Any cache in the
request/response chain between client and server will serve a cached object without
contacting the origin server. The HTTP caching model's update strategy is purely
expiration-based: once a TTL has been delivered, the respective resource cannot
be invalidated before the TTL has expired. In the literature, expiration-based
caching is also known as the *lease model* [How+88, Mog94, Vak06] and has
been proposed by Gray et al. [GC89] long before HTTP. In contrast, *invalidation-
based* caches use out-of-band protocols to receive notifications about URLs that
should be purged from the cache (e.g., non-standardized HTTP methods or separate
purging protocols). This model is in wide use for many non-HTTP caches, too
[Car13, ERR11, Lwe10, Bla+10, Lab+09]. As the literature is lacking a survey of
web caching in the light of data management, we give a concise overview of web
cache types, scalability mechanisms, and consistency aspects of expiration-based
and invalidation-based HTTP caching.

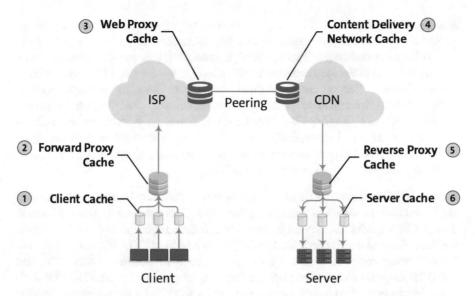

Fig. 3.2 Different types of web caches distinguished by their location. Caches 1–3 are expiration-based, while caches 4–6 are invalidation-based

3.3.1   Types of Web Caches

The closer a web cache is to the network edge, the more the network latency decreases. We distinguish between six types of web caches, based on their network *location* as shown in Fig. 3.2 (cf. [Lab+09, Nag04]):

Client Cache.   A cache can be directly embedded in the application as part of the browser, mobile app, or an HTTP library [Fie+99]. Client caches have the lowest latency, but are not shared between clients and rather limited in size.

Forward Proxy Cache.   Forward proxy caches are placed in networks as shared web caches for all clients in that network. Being very close to the application, they achieve a substantial decrease in network latency. Forward proxy caches can either be configured as explicit proxies by providing configuration information to clients through protocols such as PAC and WPAD [Gou+02] or by transparently intercepting outgoing, unencrypted TCP connections.

Web Proxy Cache.   Internet Service Providers (ISPs) deploy web proxy caches in their networks. Besides accelerating HTTP traffic for end users, this also reduces transit fees at Internet exchange points. Like client and forward proxy caches, web proxy caches are purely expiration-based.

Content Delivery Network (CDN) Cache.   CDNs provide a distributed network of web caches that can be controlled by the backend [PB07]. CDN caches are designed to be scalable and multi-tenant and can store massive amounts of cached data. Like reverse proxy caches and server caches, CDN caches are usually invalidation-based.

Reverse Proxy Cache.   Reverse proxy caches are placed in the server's network and accept incoming connections as a surrogate for the server [Kam17]. They can be extended to perform application-specific logic, for example, to check authentication information and to perform load balancing over backend servers.

Server Cache.   Server caches offload the server and its database system by caching intermediate data, query results, and shared data structures [Fit04, Nis+13, Xu+14, Can+01b, Gar+08, Bro+13]. Server caches are not based on HTTP, but explicitly orchestrated by the database system (e.g., DBCache [Bor+04]), a specialized middleware (e.g., Quaestor [Ges+17]), or the application tier (e.g., Memcache [Fit04]).

The defining characteristic of all web caches is that they transparently interpret HTTP caching metadata as *read-through* caches. This means that when a request causes a cache miss, the request is forwarded to the next cache or the origin server and then the response is cached according to the provided TTL. Web caches always forward write requests, as these come in the form of opaque POST, PUT, and DELETE requests whose semantics are implicit properties of a REST/HTTP API. The effectiveness of web caching is measured by a *cache hit ratio* that captures the percentage of all requests that were served from a cache and the *byte hit ratio* that expresses the corresponding data volume.

3.3.2   Scalability of Web Caching

To employ web caches for cloud data management, they have to support scalability. It is widely unknown in the database community that web caches scale through the same primary mechanisms as most NoSQL databases: replication and hash sharding. Figure 3.3 gives an overview of these techniques in the context of web caches. Load balancers that can work on different levels of the protocol stack forward HTTP requests to web caches using a policy like round-robin or a uniform distribution [GJP11]. In contrast to database systems, no replication protocols are required, as each replica fetches missing resources on demand. Partitioning the space of cached objects for a cluster of caches is achieved by hash sharding the space of URLs. Requests can then be forwarded to URL partitions through the Cache Array Routing Protocol (CARP) [Wan99]. Hierarchies of communicating web caches (*cache peering* [KR01]) build on query-based protocols like the Inter Cache Protocol (ICP) [Wes97], the Hypertext Caching Protocol (HTCP) [VW99], or Cache Digests [Fan+00]. The underlying idea of query-based protocols is that checking another cache replica's entries is more efficient than forwarding a request to the origin server. Finally, global meshes of web caches in CDNs can rely on inter-cluster exchanges for geo-replication [PB08]. In practice, CDN providers exploit the fact that a cache lookup of a URL maps well to a key-value interface. This allows scaling cache clusters by deploying web caches as a proxy on top of a distributed key-value store [Spa17].

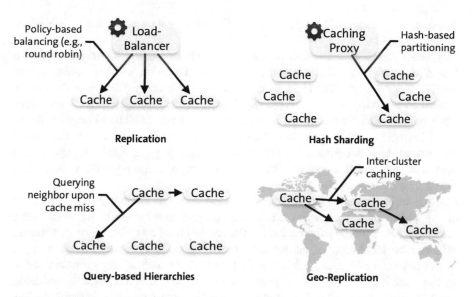

Fig. 3.3 Scalability mechanisms of web caches: replication, sharding, query-based hierarchies, and geo-replication

Web caching increases read scalability and fault tolerance, as objects can still be retrieved from web caches if the backend is temporarily unavailable [RS03]. As web caches only fetch content lazily, elasticity is easy to achieve: web cache replicas can be added at any time to scale reads.

3.3.3 Expiration-Based Web Caching

HTTP defines a Cache-Control header that both clients and servers leverage to control caching behavior. The server uses it to specify *expiration*, whereas the client employs it for *validation*.

Expirations are provided as TTLs at the granularity of seconds in order to be independent from clock synchronization. Additionally an Age header indicates how much time has passed since the original request, to preserve correct expirations when caches communicate with each other. The actual expiration time t_{exp} is then computed using the local clock's timestamp at the moment the response was received $now_{res}()$, giving $t_{exp} = now_{res}() + TTL - Age$. The server can set separate expirations for shared web caches (s-max-age) and client caches (max-age). Furthermore, it can restrict that responses should not be cached at all (no-cache and must-revalidate), should only be cached in client caches (private), or should not be persisted (no-store). By default, the *cache key* that uniquely identifies a cached response consists of the URL and the host. The Vary header allows to extend the cache key through specified request headers, e.g., `Accept-Language`, in order to cache the same resource in various representations.

Clients and web caches can **revalidate** objects by asking the origin server for potential modifications of a resource based on a version number (called `ETag` in HTTP) or a `Last-Modified` date (*cache validators*). The client thus has a means to explicitly request a fresh object and to save transfer time, if resources have not changed. Revalidations are performed through conditional requests based on `If-Modified-Since` and `If-None-Match` headers. If the timestamp or version does not match for the latest resource (e.g., a database object), the server returns a full response. Otherwise, an empty response with a `304 Not Modified` status code is returned.

Figure 3.4 illustrates the steps a web cache performs when handling a request: if the object of the requested URL was not previously cached, the web cache forwards the request to the backend. If a cache hit occurs, the cache determines whether the local copy of the resource is still fresh by checking $now() > t_{exp}$. If the object is still fresh, it is returned to the client without any communication to the backend. If $now() > t_{exp}$ and the cached resource has a cache validator, the web cache revalidates the resource, otherwise, the request is forwarded. This logic is performed for any cache in the chain from the client cache to reverse proxy caches. In a revalidation, clients can furthermore bound the age of a response (`max-age` and `min-fresh`), allow expired responses (`max-stale`) or explicitly load cached versions (`only-if-cached`). CDNs and reverse proxies typically ignore revalidation requests and simply serve the latest cached copy, in order to secure the origin against revalidation attacks [PB08].

The consistency model of expiration-based caching is Δ-atomicity. The problem is that Δ is a high, fixed TTL in the order of hours to weeks [RS03], as accurate TTLs for dynamic data are impossible to determine. This makes the native caching model of HTTP unsuitable for data management and is the reason why REST APIs of DBaaS, BaaS, and NoSQL systems explicitly circumvent HTTP caching [Dep, Hoo, Par, ALS10, Amaa, Dyn, Cal+11, Bie+15, Dat].

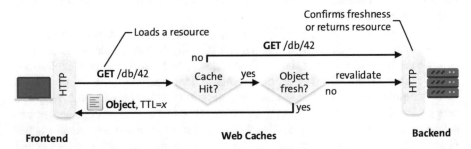

Fig. 3.4 Validation of resource freshness in expiration-based HTTP caching

3.3.4 Invalidation-Based Web Caching

CDNs and reverse proxy caches are *invalidation-based* HTTP caches. They extend
the expiration-based caching model and additionally expose (non-standardized)
interfaces for asynchronous cache invalidation. The backend has to explicitly send
an invalidation to every relevant invalidation-based cache. While CDN APIs forward
invalidations internally with efficient broadcasting protocols (e.g., bimodal multicast
[Spa17]), employing many reverse proxies can lead to a scalability problem, if many
invalidations occur. In general, an invalidation is required if a resource was updated
or deleted and invalidation-based caches have observed an expiration time greater
than the current time: $\exists t_{exp} : now() < t_{exp}$. For DBaaS/BaaS systems this condition
is non-trivial to detect, since updates may affect otherwise unrelated query results
and objects.

Besides their invalidation interfaces, CDNs (e.g., Akamai and Fastly [BPV08,
Spa17]) and reverse proxies (e.g., Varnish, Squid, Nginx, Apache Traffic Server
[Kam17, Ree08, Wes04]) often also provide further extensions to HTTP caching:

- Limited **application logic** can be executed in the cache. For example, the Varnish
  Control Language (VCL) allows to manipulate requests and responses, perform
  health checks and validate headers [Kam17].
- **Prefetching** mechanisms proactively populate the cache with resources that are
  likely to be requested in the near future.
- Edge-side **templating** languages like ESI [Tsi+01] allow to assemble responses
  from cached data and backend requests.
- By assigning tags to cacheable responses, efficient bulk invalidations of related
  resources can be performed (**tag-based invalidation**).
- Distributed **Denial of Service** (DDoS) attacks can automatically be mitigated and
  detected before the backend is compromised [PB08].
- Updated resources can be proactively pushed (**prewarming**).
- Real-time **access logs** may be used by the application for analytics and account-
  ing.
- **Stale resources** can be served while the backend is offline (`stale-on-error`)
  or during revalidations (`stale-while-revalidate`) [IET15].
- **Speed Kit**[5] [WGW+20] leverages Service Workers to control and maintain
  the client cache, reroute requests to a CDN, and apply transparent image
  optimization.

For latency, an important characteristic of invalidation-based caches is their
ability to maintain long-lived backend connections that incoming requests can be
multiplexed over. This significantly reduces the overhead of connection handshakes
as they only have to be performed over low-latency links between clients and
CDN edge nodes. In many cases, cloud services have end-to-end encryption as

---

[5]Speed Kit: https://speed-kit.com.

a requirement for authenticity, privacy, data integrity, and confidentiality. To this end, TLS certificates are deployed to CDNs and reverse proxies to terminate TLS connections on the network edge and to establish different connections to the backend. Thus, for encrypted REST APIs and websites, only client, CDN, and reverse proxy caches apply for HTTP caching, whereas forward and web proxy caches only observe encrypted traffic.

Previous research on web caching has focused on cache replacement strategies [PB03, Bre+99, Lab+09], CDN architectures [PB08, FFM04, Fre10], cache cooperation [KR01, Wes97, VW99, Fan+00], proxy and client extensions [Rab+03, Tsi+01, BR02], and changes to the caching model itself [KW97, Wor94, KW98, Bhi+02]. Further treatments of expiration-based and invalidation-based web caching are provided by Rabinovich and Spatscheck [RS03], Labrindis et al. [Lab+09], Nagaraj [Nag04], Buyya et al. [BPV08], and Grigorik [Gri13].

3.3.5   Challenges of Web Caching for Data Management

Both expiration-based and invalidation-based caching are challenging for data management, as they interfere with the consistency mechanisms of database systems. Figure 3.5 gives an example of how web caching affects consistency.

1. On the first request, the server has to set a TTL for the response. If the TTL is too low, caching has no effect. If it is too high, clients will experience many stale reads. Due to the dynamic nature of query results and objects in data management, TTLs are not known in advance.
2. When a second client updates the previously read object before its TTL expired, caches are in an inconsistent state. Even if the server could issue an invalidation (which is usually impossible for query results), the invalidation is asynchronous and only takes effect at some later point in time.
3. Reads that happen between the completed update and the initially provided expiration time will cause stale reads at expiration-based caches.

In conclusion, web caching for data management is considerably restricted because of several challenges:

- **Expiration-based caching** either degrades consistency (high TTLs) or causes very high cache miss rates (low TTLs).
- **Cache coherence** for DBaaS and BaaS REST APIs is currently achieved by marking all types of dynamic data as uncacheable.
- Currently, **TTL estimation** is a manual and error-prone process leading to low caching efficiency as TTLs do not adapt to changing workloads and differences between individual query responses.
- **Cache invalidation** requires detecting changes to files, objects, and query results in real-time based on the updates performed against the data management API.

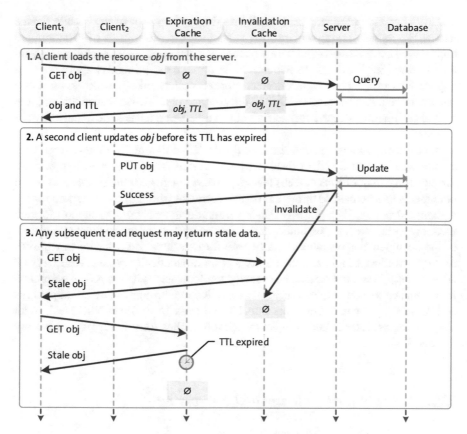

Fig. 3.5 Cache coherence problems of web caches for data management caused by access of two different clients

- Fetching **dynamic data** (e.g., query results) via REST/HTTP requires contacting a remote server, which involves the full end-to-end latency from the client to the server.
- With standard HTTP caching, clients cannot control **consistency requirements** on a per-user, per-session, or per-operation basis, as the server provides the HTTP caching metadata used by intermediate caches.

3.4   The Client Perspective: Processing, Rendering, and Caching for Mobile and Web Applications

Frontend performance is concerned with how fast data can be rendered and computations be performed at the client side. Incidentally, the frontend is often not considered during the design of a data management solution. However, as the SDK and API layer of a DBaaS/BaaS reach into the environment of the mobile device and utilize its networking and caching capabilities, some aspects of browsers are highly relevant for end-to-end performance. We will specifically examine frontend performance for browsers. In native mobile apps, most principles apply too, but applications can choose from different storage options like the files system and embedded relational databases. Due to the absence of a browser cache, though, the task of maintaining cache consistency with remote storage has to be handled by the application.

As of 2018, an average website downloads 107 different HTTP resources with a total size of over 3 MB of data to be transferred [Arc]. The web has evolved through three major forms of websites. **Hypertext documents** are simple text-based documents interconnected through links and formatted through basic markup for the content's structure. **Web pages** enrich hypertext documents through support for rich media types such as images, audio, and video, as well as complex layout and styling of the document's appearance. Finally, **web applications** add behavior to websites through JavaScript logic and the ability to programmatically request REST/HTTP APIs (Ajax). Web applications are usually implemented with single-page application frameworks that help to structure the application through architectural patterns and templating for rendering data into UI elements [Ang, Emb, Vue, Rea]. With the growing prevalence and complexity of web applications, the impact of latency increases.

3.4.1   Client-Side Rendering and Processing

The **critical rendering path** (CRP) describes the process that a browser performs in order to render a website from HTML, JavaScript, and CSS resources [Fir16, Gri13]. The dependency graph between these critical resources, i.e., files required for the initial paint, determines the length, size, and weight of the CRP. The *length* of the CRP is the minimum number of network round-trips required to render the web page. The *size* of the CRP is the number of critical resources that are loaded. The *weight* (also called "critical bytes") of the CRP is the combined size of all critical resources measured in bytes.

The execution of the CRP is illustrated in Fig. 3.6. After receiving the HTML from the network, the browser starts parsing it into a Document Object Model (DOM). If the HTML references CSS and JavaScript resources, the parser (respectively its look-ahead heuristics) will trigger their background download as soon as they are discovered. The CSS stylesheet is parsed into a CSS object model (CSSOM). CSS is *render-blocking*, as rendering can only proceed when the CSSOM is fully constructed and thus all styling information available. JavaScript can modify and read from both the DOM and CSSOM. It is *parser-blocking* as the HTML parser blocks until the discovered JavaScript is executed. Furthermore, JavaScript execution blocks until the CSSOM is available causing a chain of interdependencies. Only when the DOM and the CSSOM are constructed, and JavaScript is executed,

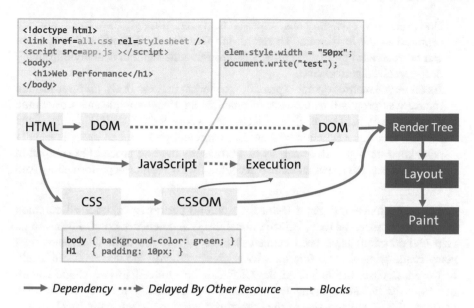

Fig. 3.6   The critical rendering path as a model for frontend performance

the browser starts to combine styling and layout information into a render tree, computes a layout, and paints the page on the screen.

The process of frontend performance optimization involves reducing the size, length, and weight of the CRP. Typical steps are loading JavaScript asynchronously, deferring its parsing, preconnecting and preloading critical resources, inlining critical CSS, applying compression, minification, and concatenation, optimizing JavaScript execution and CSS selector efficiency, and loading "responsive" images based on screen size [Wag17]. HTTP/2 eliminates the necessity for many common performance workarounds that negatively impact cacheability, for example, concatenation of resources [IET15].

End-user performance can be measured using different web performance metrics:

- Browsers implement events that indicate the completeness of the rendering process. The **DomContentLoaded** event is fired once the DOM has been constructed and no stylesheets block JavaScript execution.
- The **first paint** occurs when the browser renders the page for the first time. Depending on the structure of the CRP this can, for example, be a blank page with a background color or a visually complete page. The first paint metric can be refined to the *first meaningful paint* [Sak17] which is defined through the paint that produces the largest change in the visual layout.
- Once all resources of the website (in particular images, JavaScript and stylesheets) have been downloaded and processed, the **load** event is fired. The event indicates the completion of loading from an end user's perspective.

However, any asynchronous requests triggered through JavaScript are not captured in the load event. Therefore, the DomContentLoaded and load event can be decreased by loading resources through code without actually improving user-perceived performance.

- As all above metrics do not capture the rendering process itself, the **speed index** metric was proposed as a means of quantifying visual completeness over time [Mee12]. It is defined as $\int_0^\infty 1 - VC(t)\,dt$, where $VC(t) \in [0, 1]$ is the visual completeness as a function of time. Experimentally, the speed index is usually calculated through video analysis of a browser's loading process. In contrast to other metrics, the speed index also accounts for API requests performed by web applications.

Latency remains the major factor for frontend performance, once all common frontend optimizations (e.g., inlined critical CSS) and network optimizations (e.g., gzip compression) have been applied. The length of the CRP determines how many round-trips occur before the user is presented with the first rendered result. In the ideal case, the length of the CRP can be reduced to one single round-trip by only including asynchronous JavaScript and inlining CSS. In practice, however, the length and size of the critical rendering path is usually much longer [Wag17, Fir16]. The increasing predominance of web applications based on rich client-side JavaScript frameworks that consume data via API requests extends the impact of latency beyond the CRP. During navigation and rendering, the latency of asynchronously fetched resources is crucial to display data quickly and to apply user interactions without perceptible delay.

3.4.2   Client-Side Caching and Storage

In recent years, it became evident that moving more application logic into the client also requires **persistence** options to maintain application state within and across user sessions. Several client-side storage and caching APIs have been standardized and implemented in browsers. A comprehensive overview of client-side storage mechanisms is provided by Camden [Cam16]. In the following, we provide an overview of storage technologies relevant for this book:

HTTP Browser Cache.   The browser cache [IET15, Fie+99] works similar to other HTTP caches, except that it is exclusive to one user. Its main advantage is that it transparently operates on any HTTP resource. On the other hand, however, it cannot be programmatically controlled by the JavaScript application and operates purely expiration-based. Also, cached data can be evicted at any time making it impossible to build application logic on the presence of cached client-side data.

Cookies.   Through the HTTP `Cookie` header, the server can store strings in the client. Cookie values are automatically attached to each client request [IET15]. Cookies are very limited in control, size, and flexibility and therefore mainly used for session state management and user tracking. Cookies frequently cause performance problems as they can only be accessed synchronously and have to be transferred with each request.

Web SQL.   The goal of the WebSQL specification is to provide SQL-based access to an embedded relational database (e.g., SQLite) [Cam16]. However, as browser support is lacking, the development of WebSQL has mostly ceased in favor of the IndexedDB API.

IndexedDB.   The IndexedDB specification [AA17] describes a low-level database API that offers key-value storage, cursors over indices, and transactions. Despite its lack of a declarative query language, it can be used to implement an embedded database system in the client. In contrast to the browser cache, storage is persistent and controlled via an API. However, this implies that custom cache coherence or replication is required if IndexedDB is used to store a subset of the backend database.

Service Worker Cache.   Service Workers are background processes that can intercept, modify, and process HTTP requests and responses of a website [Ama16]. This allows implementing advanced network behavior such as an offline mode that continues serving responses even though the user lacks a mobile network connection. The Service Worker cache is a persistent, asynchronous map storing pairs of HTTP requests and responses. The default cache coherence mechanism is to store data indefinitely. However, the JavaScript code of the Service Worker can modify this behavior and implement custom cache maintenance strategies.

Local and Session Storage.   The DOM storage APIs [Cam16] allow persisting key-value pairs locally for a single session (`SessionStorage`) or across sessions (`LocalStorage`). The API only allows blocking `get` and `set` operations on keys and values. Due to its synchronous nature, the API is not accessible in background JavaScript processes (e.g., Service Workers).

The central problem of client-side storage and caching abstractions is that they have to be **manually controlled** by the application. Besides first attempts, there is furthermore no coupling between query languages and persistence APIs employed in the client and the DBaaS/BaaS [ALS10, Go+15, Lak+16]. This forces application developers to duplicate data-centric business logic and maintain cache consistency manually. The error-prone and complex task of manual cache maintenance prevents many applications from incorporating client-side storage into the application's data management. Client-side caching and storage standards potentially enable serving web applications in the absence of network connectivity (offline mode). However, this also requires new mechanisms for cache coherence of reads and query results as well as synchronization and concurrency control for updates made while being offline.

3.5   Challenges and Opportunities: Using Web Caching for Cloud Data Management

The network and the protocols involved in communication with cloud services are the fundamental cause of high latency. In this chapter, we discussed how most aspects of networking can be optimized, leaving end-to-end latency resulting from physical distance as the major remaining performance challenge. Even though REST and HTTP are widely used for DBaaS, BaaS, and NoSQL systems, their caching model is not easy to combine with the requirements of data management: Expiration-based caches interfere with the consistency guarantees of database systems, whereas invalidation-based caching requires non-trivial change detection for dynamic data. Frontend performance is defined by the highly latency-dependent critical rendering path. Modern browsers potentially allow latency reduction for data-centric API requests through storage abstractions. However, cache coherence needs to be solved in order to avoid sacrificing consistency for reduced latency. While latency reduction through HTTP caching is a mostly open problem for cloud data management, there are approaches (e.g. the Cache Sketch [Ges+15]) that consolidate expiration-based caching with data management in transparent fashion while preserving invariants such as consistency guarantees and correctness of query results. At the time of writing, however, Baqend[6] is the only commercial implementation of such an approach.

In the upcoming chapters, we will address the latency, scalability, and consistency challenges across the data management stack to achieve better performance for a wide spectrum of web and mobile applications.

References

[AA17] Joshua Bell Ali Alabbas. *Indexed Database API 2.0.* https://w3c.github.io/ IndexedDB/. (Accessed on 07/14/2017). 2017.

[All10] Subbu Allamaraju. *Restful web services cookbook: solutions for improving scalability and simplicity.* "O'Reilly Media, Inc.", 2010.

[Alo+04] Gustavo Alonso et al. "Web services". In: *Web Services.* Springer, 2004, pp. 123–149.

[ALS10] J. Chris Anderson, Jan Lehnardt, and Noah Slater. *CouchDB - The Definitive Guide: Time to Relax.* O'Reilly, 2010. ISBN: 978-0-596-15589-6. URL: http://www.oreilly.de/ catalog/9780596155896/index.html.

[Amaa] *Amazon Simple Storage Service (S3).* //aws.amazon.com/documentation/s3/. (Accessed on 07/28/2017). 2017. URL: //aws.amazon.com/documentation/s3/ (visited on 02/18/2017).

[Ama16] Sean Amarasinghe. *Service worker development cookbook.* English. OCLC: 958120287. 2016. ISBN: 978-1-78646-952-6. URL: http://lib.myilibrary.com?id= 952152 (visited on 01/28/2017).

---

[6]Baqend: https://www.baqend.com/.

[Amu17] Mike Amundsen. *RESTful Web Clients: Enabling Reuse Through Hypermedia*. 1st ed. O'Reilly Media, Feb. 2017. ISBN: 9781491921906. URL: http://amazon.com/o/ASIN/ 1491921900/.

[Ang] *Angular Framework*. https://angular.io/. (Accessed on 05/26/2017). 2017.

[Arc] *HTTP Archive*. http://httparchive.org/trends.php. Accessed: 2018-07-14. 2018.

[Bhi+02] Manish Bhide et al. "Adaptive push-pull: Disseminating dynamic web data". In: *IEEE Transactions on Computers* 51.6 (2002), pp. 652–668.

[Bie+15] Christopher D Bienko et al. *IBM Cloudant: Database as a Service Advanced Topics*. IBM Redbooks, 2015.

[Bla+10] Roi Blanco et al. "Caching search engine results over incremental in- dices". In: *Proceedings of the 33rd international ACM SIGIR conference on Research and development in information retrieval*. ACM, 2010, pp. 82–89. URL: http://dl.acm.org/ citation.cfm?id=1835466 (visited on 04/24/2015).

[Bor+04] C. BornhÃüvd et al. "Adaptive database caching with DBCache". In: *Data Engineering* 27.2 (2004), pp. 11–18. URL: http://sipew.org/staff/bornhoevd/IEEEBull'04.pdf (visited on 06/28/2012).

[BPV08] Rajkumar Buyya, Mukaddim Pathan, and Athena Vakali, eds. *Content Delivery Networks (Lecture Notes in Electrical Engineering)*. 2008th ed. Springer Sept. 2008. ISBN: 9783540778868. URL: http://amazon.com/o/ASIN/3540778861/.

[BR02] Laura Bright and Louiqa Raschid. "Using Latency-Recency Profiles for Data Delivery on the Web". In: *VLDB 2002, Proceedings of 28th International Conference on Very Large Data Bases, August 20–23, 2002, Hong Kong, China*. Morgan Kaufmann, 2002, pp. 550–561. URL: http://www.vldb.org/conf/2002/S16P01.pdf.

[Bre+99] Lee Breslau et al. "Web caching and Zipf-like distributions: Evidence and implications". In: *INFOCOM'99. Eighteenth Annual Joint Conference of the IEEE Computer and Communications Societies. Proceedings. IEEE*. Vol. 1. IEEE. IEEE, 1999, pp. 126–134. URL: http://ieeexplore.ieee.org/xpls/abs_all.jsp?arnumber=749260 (visited on 01/03/2015).

[Bro+13] Nathan Bronson et al. "TAO: Facebook's Distributed Data Store for the Social Graph." In: *USENIX Annual Technical Conference*. 2013, pp. 49–60. URL: http://dl.frz.ir/ FREE/papers-we-love/datastores/tao-facebook-distributed-datastore.pdf (visited on 09/28/2014).

[Cal+11] Brad Calder et al. "Windows Azure Storage: a highly available cloud storage service with strong consistency". In: *Proceedings of the Twenty-Third ACM Symposium on Operating Systems Principles*. ACM. ACM, 2011, pp. 143–157. URL: http://dl.acm. org/citation.cfm?id=2043571 (visited on 04/16/2014).

[Cam16] Raymond Camden. *Client-side data storage: keeping it local*. First edition. OCLC: ocn935079139. Beijing: O'Reilly, 2016. ISBN: 978-1-4919-3511-8.

[Can+01b] K. SelÃğuk Candan et al. "Enabling Dynamic Content Caching for Database-driven Web Sites". In: *SIGMOD*. New York, NY, USA: ACM, 2001, pp. 532–543. ISBN: 1-58113-332-4. DOI: 10.1145/375663.375736. URL: http://doi.acm.org/10. 1145/375663.375736 (visited on 10/04/2014).

[Car13] Josiah L. Carlson. *Redis in Action*. Greenwich, CT, USA: Manning Publications Co., 2013. ISBN: 1617290858, 9781617290855.

[Che+14] Yuchung Cheng et al. *Tcp fast open*. Tech. rep. 2014.

[Chu+13] Jerry Chu et al. "Increasing TCP's initial window". In: (2013).

[Dat] *Google Cloud Datastore*. https://cloud.google.com/datastore/docs/concepts/overview. (Accessed on 05/20/2017). 2017. URL: https://cloud.google.com/datastore/docs/ concepts/overview (visited on 02/18/2017).

[Dep] *Deployd: a toolkit for building realtime APIs*. https://github.com/deployd/deployd. (Accessed on 05/20/2017). 2017. URL: https://github.com/deployd/deployd (visited on 02/19/2017).

[DFR15b] Akon Dey, Alan Fekete, and Uwe Rohm. "REST+T: Scalable Transactions over HTTP". In: IEEE, Mar 2015, pp. 36–41. ISBN: 978-1-4799-8218-9. DOI:

[Nis+13] Rajesh Nishtala et al. "Scaling Memcache at Facebook". In: *NSDI*. USENIX Association, 2013, pp. 385–398.

[Ope]   *Open API Initiative*. https://www.openapis.org/. (Accessed on 07/28/2017). 2017.

[Par]   *Parse Server*. http://parseplatform.github.io/docs/parse-server/guide/. (Accessed on 07/28/2017). 2017. URL: http://parseplatform.github.io/docs/parse-server/guide/ (visited on 02/19/2017).

[PB03] Stefan Podlipnig and László Böszörményi. "A survey of Web cache replacement strategies". In: *ACM Comput. Surv.* 35.4 (2003), pp. 374–398. DOI: 10.1145/954339.954341.

[PB07] Al-Mukaddim Khan Pathan and Rajkumar Buyya. "A taxonomy and survey of content delivery networks". In: *Grid Computing and Distributed Systems Laboratory, University of Melbourne, Technical Report* (2007), p. 4. URL: http://cloudbus.org/reports/CDN-Taxonomy.pdf (visited on 09/28/2014).

[PB08] Mukaddim Pathan and Rajkumar Buyya. "A Taxonomy of CDNs". English. In: *Content Delivery Networks*. Ed. by Rajkumar Buyya, Mukaddim Pathan, and Athena Vakali. Vol. 9. Lecture Notes Electrical Engineering. Springer Berlin Heidelberg, 2008, pp. 33–77. ISBN: 978-3-540-77886-8. URL: http://dx.doi.org/10.1007/978-3-540-77887-5_2.

[Pos]   *PostgreSQL: Documentation: 9.6: High Availability, Load Balancing, and Replication*. https://www.postgresql.org/docs/9.6/static/high-availability.html (Accessed on 07/28/2017). 2017. URL: https://www.postgresql.org/docs/9.6/static/high-availability.html (visited on 02/04/2017).

[Pos81] Jon Postel. "Transmission control protocol". In: (1981).

[Rab+03] Michael Rabinovich et al. "Moving Edge-Side Includes to the Real Edge - the Clients". In: *4th USENIX Symposium on Internet Technologies and Systems, USITS'03, Seattle, Washington, USA, March 26–28, 2003*. Ed. by Steven D. Gribble. USENIX, 2003. URL: http://www.usenix.org/events/usits03/tech/rabinovich.html.

[RAR13] Leonard Richardson, Mike Amundsen, and Sam Ruby. *RESTful Web APIs: Services for a Changing World*. "O'Reilly Media, Inc.", 2013.

[Rea]   *React - A JavaScript library for building user interfaces*. https://facebook.github.io/react/. (Accessed on 05/26/2017). 2017.

[Ree08] Will Reese. "Nginx: the high-performance web server and reverse proxy". In: *Linux Journal* 2008.173 (2008), p. 2.

[Res17] E. Rescorla. *The Transport Layer Security (TLS) Protocol Version 1.3 (Draft)*. https://tools.ietf.org/html/draft-ietf-tls-tls13-21. (Accessed on 07/29/2017). 2017.

[RS03] M. Rabinovich and O. Spatscheck. "Web caching and replication". In: *SIGMOD Record* 32.4 (2003), p. 107. URL: http://www.sigmod-org/publications/sigmod.record/0312/20.WebCachingReplication2.pdf (visited on 06/28/2012).

[Sak17] Kunihiko Sakamoto. *Time to First Meaningful Paint: a layout-based approach*. https://docs.google.com/document/d/1BR94tJdZLsin5poeet0XoTW60M0SjvOJQttKT-JK8HI/. (Accessed on 07/16/2017). 2017.

[Spa17] Bruce Spang. *Building a Fast and Reliable Purging System* https://www.fastly.com/blog/building-fast-and-reliable-purging-system/ (Accessed on 07/30/2017). Feb 2017.

[Tsi+01] Mark Tsimelzon et al. "ESI language specification 1.0". In: *Akamai Technologies, Inc. Cambridge, MA, USA, Oracle Corporation, Redwood City, CA, USA* (2001), pp. 1–0.

[TW11] Andrew S. Tanenbaum and David Wetherall. *Computer networks, 5th Edition*. Pearson, 2011. ISBN: 0132553171. URL: http://www.worldcat.org/oclc/698581231.

[Usa]   *Usage Statistics of HTTP/2 for Websites, July 2017*. https://w3techs.com/technologies/details/ce-http2/all/all (Accessed on 07/29/2017). 2017.

[Vak06] Athena Vakali. *Web Data Management Practices: Emerging Techniques and Technologies: Emerging Techniques and Technologies*. IGI Global, 2006.

[Vue]   *Vue.js*. https://vuejs.org/. (Accessed on 05/26/2017). 2017.

[VW99] Paul Vixie and Duane Wessels. *Hyper Text Caching Protocol (HTCP/0.0)*. Tech. rep. 1999.

[Wag17] Jeremy Wagner. *Web Performance in Action: Building Faster Web Pages.* Manning Publications, 2017. ISBN: 1617293776. URL: https://www.amazon. com/Web-Performance-Action-Building-Faster/dp/1617293776?SubscriptionId= 0JYN1NVW651KCA56C102&tag=techkie-20&linkCode=xm2&camp=2025& creative=165953&creativeASIN=1617293776.

[Wan99] J. Wang. "A survey of web caching schemes for the internet". In: *ACM SIGCOMM Computer Communication Review* 29.5 (1999), pp. 36–46. URL: http://dl.acm.org/ citation.cfm?id=505701 (visited on 06/28/2012).

[WDM01] Jörg Widmer, Robert Denda, and Martin Mauve. "A survey on TCP-friendly congestion control". In: *IEEE network* 15.3 (2001), pp. 28–37.

[Wes04] Duane Wessels. *Squid - the definitive guide: making the most of your internet.* O'Reilly, 2004. ISBN: 978-0-596-00162-9. URL: http://www.oreilly.de/catalog/squid/ index.html.

[Wes97] Duane Wessels. "Application of internet cache protocol (ICP), version 2". In: (1997).

[WGW+20] Wolfram Wingerath, Felix Gessert, Erik Witt, et al. "Speed Kit: A Polyglot & GDPR-Compliant Approach For Caching Personalized Content". In: *36th IEEE International Conference on Data Engineering, ICDE 2020, Dallas, Texas, April 20–24, 2020.* 2020.

[Wor94] Kurt Jeffery Worrell. "Invalidation in Large Scale Network Object Caches". In: (1994).

[WP11] Erik Wilde and Cesare Pautasso. *REST: from research to practice.* Springer Science & Business Media, 2011.

[WPR10] Jim Webber, Savas Parastatidis, and Ian Robinson. *REST in practice: Hypermedia and systems architecture.* "O'Reilly Media, Inc.", 2010.

[Xu+14] Yuehai Xu et al. "Characterizing Facebook's Memcached Workload". In: *IEEE Internet Computing* 18.2 (2014), pp. 41–49.

[IET15] IETF. "RFC 7540 - Hypertext Transfer Protocol Version 2 (HTTP/2)". In: (2015).

Chapter 4
Systems for Scalable Data Management

Irrespective of the server-side architecture, scalable data management is the primary challenge for high performance. Business and presentation logic can be designed to scale by virtue of stateless processing or by offloading the problem of state to a shared data store. Therefore, the requirements of high availability and elastic scalability depend on database systems.

Today, data is produced and consumed at a rapid pace. This has led to novel approaches for scalable data management subsumed under the term "NoSQL" database systems to handle the ever-increasing data volume and request loads. However, the heterogeneity and diversity of the numerous existing systems impede the well-informed selection of a data store appropriate for a given application context. In this section, we will provide a high-level overview of the current NoSQL landscape. In Chap. 8, we will furthermore survey commonly used techniques for sharding, replication, storage management, and query processing in these systems to derive a classification scheme for NoSQL databases. A straightforward and abstract decision model for restricting the choice of appropriate NoSQL systems based on application requirements concludes the book in Chap. 9.

4.1 NoSQL Database Systems

Traditional relational database management systems (RDBMSs) provide robust mechanisms to store and query structured data under strong consistency and transaction guarantees and have reached an unmatched level of reliability, stability, and support through decades of development. In recent years, however, the amount of useful data in some application areas has become so vast that it cannot be stored or processed by traditional database solutions. User-generated content in social networks and data retrieved from large sensor networks are only two examples of this phenomenon commonly referred to as **Big Data** [Lan01]. A class of novel

© Springer Nature Switzerland AG 2020
F. Gessert et al., *Fast and Scalable Cloud Data Management*,
https://doi.org/10.1007/978-3-030-43506-6_4

data storage systems able to cope with the management of Big Data are subsumed under the term **NoSQL databases**, many of which offer horizontal scalability and higher availability than relational databases by sacrificing querying capabilities and consistency guarantees. These trade-offs are pivotal for service-oriented computing and "as-a-service" models since any stateful service can only be as scalable and fault-tolerant as its underlying data store.

Please note, that throughout this book, we address Big Data management, i.e., database and application techniques for dealing with data at high velocity, volume, and variety (coined as the "three Vs" [ZS17]). We only cover Big Data analytics, where it directly concerns the design of our low-latency methodology for data management and refer to our tutorials for further background on systems and approaches for analytics [GR15, GR16, GWR17, WGR+18, WGR19].

There are dozens[1] of NoSQL database systems and it is hard for practitioners and researchers to keep track of where they excel, where they fail or even where they differ, as implementation details change quickly and feature sets evolve over time. In this section, we therefore aim to provide an overview of the NoSQL landscape by discussing employed concepts rather than system specificities and explore the requirements typically posed to NoSQL database systems, the techniques used to fulfill these requirements and the trade-offs that have to be made in the process. Our focus lies on key-value, document, and wide-column stores since these NoSQL categories cover the most relevant techniques and design decisions in the space of scalable data management and are well suitable for the context of scalable cloud data management.

In order to abstract from implementation details of individual NoSQL systems, high-level classification criteria can be used to group similar data stores into categories. As shown in Fig. 4.1, we will describe how NoSQL systems can be cat-

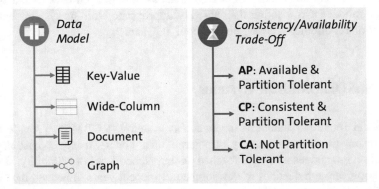

Fig. 4.1 The two high-level approaches of categorizing NoSQL systems according to data models and consistency-availability trade-offs

---

[1] An extensive list of NoSQL database systems can be found at http://nosql-database.org/.

egorized by their data model (key-value stores, document stores, and wide-column stores) and the safety-liveness trade-offs in their design (CAP and PACELC).

4.2 Data Models: Key-Value, Wide-Column and Document Stores

The most commonly employed distinction between NoSQL databases is the way they store and allow access to data. Each system covered in this overview can be categorized as either a key-value store, document store, or wide-column store.

4.2.1 Key-Value Stores

A key-value store consists of a set of key-value pairs with unique keys. Due to this simple structure, it only supports get and put operations. As the nature of the stored value is transparent to the database, pure key-value stores do not support operations beyond simple CRUD (Create, Read, Update, Delete). Key-value stores are therefore often referred to as **schemaless** [SF12]: any assumptions about the structure of stored data are implicitly encoded in the application logic (*schema-on-read* [Kle17]) and not explicitly defined through a data definition language (*schema-on-write*).

The obvious advantages of this data model lie in its simplicity. The very simple abstraction makes it easy to partition and query data so that the database system can achieve low latency as well as high throughput. However, if an application demands more complex operations, e.g., range queries, this data model is not powerful enough. Figure 4.2 illustrates how user account data and settings might be stored in a key-value store. Since queries more complex than simple lookups are not supported, data has to be analyzed inefficiently in application code to extract information like whether cookies are supported or not (`cookies: false`).

Fig. 4.2 Key-value stores offer efficient storage and retrieval of arbitrary values

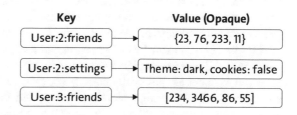

Fig. 4.3 Document stores are
aware of the internal structure
of the stored entity and thus
can support queries

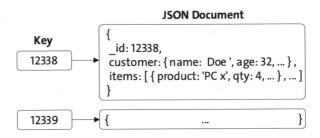

4.2.2 Document Stores

A document store is a key-value store that restricts values to semi-structured formats
such as JSON documents like the one illustrated in Fig. 4.3. This restriction in
comparison to key-value stores brings great flexibility in accessing the data. It is not
only possible to fetch an entire document by its ID, but also to retrieve only parts
of a document, e.g., the age of a customer, and to execute queries like aggregations,
query-by-example or even full-text search.

4.2.3 Wide-Column Stores

Wide-column stores inherit their name from the image that is often used to explain
the underlying data model: a relational table with many sparse columns. Technically,
however, a wide-column store is closer to a distributed multi-level[2] sorted map: the
first-level keys identify rows which themselves consist of key-value pairs. The first-
level keys are called **row keys**, the second-level keys are called **column keys**. This
storage scheme makes tables with arbitrarily many columns feasible because there
is no column key without a corresponding value. Hence, null values can be stored
without any space overhead. The set of all columns is partitioned into so-called
column families to co-locate columns on disk that are usually accessed together.

On disk, wide-column stores do not co-locate all data from each row, but instead,
values of the same column family *and* from the same row. Hence, an entity (a
row) cannot be retrieved by one single lookup as in a document store but has to be
joined from the columns of all column families. However, this storage layout usually
enables highly efficient data compression and makes retrieving only a portion of an
entity fast. All data is stored in lexicographic order of the keys, so that rows that are
accessed together are physically co-located, given a careful key design. As all rows
are distributed into contiguous ranges (so-called **tablets**) among different **tablet
servers**, row scans only involve few servers and thus are very efficient.

---

[2]In some systems (e.g., BigTable and HBase), multi-versioning is implemented by adding a
timestamp as a third-level key.

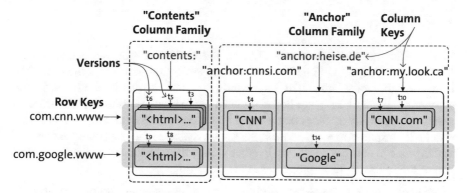

Fig. 4.4 Data in a wide-column store

Bigtable [Cha+08], which pioneered the wide-column model, was specifically developed to store a large collection of web pages as illustrated in Fig. 4.4. Every row in the table corresponds to a single web page. The row key is a concatenation of the URL components in reversed order, and every column key is composed of the column family name and a column qualifier, separated by a colon. There are two column families: the "contents" column family with only one column holding the actual web page and the "anchor" column family holding links to each web page, each in a separate column. Every cell in the table (i.e., every value accessible by the combination of row and column key) can be versioned by timestamps or version numbers. It is important to note that much of the information of an entity lies in the keys and not only in the values [Cha+08].

4.3   Pivotal Trade-Offs: Latency vs. Consistency vs. Availability

Another defining property of a database apart from how data is stored and how it can be accessed is the level of consistency that is provided. Some databases are built to guarantee strong consistency and serializability (ACID[3].), while others favor availability (BASE[4].). This trade-off is inherent to every distributed database system and the huge number of different NoSQL systems shows that there is a wide spectrum between the two paradigms. In the following, we explain the two theorems CAP and PACELC according to which database systems can be categorized by their respective positions in this spectrum.

---

[3]ACID [HR83]: **A**tomicity, **C**onsistency, **I**solation, **D**urability.
[4]BASE [Pri08]: **B**asically **A**vailable, **S**oft-state, **E**ventually consistent.

4.3.1   CAP

Like the famous FLP Theorem[5] [FLP85], the CAP Theorem, presented by Eric
Brewer at PODC 2000 [Bre00] and later proven by Gilbert and Lynch [GL02],
is one of the most influential impossibility results in the field of distributed
computing. It places an upper bound on what can be accomplished by a distributed
system. Specifically, it states that a sequentially consistent read/write register[6] that
eventually responds to every request, cannot be realized in an asynchronous system
that is prone to network partitions. In other words, the register can guarantee at most
two of the following three properties at the same time:

- **Consistency (C)**. Reads and writes are always executed atomically and are
  strictly consistent (linearizable [HW90]). Put differently, all clients have the same
  view on the data at all times.
- **Availability (A)**. Every non-failing node in the system can always accept read
  and write requests from clients and will eventually return with a meaningful
  response, i.e., not with an error message.
- **Partition-tolerance (P)**. The system upholds the previously displayed consistency guarantees and availability in the presence of message loss between the
  nodes or partial system failure.

Brewer argues that a system can be both available and consistent in normal operation, but in the presence of a network partition, this is not possible: if the system
continues to work in spite of the partition, there is some non-failing node that has
lost contact to the other nodes and thus has to decide to either continue processing
client requests to preserve availability (AP, **eventually consistent systems**) or to
reject client requests in order to uphold consistency guarantees (CP). The first option
violates consistency because it might lead to stale reads and conflicting writes,
while the second option obviously sacrifices availability. There are also systems
that usually are available and consistent but fail completely when there is a partition
(CA), for example, single-node systems. It has been shown that the CAP-theorem
holds for any consistency property that is at least as strong as causal consistency,
which also includes any recency bounds on the permissible staleness of data (Δ-
atomicity) [MAD+11]. Serializability as the correctness criterion of transactional
isolation does not require strong consistency. However, similar to consistency,
serializability cannot be achieved under network partitions either [DGMS85].

The classification of NoSQL systems as either AP, CP or CA vaguely reflects
the individual systems' capabilities and hence is widely accepted as a means for
high-level comparisons. However, it is important to note that the CAP Theorem

---

[5]The FLP theorem states, that in a distributed system with asynchronous message delivery, no
algorithm can guarantee to reach a *consensus* between participating nodes if one or more of them
can fail by stopping.

[6]A read/write register is a data structure with only two operations: setting a specific value (`set`)
and returning the latest value that was set (`get`).

actually does not state anything on normal operation; it merely expresses whether a system favors availability or consistency *in the face of a network partition*. In contrast to the FLP-Theorem, the CAP theorem assumes a failure model that allows arbitrary messages to be dropped, reordered or delayed indefinitely. Under the weaker assumption of reliable communication channels (i.e., messages always arrive but asynchronously and possibly reordered) a CAP-system is in fact possible using the Attiya, Bar-Noy, Dolev algorithm [ABN+95], as long as a majority of nodes are up.[7]

4.3.2 PACELC

The shortcomings of the CAP Theorem were addressed by Abadi [Aba12] who points out that the CAP Theorem fails to capture the trade-off between latency and consistency during *normal* operation, even though it has proven to be much more influential on the design of distributed systems than the availability-consistency trade-off in failure scenarios. He formulates PACELC which unifies both trade-offs and thus portrays the design space of distributed systems more accurately. From PACELC, we learn that in case of a Partition, there is an Availability-Consistency trade-off; Else, i.e., in normal operation, there is a Latency-Consistency trade-off.

This classification offers two possible choices for the partition scenario (A/C) and also two for normal operation (L/C) and thus appears more fine-grained than the CAP classification. However, many systems cannot be assigned exclusively to one single PACELC class and one of the four PACELC classes, namely PC/EL, can hardly be assigned to any system.

In summary, NoSQL database systems support applications in achieving horizontal scalability, high availability and backend performance through differentiated trade-offs in functionality and consistency.

4.4 Relaxed Consistency Models

CAP and PACELC motivate that there is a broad spectrum of choices regarding consistency guarantees and that the strongest guarantees are irreconcilable with high availability. In the following, we examine different consistency models that fulfill two requirements needed in modern application development. First, the models must exhibit sufficient *power* to precisely express latency-consistency trade-offs

---

[7]Therefore, consensus as used for coordination in many NoSQL systems either natively [Bak+11] or through coordination services like Chubby and Zookeeper [Hun+10] is considered a "harder" problem than strong consistency, as it cannot even be guaranteed in a system with reliable channels [FLP85].

introduced by caching and replication. Second, the consistency models must have
the *simplicity* to allow easy reasoning about application behavior for developers and
system architects.

As summarized in Fig. 4.5, NoSQL systems exhibit various relaxed consistency
guarantees that are usually a consequence of replication and caching. **Eventual
consistency** is a commonly used term to distinguish between strongly consistent
(linearizable) systems and systems with relaxed guarantees. Eventual consistency
is slightly stronger than weak consistency, as it demands that in the absence of
failures, the system converges to a consistent state. The problem with eventual
consistency is that it purely represents a *liveness* guarantee, i.e., it asserts that
some property is eventually reached [Lyn96]. However, it lacks a *safety* guarantee:
eventual consistency does not prescribe which state the database converges to
[Bai15, p. 20]. For example, the database could eventually converge to a null value
for every data item and would still be eventually consistent. For this reason, more
specific relaxed consistency models provide a framework for reasoning about safety
guarantees that are weaker than strong, immediate consistency.

The idea of **relaxing correctness guarantees** is wide-spread in the database
world. Even in single-node systems, providing ACID and in particular serializability incurs performance penalties through limited concurrency and contention,
especially on multi-core hardware [Gra+76]. As a consequence, weak isolation
models relax the permissible transaction schedules by allowing certain concurrency
anomalies that are not present under serializability. Bailis et al. [Bai+13b] surveyed

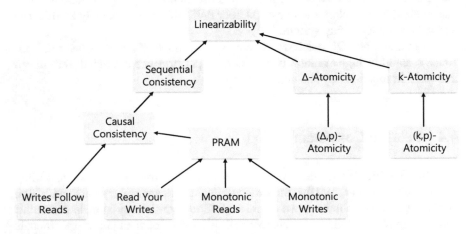

Fig. 4.5 An overview of selected consistency models. Arrows indicate which models are subsumed by a stronger model

18 representative systems claiming to provide ACID or "NewSQL"[8] guarantees. Of these systems, only three provided serializability by default, and eight did not offer serializable isolation at all.

4.4.1 Strong Consistency Models

The strongest consistency guarantee in a concurrent system is linearizability (see Definition 4.1) introduced by Herlihy and Wing [HW90]. A linearizable system behaves analogously to a single-node system, i.e., each read and write appears to be applied at one defined point in time between invocation and response. While linearizability is the gold standard for correctness, it is not only subject to the CAP theorem, but also hard to implement at scale [Lee+15, Ajo+15, Bal+15, DGMS85, Kra+13, Ter+13, BK13, BT11, Wad+11].

Definition 4.1 An execution satisfies **linearizability**, if all operations are totally ordered by their arrival time. Any read with an invocation time larger than the response time of a preceding write is able to observe its effects. Concurrent operations must guarantee sequential consistency, i.e., overlapping write operations become visible to all reads in a defined global order.

Sequential consistency (see Definition 4.2) is a frequently used model in operating system and hardware design that is slightly weaker than linearizability. It does not guarantee any recency constraints, but it ensures that writes become visible for each client in the same order. So in contrast to linearizability, the global ordering of operations is not required to respect real-time ordering, only the local real-time ordering for each client is preserved.

Definition 4.2 An execution satisfies **sequential consistency**, if there is a global order of read and write operations that is consistent with the local order in which they were submitted by each client.

Consistency in replicated systems is sometimes confused with consistency in ACID transactions. With respect to ACID, consistency implies that no integrity constraints are violated, e.g., foreign key constraints. In distributed, replicated systems, consistency is an ordering guarantee for reads and writes that are potentially executed concurrently and on different copies of the data. The main correctness criterion for transactional isolation is serializability, which does not require strong consistency. If conflict serializability is combined with strong consistency, it is

---

[8]The term NewSQL was coined by relational database vendors seeking to provide similar scalability and performance as NoSQL databases while maintaining well-known abstractions such as SQL as a query language and ACID guarantees [Gro+13]. This is achieved by introducing trade-offs that are mostly similar to that of NoSQL databases. Examples are H-Store [Kal+08], VoltDB [SW13], Clustrix [Clu], NuoDB [Nuo], and Calvin [Tho+12] that are discussed in Chap. 6.

referred to as strict (or strong) serializability (e.g., in Spanner [Coo13]) or commit order-preserving conflict serializability (COCSR) [WV02]. Just as linearizability, serializability is also provably irreconcilable with high availability [Bai+13c].

4.4.2　Staleness-Based Consistency Models

To increase efficiency, staleness-based models allow *stale reads*, i.e., returning outdated data. The two common measures for quantifying staleness are (wall-clock) *time* and object *versions*. In contrast, k-atomicity (see Definition 4.3) [AAB05] bounds staleness by only allowing reads to return a value written by one of the k preceding updates. Thus k-atomicity with $k = 1$ is equivalent to linearizability.

Definition 4.3 An execution satisfies k-**atomicity**, if any read returns one of the versions written by the k preceding, completed writes that must have a global order that is consistent with real-time order.

Δ-atomicity (see Definition 4.4) introduced by Golab et al. [GLS11] expresses a time-based recency guarantee. Intuitively, Δ is the upper bound on staleness observed for any read in the system, i.e., it never happens that the application reads data that has been stale for longer than Δ time units.

Definition 4.4 An execution satisfies Δ-**atomicity**, if any read returns either the latest preceding write or the value of a write that returned at most Δ time units ago.

Δ-atomicity is a variant of the influential *atomic* semantics definition introduced by Lamport in the context of inter-process communication [Lam86b, Lam86a]. Atomicity and linearizability are equivalent [VV16], i.e., they demand that there is a logical **point of linearization** between invocation and response for each operation at which it appears to be applied instantaneously [HW90]. An execution is Δ-atomic, if by decreasing the start time of each read operation by Δ produces an atomic execution. Lamport also introduced two relaxed properties of *regular* and *safe* semantics that are still often used in the literature. In the absence of a concurrent write, regular and safe reads behave exactly like atomic reads. However, during concurrent writes, safe reads are allowed to return arbitrary values.[9] A read under regular semantics returns either the latest completed write or the result of any concurrent write. The extension of safety and regularity to Δ-safety, Δ-regularity, k-safety, and k-regularity is straightforward [AAB05, GLS11, Bai+14b].

Other time-based staleness models from the literature are very similar to Δ-atomicity. Delta consistency by Singla et al. [SRH97], timed consistency by Torres-Rojas et al. [TAR99], and bounded staleness by Mahajan et al. [Mah+11] all express that a write should become visible before a defined maximum delay.

---

[9]The usefulness of this property has been criticized for database systems, as no typical database would return values that have never been written, even under concurrent writes [Ber14].

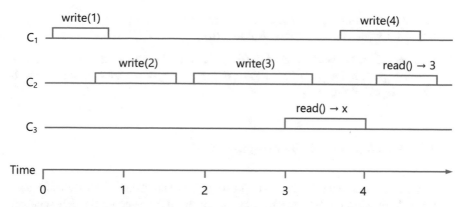

Fig. 4.6 An example execution of interleaved reads and writes from three clients that yields different read results depending on the consistency model. Brackets indicate the time between invocation and response of an operation

Δ-atomicity is hard to measure experimentally due to its dependency on a global time. Golab et al. [Gol+14] proposed Γ-atomicity as a closely related alternative that is easier to capture in benchmarks. The central difference is that the Γ parameter also allows writes to be reordered with a tolerance of Γ time units, whereas Δ-atomicity only considers earlier starting points for reads, while maintaining the order of writes. With NoSQLMark, we proposed an experimental methodology to measure lower and upper staleness bounds [Win+15].

For illustration of these models, please consider the example execution in Fig. 4.6. The result x of the read operation performed by client C_3 depends on the consistency model:

- With *atomicity* (including $k = 1$ and $\Delta = 0$) or *linearizability*, x can be either 2 or 3. x cannot be 4 since the later read of 3 by client C_2 would then violate linearizability.
- Under *sequential consistency* semantics, x can be 0 (the initial value), 1, 2, 3, or 4. As C_3 only performs a read, no local order has to be maintained. It can be serialized to the other clients' operations in any order.
- Given *regular* semantics, x can be either 2, 3, or 4.
- Under *safe* semantics, x can be any value.
- For Δ-*atomicity* with $\Delta = 1$, x can be 2 or 3. With $\Delta = 2$, x can be 1, 2, or 3: if the begin of the read was stretched by $\Delta = 2$ time units to begin at time 1, then 1, 2, and 3 would be reads satisfying atomicity.
- For k-*atomicity* with $k = 2$, x can be 1, 2, or 3: compared to atomicity, a lag of one older object version is allowed.

Δ-atomicity and k-atomicity can be extended to the probabilistic guarantees (Δ, p)-atomicity and (k, p)-atomicity (see Definition 4.5) [Bai+14b]. This allows expressing the average time or version-based lag as a distribution. For consistency benchmarks and simulations, these values are preferable, as they express more details than Δ-atomicity and k-atomicity which are just bounded by the maximum encountered values [BWT17, Ber14, Bai+14b].

Definition 4.5 An execution satisfies (Δ, p)-**atomicity**, if reads are Δ-atomic with probability p. Similarly, an execution satisfies (k, p)-**atomicity**, if reads are k-atomic with probability p.

4.4.3   Session-Based Consistency Models

Data-centric consistency models like linearizability and Δ-atomicity describe consistency from the provider's perspective, i.e., in terms of synchronization schemes to provide certain guarantees. Client-centric or session-based models take the perspective of clients interacting with the database and describe guarantees an application expects within a session.

Monotonic writes consistency (see Definition 4.6) guarantees that updates from a client do not get overwritten or reordered. Systems that lack this guarantee make it hard to reason about how updates behave, as they can be seen by other clients in a different order [Vog09]. For example, in a social network without monotonic write consistency, posts by a user could be observed in a different, potentially nonsensical order by other users.

Definition 4.6 A session satisfies **monotonic writes consistency**, if the order of all writes from that session is maintained for reads.

Monotonic reads consistency (see Definition 4.7) guarantees that if a client has read version n of an object, it will later only see versions $\geq n$ [TS07]. For example on a content website, this would prevent a user from first seeing a revised edition of an article and then upon a later return to the page reading the unrevised article.

Definition 4.7 A session satisfies **monotonic reads consistency**, if reads return versions in a monotonically increasing order.

With read your writes consistency (see Definition 4.8) clients are able to observe their own interactions. For example, in a web application with user-generated content, a user could reload the page and still see the update he applied.

Definition 4.8 A session satisfies **read your writes consistency**, if reads return a version that is equal to or higher than the latest version written in that session.

Combining the above three session guarantees yields the PRAM consistency level (see Definition 4.9) [LS88a]. It prescribes that all clients observe writes from different processes in their local order, i.e., as if the writes were in a pipeline. However, in contrast to sequential consistency, there is no global order for writes.

Definition 4.9 If monotonic writes consistency, monotonic reads consistency, and read your writes consistency are guaranteed, **pipelined random access memory (PRAM) consistency** is satisfied.

With writes follow reads consistency (see Definition 4.10), applications get the guarantee that their writes will always be accompanied by the relevant information that might have influenced the write. For example, writes follow reads (also called session causality) prevents the anomaly of a user responding to a previous post or comment on a website where other users would observe the response without seeing the original post it is based on.

Definition 4.10 A session satisfies **writes follow reads consistency**, if its writes are ordered after any other writes that were observed by previous reads in the session.

Causal consistency (see Definition 4.11) [Ady99, Bai+13c] combines the previous session guarantees. It is based on the concept of potential causality introduced through Lamport's *happened-before* relation in the context of message passing [Lam78]. An operation a causally depends on an operation b, if [HA90]:

1. a and b were issued by the same client and the database received b before a,
2. a is a read that observed the write b, or
3. a and b are connected transitively through condition 1. and/or 2.

In distributed systems, causality is often tracked using *vector clocks* [Fid87]. Causal consistency can be implemented through a middleware or directly in the client by tracking causal dependencies and only revealing updates when their causal dependencies are visible, too [Bai+13a, Ber+13]. Causal consistency is the strongest guarantee that can be achieved with high availability in the CAP theorem's system model of unreliable channels and asynchronous messaging [MAD+11]. The reason for causal consistency being compatible with high availability is that causal consistency does not require **convergence** of replicas and does not imply staleness bounds [GH02]. Replicas can be in completely different states, as long as they only return writes where causal dependencies are met.

Bailis et al. [Bai+13a] argued that **potential causality** leads to a high fan-out of potentially relevant data. Instead, application-defined causality can help to minimize the actual dependencies. In practice, however, potential causality can be determined automatically through dependency tracking (e.g., in COPS [Llo+11]), while explicit causality forces application developers to declare dependencies.

Causal consistency can be combined with a timing constraint demanding that the global ordering respects causal consistency with tolerance Δ for each read, yielding a model called *timed causal consistency* [TM05]. This model is weaker than Δ-atomicity: timed causal consistency with $\Delta = 0$ yields causal consistency, while Δ-atomicity with $\Delta = 0$ yields linearizability.

Definition 4.11 If both PRAM and writes follow reads are guaranteed, **causal consistency** is satisfied.

Besides the discussed consistency models, many different deviations have been proposed and implemented in the literature. Viotti and Vukolic [VV16] give a comprehensive survey and formal definitions of consistency models. In particular, they review the overlapping definitions used in different lines of work across the distributed systems, operating systems, and database research community.

While strong guarantees are a sensible default for application developers, consistency guarantees are often relaxed in practice to shift the trade-off towards non-functional availability and performance requirements.

4.5   Offloading Complexity to the Cloud: Database- and Backend-as-a-Service

Cloud data management is the research field tackling the design, implementation, evaluation and application implications of database systems in cloud environments [GR15, GR16, GWR17, WGR+18, WGR19, WGW+20]. We group cloud data management systems into two categories: **Database-as-a-Service** (DBaaS) and **Backend-as-a-Service** (BaaS). In the DBaaS model, only data management is covered. Therefore, application logic in a two- and three-tier architecture has to employ an additional IaaS or PaaS cloud. BaaS combines a DBaaS with custom application logic and standard APIs for web and app development. BaaS is a form of *serverless* computing, an architectural approach that describes applications which mostly rely on cloud services for both application logic and storage [Rob16]. Besides the BaaS mode, serverless architectures can also make use of **Function-as-a-Service** (FaaS) providers, that provide scalable and stateless execution of business logic functions in a highly elastic environment (e.g., AWS Lambda, and Google Cloud Functions). BaaS combines the concepts of DBaaS with a FaaS execution layer for business logic.

4.5.1   Database-as-a-Service

Hacigumus et al. [HIM02] introduced DBaaS as an approach to run databases without acquiring hardware or software. As the landscape of DBaaS systems has become a highly heterogeneous ecosystem, we propose a two-dimensional classification as shown in Fig. 4.7. The first dimension is the data model ranging from structured relational systems over semi-structured or schema-free data to completely unstructured data. The second dimension describes the deployment model.

Cloud-deployed databases use an IaaS or PaaS cloud to provision an operating system and the database software as an opaque application. Cloud providers usually maintain a repository of pre-built machine images containing RDBMSs, NoSQL databases, or analytics platforms that can be deployed as a virtual machine (VM) [Bar+03]. While cloud-deployed systems allow for a high degree of customization,

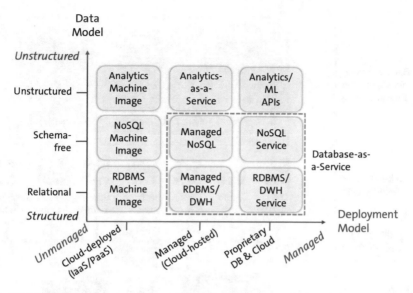

Fig. 4.7 Classes of cloud databases and DBaaS systems according to their data model and deployment model

maintenance (e.g., operating system and database updates), as well as operational duties (e.g., scaling in and out) have to be implemented or performed manually.

In **managed** cloud databases, the service provider is responsible for configuration, scaling, provisioning, monitoring, backup, privacy, and access control [Cur+11a]. Many commercial DBaaS providers offer standard database systems (e.g., MongoDB, Redis, and MySQL) as a managed service. For example MongoDB Atlas provides a managed NoSQL database [Mon], Amazon Elastic Map-Reduce [Amab] is an Analytics-as-a-Service based on managed Hadoop clusters, and Azure SQL Server offers a managed RDBMS [Muk+11].

DBaaS providers can also specifically develop a **proprietary database or cloud infrastructure** to achieve scalability and efficiency goals that are harder to implement with standard database systems. A proprietary architecture enables co-design of the database or analytics system with the underlying cloud infrastructure. For example, Amazon DynamoDB provides a large-scale, multi-tenant NoSQL database loosely based on the Dynamo architecture [Dyn], and Google provides machine learning (ML) APIs for a variety of classification and clustering tasks [Goob].

We refer to Chap. 7 for a discussion of DBaaS deployments in the context of polyglot persistence and to Lehner and Sattler [LS13] and Zhao et al. [Zha+14] for a more comprehensive overview on DBaaS research.

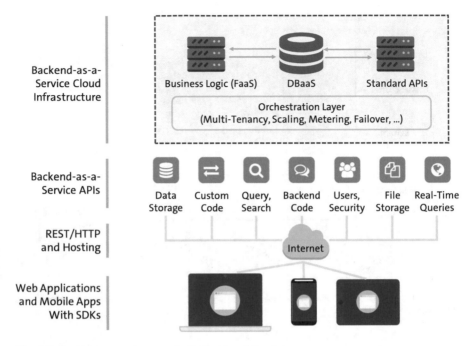

Backend-as-a-
Service Cloud
Infrastructure

Backend-as-a-
Service APIs

REST/HTTP
and Hosting

Web Applications
and Mobile Apps
With SDKs

Fig. 4.8 Architecture and usage of a Backend-as-a-Service

4.5.2 Backend-as-a-Service

Many data access and application patterns are very similar across different web and mobile applications and can therefore be standardized. This was recognized by the industry and led to BaaS systems that integrate DBaaS with application logic and predefined building blocks, e.g., for push notifications, user login, static file delivery, etc. BaaS is a rather recent trend and similar to early cloud computing and Big Data processing, progress is currently driven by industry projects, while structured research has yet to be established [Use, Par, Dep].

Figure 4.8 gives an overview of a generic BaaS architecture as similarly found in commercial services (e.g., Azure Mobile Services, Firebase, Kinvey, and Baqend [Baq]) as well as open-source projects (e.g., Meteor [HS16], Deployd [Dep], Hoodie [Hoo], Parse Server [Par], BaasBox [Bas], and Apache UserGrid [Use]).

The BaaS cloud infrastructure consists of three central components. The DBaaS component is responsible for data storage and retrieval. Its abstraction level can range from structured relational, over semi-structured JSON to opaque files. The FaaS component is concerned with the execution of server-side business logic, for example, to integrate third-party services and perform data validation. It can either be invoked as an explicit API or be triggered by DBaas operations. The standard API component offers common application functionality in a convention-over-configuration style, i.e., it provides defaults for tasks such as user login, push notifications, and messaging that are exposed for each tenant individually. The cloud infrastructure is orchestrated by the BaaS provider to ensure isolated multi-tenancy, scalability, availability, and monitoring.

The BaaS is accessed through a REST API [Dep, Hoo, Par, Bas, Use] (and sometimes WebSockets [HS16]) for use with different client technologies. To handle not only native mobile applications but also websites, BaaS systems usually provide file hosting to deliver website assets like HTML and script files to browsers. The communication with the BaaS is performed through SDKs employed in the frontend. The SDKs provide high-level abstractions to application developers, for example, to integrate persistence with application data models [Tor+17].

A feature that has been gaining popularity in recent years is real-time queries as offered by Firebase, Meteor, Baqend, and others [WGR20]. Real-time queries are typically provided over a WebSocket connection, since they require a persistent communication channel between client and server. While the ability to have informational updates pushed to the client is highly useful for developing collaborative or other reactive applications, the major challenge for providing real-time queries lies within scalability [Win19]: At the time of writing, Baqend's real-time query engine is the only one that scales with both write throughput and query concurrency. For a detailed discussion of the current real-time database landscape, we refer to [WRG19].

BaaS systems are thus confronted with even stronger latency challenges than a DBaaS: all clients access the system via high-latency WAN network so that latency for retrieving objects, files, and query results determines application performance. Similar to DBaaS systems, BaaS APIs usually provide persistence on top of one single database technology, making it infeasible to achieve all potential functional and non-functional application requirements. The problem is even more severe when all tenants are co-located on a shared database cluster. In that case, one database system configuration (e.g., the replication protocol) prescribes the guarantees for each tenant [ADE12].

4.5.3 Multi-Tenancy

The goal of multi-tenancy in DBaaS/BaaS systems is to allow efficient resource pooling across tenants so that only the capacity for the global average resource consumption has to be provisioned and resources can be shared. There is an inherent trade-off between higher isolation of tenants and efficiency of resource sharing [ADE12]. As shown in Fig. 4.9, the boundary between tenant-specific resources and shared provider resources can be drawn at different levels of the software stack [MB16, p. 562]:

- With **private operating system (OS)** virtualization, each tenant is assigned to one or multiple VMs that execute the database process. This model achieves

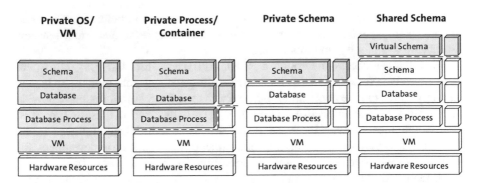

Fig. 4.9 Different approaches to multi-tenancy in DBaaS/BaaS systems. The dashed line indicates the boundary between shared and tenant-specific resources

a high degree of isolation, similar to IaaS clouds. However, resource reuse is limited as each tenant has the overhead of a full OS and database process.

- By allocating a **private process** to each tenant, the overhead of a private OS can be mitigated. To this end, the provider orchestrates the OS to run multiple isolated database processes. This is usually achieved using container technology such as Docker [Mer14] that isolates processes within a shared OS.
- Efficiency can be further increased if tenants only possess a **private schema** within a shared database process. The database system can thus share various system resources (e.g., the buffer pool) between tenants to increase I/O efficiency.
- The **shared schema** model requires all tenants to use the same application that dictates the common schema. The schema can be adapted to specific tenant requirements by extending it with additional fields or tables [KL11]. A shared schema is frequently used in SaaS applications such as Salesforce [Onl].

The major open challenge for multi-tenancy of NoSQL systems in cloud environments is database independence and the combination with multi-tenant FaaS code execution. If a generic middleware can expose unmodified data stores as a scalable, multi-tenant DBaaS/BaaS, the problems of database and service architectures are decoupled, and polyglot persistence is enabled. In Chap. 7, we will go into more detail on polyglot persistence in modern data management.

Most research efforts in the DBaaS community have been concerned with multi-tenancy and virtualization [Aul+11, Aul+08, Aul+09, KL11, SKM08, WB09, JA07], database privacy and encryption [KJH15, Gen09, Pop+11, Pop14, Kar+16, PZ13, Pop+14], workload management [Cun+07, Zha+14, ABC14, Bas12, Xio+11, Ter+13, LBMAL14, Pad+07, Sak14], resource allocation [Mad+15, Sou+09], automatic scaling [Kim+16, LBMAL14], and benchmarking [Dey+14, Coo+10, Coo+10, Pat+11, BZS13, Ber+14, BT11, BK13, BT14, Ber15, Ber14]. However, several DBaaS and BaaS challenges still require further research [Ges19]:

- **Low latency** access to DBaaS systems, to improve application performance and allow distribution of application logic and data storage

- Unified REST/HTTP access to polyglot data stores with **service level agreements** for functional and non-functional guarantees
- **Elastic scalability** of read and query workloads for arbitrary database systems
- Generic, **database-independent APIs and capabilities** for fundamental data management abstractions such as schema management, FaaS business logic, real-time queries, multi-tenancy, search, transactions, authentication, authorization, user management, and file storage for single databases and across databases.

4.6   Summary

The challenges of building low-latency applications can be attributed to three different layers in the application stack: the frontend, the backend, and the network. In Chap. 2, we started with the technical foundations of scalable cloud-based web applications and compared different architectural designs with respect to the way that data is accessed and assembled. In Chap. 3, we then explored the network performance of web applications which is determined by the design of the HTTP protocol and the constraints of the predominant REST architectural style, and we reviewed the mechanisms that HTTP provides for web caching and how they relate to the infrastructure of the Internet. In this chapter, we turned to data management and gave an overview of NoSQL system's data models, their different notions of consistency, and their use for Database- and Backend-as-a-Service cloud service models.

In the following chapters, we will continue with a focus on data management by surveying today's caching technology in Chap. 5, transactional semantics in distributed systems in Chap. 6, and approaches for polyglot persistence in Chap. 7. In Chaps. 8 and 9, we will conclude with a classification of today's NoSQL landscape and a projection of possible future developments, respectively.

References

[AAB05] Amitanand S. Aiyer, Lorenzo Alvisi, and Rida A. Bazzi. "On the Availability of Non-strict Quorum Systems". In: *Distributed Computing, 19th International Conference, DISC 2005, Cracow, Poland, September 26–29, 2005, Proceedings*. Ed. by Pierre Fraigniaud. Vol. 3724. Lecture Notes in Computer Science. Springer, 2005, pp. 48–62. DOI: 10.1007/11561927_6.

[Aba12] D. Abadi. "Consistency tradeoffs in modern distributed database system design: CAP is only part of the story". In: *Computer* 45.2 (2012), pp. 37–42. URL: http://ieeexplore. ieee.org/xpls/abs_all.jsp?arnumber=6127847 (visited on 10/10/2012).

[ABC14] Ioannis Arapakis, Xiao Bai, and B. Barla Cambazoglu. "Impact of Response Latency on User Behavior in Web Search". In: *Proceedings of the 37th International ACM SIGIR Conference on Research & Development in Information Retrieval*. SIGIR '14. Gold Coast, Queensland, Australia: ACM, 2014, pp. 103–112. ISBN: 978-1-4503-2257-7. DOI: 10.1145/2600428.2609627. URL: http://doi.acm.org/10.1145/2600428. 2609627.

[ABN+95] H. Attiya, A. Bar-Noy, et al. "Sharing memory robustly in message-passing systems". In: *JACM* 42.1 (1995).

[ADE12] Divyakant Agrawal, Sudipto Das, and Amr El Abbadi. *Data Management in the Cloud: Challenges and Opportunities*. Synthesis Lectures on Data Management. Morgan & Claypool Publishers, 2012. DOI: 10.2200/S00456ED1V01Y201211DTM032.

[Ady99] Atul Adya. "Weak consistency: a generalized theory and optimistic implementations for distributed transactions". PhD thesis. Massachusetts Institute of Technology, 1999. URL: http://www.csd.uoc.gr/~hy460/pdf/adya99weak.pdf (visited on 01/03/2015).

[Ajo+15] Phillipe Ajoux et al. "Challenges to adopting stronger consistency at scale". In: *15th Workshop on Hot Topics in Operating Systems (HotOS XV)*. 2015. URL: https://www.usenix.org/conference/hotos15/workshop-program/presentation/ajoux (visited on 11/28/2016).

[Amab] *Amazon Web Services AWS â Server Hosting & Cloud Services*. https://aws.amazon.com/de/. (Accessed on 05/20/2017). 2017.

[Aul+08] S. Aulbach et al. "Multi-tenant databases for software as a service: schema-mapping techniques". In: *Proceedings of the 2008 ACM SIGMOD international conference on Management of data*. 2008, pp. 1195–1206. URL: http://dl.acm.org/citation.cfm?id=1376736 (visited on 11/15/2012).

[Aul+09] Stefan Aulbach et al. "A comparison of flexible schemas for software as a service". In: *Proceedings of the ACM SIGMOD International Conference on Management of Data, SIGMOD 2009, Providence, Rhode Island, USA, June 29 - July 2, 2009*. Ed. by Ugur Çetintemel et al. ACM, 2009, pp. 881–888. DOI: 10.1145/1559845.1559941.

[Aul+11] Stefan Aulbach et al. "Extensibility and Data Sharing in evolving multitenant databases". In: *Proceedings of the 27th International Conference on Data Engineering, ICDE 2011, April 11–16, 2011, Hannover, Germany*. Ed. by Serge Abiteboul et al. IEEE Computer Society, 2011, pp. 99–110. DOI: 10.1109/ICDE.2011.5767872.

[Bai+13a] Peter Bailis et al. "Bolt-on Causal Consistency". In: *Proceedings of the 2013 ACM SIGMOD International Conference on Management of Data*. SIGMOD '13. New York, New York, USA: ACM, 2013, pp. 761–772.

[Bai+13b] Peter Bailis et al. "HAT, not CAP: Highly available transactions". In: *Workshop on Hot Topics in Operating Systems*. 2013.

[Bai+13c] Peter Bailis et al. "Highly Available Transactions: Virtues and Limitations". In: *Proceedings of the VLDB Endowment* 7.3 (2013). 00001.

[Bai+14b] Peter Bailis et al. "Quantifying eventual consistency with PBS". en. In: *The VLDB Journal* 23.2 (Apr. 2014), pp. 279–302. ISSN: 1066-8888, 0949-877X. DOI: 10.1007/s00778-013-0330-1. URL: http://link.springer.com/10.1007/s00778-013-0330-1 (visited on 01/03/2015).

[Bai15] Peter Bailis. "Coordination Avoidance in Distributed Databases". PhD thesis. University of California, Berkeley, USA, 2015. URL: http://www.escholarship.org/uc/item/8k8359g2.

[Bak+11] J. Baker et al. "Megastore: Providing scalable, highly available storage for interactive services". In: *Proc. of CIDR*. Vol. 11. 2011, pp. 223–234.

[Bal+15] Valter Balegas et al. "Putting consistency back into eventual consistency". en. In: ACM Press, 2015, pp. 1–16. ISBN: 978-1-4503-3238-5. DOI: 10.1145/2741948.2741972. URL: http://dl.acm.org/citation.cfm?doid=2741948.2741972 (visited on 11/25/2016).

[Baq] *News BaaS Benchmark*. https://github.com/Baqend/news-benchmark (Accessed on 09/08/2018). 2018.

[Bar+03] P. Barham et al. "Xen and the art of virtualization". In: *ACM SIGOPS Operating Systems Review*. Vol. 37. 2003, pp. 164–177. URL: http://dl.acm.org/citation.cfm?id=945462%7C (visited on 10/09/2012).

[Bas] *The BaasBox server*. https://github.com/baasbox/baasbox. (Accessed on 05/20/2017). 2017. URL: https://github.com/baasbox/baasbox (visited on 02/19/2017).

[Bas12] Salman A. Baset. "Cloud SLAs: present and future". In: *ACM SIGOPS Operating Systems Review* 46.2 (2012), pp. 57–66. URL: http://dl.acm.org/citation.cfm?id=2331586 (visited on 01/03/2015).

[Ber+13] David Bermbach et al. "A Middleware Guaranteeing Client-Centric Consistency on Top of Eventually Consistent Datastores". In: *2013 IEEE International Conference on Cloud Engineering, IC2E 2013, San Francisco, CA, USA, March 25–27, 2013.* IEEE Computer Society, 2013, pp. 114–123. DOI: 10.1109/IC2E.2013.32.

[Ber+14] David Bermbach et al. "Towards an Extensible Middleware for Database Benchmarking". In: *Performance Characterization and Bench-marking. Traditional to Big Data - 6th TPC Technology Conference, TPCTC 2014, Hangzhou, China, September 1–5, 2014. Revised Selected Papers.* Ed. by Raghunath Nambiar and Meikel Poess. Vol. 8904. Lecture Notes in Computer Science. Springer, 2014, pp. 82–96. DOI: 10.1007/978-3-319-15350-6_6.

[Ber14] David Bermbach. *Benchmarking Eventually Consistent Distributed Storage Systems.* eng. Karlsruhe, Baden: KIT Scientific Publishing, 2014. ISBN: 978-3-7315-0186-2 3-7315-0186-4 978-3-7315-0186-2.

[Ber15] David Bermbach. "An Introduction to Cloud Benchmarking". In: *2015 IEEE International Conference on Cloud Engineering, IC2E 2015, Tempe, AZ, USA, March 9–13, 2015.* IEEE Computer Society, 2015, p. 3. DOI: 10.1109/IC2E.2015.65.

[BK13] David Bermbach and Jörn Kuhlenkamp. "Consistency in Distributed Storage Systems - An Overview of Models, Metrics and Measurement Approaches". In: *Networked Systems - First International Conference, NETYS 2013, Marrakech, Morocco, May 2–4, 2013, Revised Selected Papers.* Ed. by Vincent Gramoli and Rachid Guerraoui. Vol. 7853. Lecture Notes in Computer Science. Springer, 2013, pp. 175–189. DOI: 10.1007/978-3-642-40148-0_13.

[Bre00] Eric A. Brewer. *Towards Robust Distributed Systems.* 2000.

[BT11] David Bermbach and Stefan Tai. "Eventual consistency: How soon is eventual? An evaluation of Amazon S3's consistency behavior". In: *Proceedings of the 6th Workshop on Middleware for Service Oriented Computing, MW4SOC 2011, Lisbon, Portugal, December 12–16, 2011.* Ed. by Karl M. Göschka, Schahram Dustdar, and Vladimir Tosic. ACM, 2011, p. 1. DOI: 10.1145/2093185.2093186.

[BT14] David Bermbach and Stefan Tai. "Benchmarking Eventual Consistency: Lessons Learned from Long-Term Experimental Studies". In: *2014 IEEE International Conference on Cloud Engineering, Boston, MA, USA, March 11–14, 2014.* IEEE Computer Society, 2014, pp. 47–56. DOI: 10.1109/IC2E.2014.37.

[BWT17] David Bermbach, Erik Wittern, and Stefan Tai. *Cloud Service Benchmarking - Measuring Quality of Cloud Services from a Client Perspective.* Springer, 2017. ISBN: 978-3-319-55482-2. DOI: 10.1007/978-3-319-55483-9.

[BZS13] David Bermbach, Liang Zhao, and Sherif Sakr. "Towards Comprehensive Measurement of Consistency Guarantees for Cloud-Hosted Data Storage Services". In: *Performance Characterization and Benchmarking - 5th TPC Technology Conference, TPCTC 2013, Trento, Italy, August 26, 2013, Revised Selected Papers.* Ed. by Raghunath Nambiar and Meikel Poess. Vol. 8391. Lecture Notes in Computer Science. Springer, 2013, pp. 32–47. DOI: 10.1007/978-3-319-04936-6_3.

[Cha+08] Fay Chang et al. "Bigtable: A distributed storage system for structured data". In: *ACM Transactions on Computer Systems (TOCS)* 26.2 (2008), p. 4.

[Clu] *Clustrix: A New Approach to Scale-Out RDBMS.* http://www.clustrix.com/wp-content/uploads/2017/01/Whitepaper-ANewApproachtoScaleOutRDBMS.pdf. (Accessed on 05/20/2017). 2017. URL: http://www.clustrix.com/wp-content/uploads/2017/01/Whitepaper-ANewApproachtoScaleOutRDBMS.pdf (visited on 02/18/2017).

[Coo+10] Brian F. Cooper et al. "Benchmarking cloud serving systems with YCSB". In: *Proceedings of the 1st ACM symposium on Cloud computing.* ACM, 2010, pp. 143–154. URL: http://dl.acm.org/citation.cfm?id=1807152 (visited on 11/26/2016).

[Coo13] Brian F. Cooper. "Spanner: Google's globally-distributed database". In: *6th Annual International Systems and Storage Conference, SYSTOR '13, Haifa, Israel - June 30 - July 02, 2013*. Ed. by Ronen I. Kat, Mary Baker, and Sivan Toledo. ACM, 2013, p. 9. DOI: 10.1145/2485732.2485756.

[Cun+07] Ítalo S. Cunha et al. "Self-Adaptive Capacity Management for Multi-Tier Virtualized Environments". In: *Integrated Network Management, IM 2007. 10th IFIP/IEEE International Symposium on Integrated Network Management, Munich, Germany, 21–25 May 2007*. IEEE, 2007, pp. 129–138. DOI: 10.1109/INM.2007.374777.

[Cur+11a] Carlo Curino et al. "Relational Cloud: A Database-as-a-Service for the Cloud". In: *Proc. of CIDR*. 2011. URL: http://dspace.mit.edu/handle/1721.1/62241 (visited on 04/15/2014).

[Dep] *Deployd: a toolkit for building realtime APIs*. https://github.com/deployd/deployd. (Accessed on 05/20/2017). 2017. URL: https://github.com/deployd/deployd (visited on 02/19/2017).

[Dey+14] Anamika Dey et al. "YCSB+T: Benchmarking web-scale transactional databases". In: *Data Engineering Workshops (ICDEW), 2014 IEEE 30th International Conference on*. IEEE. 2014, pp. 223–230.

[DGMS85] Susan B Davidson, Hector Garcia-Molina, and Dale Skeen. "Consistency in a partitioned network: a survey". In: *ACM Computing Surveys (CSUR)* 17.3 (1985), pp. 341–370.

[Dyn] *DynamoDB*. http://docs.aws.amazon.com/amazondynamodb/latest/developerguide/Introduction.html. (Accessed on 05/20/2017). 2017. URL: http://docs.aws.amazon.com/amazondynamodb/latest/developerguide/Introduction.html (visited on 01/13/2017).

[Fid87] Colin J Fidge. "Timestamps in message-passing systems that preserve the partial ordering". In: (1987).

[FLP85] M. J. Fischer, N. A. Lynch, and M. S. Paterson. "Impossibility of distributed consensus with one faulty process". In: *Journal of the ACM (JACM)* 32.2 (1985), pp. 374–382. URL: http://dl.acm.org/citation.cfm?id=214121 (visited on 11/27/2012).

[Gen09] Craig Gentry. "A fully homomorphic encryption scheme". PhD thesis. Stanford University, 2009.

[Ges19] Felix Gessert. "Low Latency for Cloud Data Management". PhD thesis. University of Hamburg, Germany, 2019. URL: http://ediss.sub.uni-hamburg.de/volltexte/2019/9541/.

[GH02] Rachid Guerraoui and Corine Hari. "On the consistency problem in mobile distributed computing". In: *Proceedings of the 2002 Workshop on Principles of Mobile Computing, POMC 2002, October 30–31, 2002, Toulouse, France*. ACM, 2002, pp. 51–57. DOI: 1.1145/584490.584501.

[GL02] S. Gilbert and N. Lynch. "Brewer's conjecture and the feasibility of consistent, available, partition-tolerant web services". In: *ACM SIGACT News* 33.2 (2002), pp. 51–59.

[GLS11] Wojciech Golab, Xiaozhou Li, and Mehul A. Shah. "Analyzing consistency properties for fun and profit". In: *ACM PODC*. ACM, 2011, pp. 197–206. URL: http://dl.acm.org/citation.cfm?id=1993834 (visited on 09/28/2014).

[Gol+14] Wojciech M. Golab et al. "Client-Centric Benchmarking of Eventual Consistency for Cloud Storage Systems". In: *IEEE 34th International Conference on Distributed Computing Systems, ICDCS 2014, Madrid, Spain, June 30 - July 3, 2014*. IEEE Computer Society, 2014, pp. 493–502. DOI: 10.1109/ICDCS.2014.57.

[Goob] *Google Cloud Prediction API*. https://cloud.google.com/prediction/docs/. (Accessed on 06/18/2017). 2017.

[GR15] Felix Gessert and Norbert Ritter. "Skalierbare NoSQL- und Cloud-Datenbanken in Forschung und Praxis". In: *Datenbanksysteme fÃijr Business, Technologie und Web (BTW 2015) - Workshopband, 2.–3. MÃd'rz 2015, Hamburg, Germany*. 2015, pp. 271–274.

[GR16] Felix Gessert and Norbert Ritter. "Scalable Data Management: NoSQL Data Stores in Research and Practice". In: *32nd IEEE International Conference on Data Engineering, ICDE 2016*. 2016.

[Gra+76] Jim Gray et al. "Granularity of Locks and Degrees of Consistency in a Shared Data Base". In: *Modelling in Data Base Management Systems, Proceeding of the IFIP Working Conference on Modelling in Data Base Management Systems, Freudenstadt, Germany, January 5–8, 1976*. Ed. by G. M. Nijssen. North-Holland, 1976, pp. 365–394.

[Gro+13] Katarina Grolinger et al. "Data management in cloud environments: NoSQL and NewSQL data stores". en. In: *Journal of Cloud Computing: Advances, Systems and Applications* 2.1 (2013), p. 22. ISSN: 2192-113X. DOI: 10.1186/2192-113X-2-22. URL: http://www.journalofcloudcomputing.com/content/2/1/22 (visited on 01/03/2015).

[GWR17] Felix Gessert, Wolfram Wingerath, and Norbert Ritter. "Scalable Data Management: An In-Depth Tutorial on NoSQL Data Stores". In: *BTW (Workshops)*. Vol. P-266. LNI. GI, 2017, pp. 399–402.

[HA90] Phillip W Hutto and Mustaque Ahamad. "Slow memory: Weakening consistency to enhance concurrency in distributed shared memories". In: *Distributed Computing Systems, 1990. Proceedings., 10th International Conference on*. IEEE. 1990, pp. 302–309.

[HIM02] H. Hacigumus, B. Iyer, and S. Mehrotra. "Providing database as a service". In: *Data Engineering, 2002. Proceedings. 18th International Conference on*. 2002, pp. 29–38. URL: http://ieeexplore.ieee.org/xpls/abs_all.jsp?arnumber=994695 (visited on 10/16/2012).

[Hoo] *GitHub - hoodiehq/hoodie: A backend for Offline First applications.* https://github.com/hoodiehq/hoodie. (Accessed on 05/25/2017). 2017. URL: https://github.com/hoodiehq/hoodie (visited on 02/17/2017).

[HR83] Theo Haerder and Andreas Reuter. "Principles of transaction-oriented database recovery". In: *ACM Comput. Surv.* 15.4 (Dec. 1983), pp. 287–317.

[HS16] Stephan Hochhaus and Manuel Schoebel. *Meteor in action.* Manning Publ., 2016.

[Hun+10] Patrick Hunt et al. "ZooKeeper: Wait-free Coordination for Internet-scale Systems." In: *USENIX Annual Technical Conference*. Vol. 8. 2010, p. 9. URL: https://www.usenix.org/event/usenix10/tech/full_papers/Hunt.pdf (visited on 01/03/2015).

[HW90] Maurice P Herlihy and Jeannette M Wing. "Linearizability: A correctness condition for concurrent objects". In: *ACM Transactions on Programming Languages and Systems (TOPLAS)* 12.3 (1990), pp. 463–492.

[JA07] Dean Jacobs and Stefan Aulbach. "Ruminations on Multi-Tenant Data-bases". In: *Datenbanksysteme in Business, Technologie und Web (BTW 2007), 12. Fachtagung des GI-Fachbereichs "Datenbanken und Informationssysteme" (DBIS), Proceedings, 7.–9. März 2007, Aachen, Germany*. Ed. by Alfons Kemper et al. Vol. 103. LNI. GI, 2007, pp. 514–521. URL: http://subs.emis.de/LNI/Proceedings/Proceedings103/article1419.html.

[Kal+08] R. Kallman et al. "H-store: a high-performance, distributed main memory transaction processing system". In: *Proceedings of the VLDB Endowment* 1.2 (2008), pp. 1496–1499.

[Kar+16] Nikolaos Karapanos et al. "Verena: End-to-End Integrity Protection for Web Applications". In: *IEEE Symposium on Security and Privacy, SP 2016, San Jose, CA, USA, May 22–26, 2016*. IEEE Computer Society, 2016, pp. 895–913. DOI: 10.1109/SP.2016.58.

[Kim+16] In Kee Kim et al. "Empirical Evaluation of Workload Forecasting Techniques for Predictive Cloud Resource Scaling". In: *9th IEEE International Conference on Cloud Computing CLOUD 2016, San Francisco, CA, USA, June 27 - July 2, 2016*. IEEE Computer Society, 2016, pp. 1–10. DOI: 10.1109/CLOUD.2016.0011.

[KJH15] Jens Köhler, Konrad Jünemann, and Hannes Hartenstein. "Confidential database-as-a-service approaches: taxonomy and survey". In: *Journal of Cloud Computing* 4.1 (2015), p. 1. ISSN: 2192-113X. DOI: 10.1186/s13677-014-0025-1. URL: http://dx.doi.org/10.1186/s13677-014-0025-1.

[KL11] Tim Kiefer and Wolfgang Lehner "Private Table Database Virtualization for DBaaS". In: *IEEE 4th International Conference on Utility and Cloud Computing, UCC 2011, Melbourne, Australia, December 5–8, 2011*. IEEE Computer Society, 2011, pp. 328–329. DOI: 10.1109/UCC.2011.52.

[Kle17] Martin Kleppmann. *Designing Data-Intensive Applications*. English. 1 edition. O'Reilly Media, Jan. 2017. ISBN: 978-1-4493-7332-0.

[Kra+13] Tim Kraska et al. "MDCC: Multi-data center consistency". In: *EuroSys*. ACM, 2013, pp. 113–126. URL: http://dl.acm.org/citation.cfm?id=2465363 (visited on 04/15/2014).

[Lam78] Leslie Lamport. "Time, Clocks, and the Ordering of Events in a Distributed System". In: *Commun. ACM* 21.7 (1978), pp. 558–565. DOI: 10.1145/359545.359563.

[Lam86a] Leslie Lamport. "On Interprocess Communication. Part I: Basic Formalism". In: *Distributed Computing* 1.2 (1986), pp. 77–85. DOI: 10.1007/BF01786227.

[Lam86b] Leslie Lamport. "On Interprocess Communication. Part II: Algorithms". In: *Distributed Computing* 1.2 (1986), pp. 86–101. DOI: 10.1007/BF01786228.

[Lan01] Douglas Laney. *3D Data Management: Controlling Data Volume, Velocity, and Variety*. Tech. rep. META Group, Feb 2001.

[LBMAL14] Tania Lorido-Botran, Jose Miguel-Alonso, and JoseA. Lozano. "A Review of Auto-scaling Techniques for Elastic Applications in Cloud Environments". English. In: *Journal of Grid Computing* 12.4 (2014), pp. 559–592. ISSN: 1570-7873. DOI: 10.1007/s10723-014-9314-7. URL: http://dx.doi.org/10.1007/s10723-014-9314-7.

[Lee+15] Collin Lee et al. "Implementing linearizability at large scale and low latency". In: *Proceedings of the 25th Symposium on Operating Systems Principles, SOSP 2015, Monterey, CA, USA, October 4–7, 2015*. Ed. by Ethan L. Miller and Steven Hand. ACM, 2015, pp. 71–86. DOI: 10.1145/2815400.2815416.

[Llo+11] Wyatt Lloyd et al. "Don't settle for eventual: scalable causal consistency for wide-area storage with COPS". In: *Proceedings of the Twenty-Third ACM Symposium on Operating Systems Principles*. ACM, 2011, pp. 401–416. URL: http://dl.acm.org/citation.cfm?id=2043593 (visited on 01/03/2015).

[LS13] Wolfgang Lehner and Kai-Uwe Sattler. *Web-Scale Data Management for the Cloud*. Englisch. Auflage: 2013. New York: Springer, Apr. 2013. ISBN: 978-1-4614-6855-4.

[LS88a] Richard J Lipton and Jonathan S Sandberg. *PRAM: A scalable shared memory*. Princeton University, Department of Computer Science, 1988.

[Lyn96] Nancy A. Lynch. *Distributed Algorithms*. Morgan Kaufmann, 1996. ISBN: 1-55860-348-4.

[MAD+11] Prince Mahajan, Lorenzo Alvisi, Mike Dahlin, et al. "Consistency, availability, and convergence". In: *University of Texas at Austin Tech Report* 11 (2011).

[Mad+15] Gabor Madl et al. "Account clustering in multi-tenant storage management environments". In: *2015 IEEE International Conference on Big Data, Big Data 2015, Santa Clara, CA, USA, October 29 - November 1, 2015*. IEEE, 2015, pp. 1698–1707. DOI: 10.1109/BigData.2015.7363941.

[Mah+11] Prince Mahajan et al. "Depot: Cloud Storage with Minimal Trust". In: *ACM Trans. Comput. Syst.* 29.4 (2011), 12:1–12:38. DOI: 10.1145/2063509.2063512.

[MB16] San Murugesan and Irena Bojanova. *Encyclopedia of Cloud Computing*. John Wiley & Sons, 2016.

[Mer14] Dirk Merkel. "Docker: lightweight linux containers for consistent development and deployment". In: *Linux Journal* 2014.239 (2014), p. 2.

[Mon] *MongoDB*. https://www.mongodb.com/. (Accessed on 06/18/2017). 2017.

[Muk+11] Kunal Mukerjee et al. "SQL Azure as a Self-Managing Database Service: Lessons Learned and Challenges Ahead." In: *IEEE Data Eng. Bull.* 34.4 (2011), pp. 61–70. URL: http://sites.computer.org/debull/A11dec/azure2.pdf (visited on 01/03/2015).

[Nuo] *NuoDB: Emergent Architecture.* http://go.nuodb.com/rs/nuodb/images/Greenbook_Final.pdf. (Accessed on 04/30/2017). 2017. URL: http://go.nuodb.com/rs/nuodb/images/Greenbook_Final.pdf (visited on 02/18/2017).

[Onl] *Salesforce Online CRM.* https://www.salesforce.com/en. (Accessed on 06/05/2017). 2017.

[Pad+07] Pradeep Padala et al. "Adaptive control of virtualized resources in utility computing environments". In: *Proceedings of the 2007 EuroSys Conference, Lisbon, Portugal, March 21–23, 2007.* Ed. by Paulo Ferreira, Thomas R. Gross, and Luís Veiga. ACM, 2007, pp. 289–302. DOI: 10.1145/1272996.1273026.

[Par] *Parse Server.* http://parseplatform.github.io/docs/parse-server/guide/. (Accessed on 07/28/2017). 2017. URL: http://parseplatform.github.io/docs/parse-server/guide/ (visited on 02/19/2017).

[Pat+11] Swapnil Patil et al. "YCSB++: benchmarking and performance debugging advanced features in scalable table stores". In: *ACM Symposium on Cloud Computing in conjunction with SOSP 2011, SOCC '11, Cascais, Portugal, October 26–28, 2011.* Ed. by Jeffrey S. Chase and Amr El Abbadi. ACM, 2011, p. 9. DOI: 10.1145/2038916.2038925.

[Pop+11] R. A. Popa et al. "CryptDB: protecting confidentiality with encrypted query processing". In: *Proceedings of the Twenty-Third ACM Symposium on Operating Systems Principles.* 00095.2011, pp. 85–100. URL: http://dl.acm.org/citation.cfm?id=2043566 (visited on 11/16/2012).

[Pop+14] Raluca Ada Popa et al. "Building Web Applications on Top of Encrypted Data Using Mylar". In: *Proceedings of the 11th USENIX Symposium on Networked Systems Design and Implementation, NSDI 2014, Seattle, WA, USA, April 2–4, 2014.* Ed. by Ratul Mahajan and Ion Stoica. USENIX Association, 2014, pp. 157–172. URL: https://www.usenix.org/conference/nsdi14/technical-sessions/presentation/popa.

[Pop14] Raluca Ada Popa. "Building practical systems that compute on encrypted data". PhD thesis. Massachusetts Institute of Technology, 2014.

[Pri08] Dan Pritchett. "BASE: An Acid Alternative". In: *Queue* 6.3 (May 2008), pp. 48–55.

[PZ13] Raluca A. Popa and Nickolai Zeldovich. "Multi-Key Searchable Encryption". In: *IACR Cryptology ePrint Archive* 2013 (2013), p. 508. URL: http://eprint.iacr.org/2013/508.

[Rob16] Mike Roberts. *Serverless Architectures.* https://martinfowler.com/articles/serverless.html. (Accessed on 07/28/2017). 2016. URL: https://martinfowler.com/articles/serverless.html (visited on 02/19/2017).

[Sak14] Sherif Sakr. "Cloud-hosted databases: technologies, challenges and opportunities". In: *Cluster Computing* 17.2 (2014), pp. 487–502. URL: http://link.springer.com/article/10.1007/s10586-013-0290-7 (visited on 07/16/2014).

[SF12] Pramod J. Sadalage and Martin Fowler. *NoSQL distilled: a brief guide to the emerging world of polyglot persistence.* Pearson Education, 2012.

[SKM08] Aameek Singh, Madhukar R. Korupolu, and Dushmanta Mohapatra. "Server-storage virtualization: integration and load balancing in data centers". In: *Proceedings of the ACM/IEEE Conference on High Performance Computing, SC 2008, November 15–21, 2008, Austin, Texas, USA.* IEEE/ACM, 2008, p. 53. DOI: 10.1145/1413370.1413424.

[Sou+09] Gokul Soundararajan et al. "Dynamic Resource Allocation for Database Servers Running on Virtual Storage". In: *7th USENIX Conference on File and Storage Technologies, February 24–27, 2009, San Francisco, CA, USA. Proceedings.* Ed. by Margo I. Seltzer and Richard Wheeler. USENIX, 2009, pp. 71–84. URL: http://www.usenix.org/events/fast09/tech/full_papers/soundararajan/soundararajan.pdf.

[SRH97] Aman Singla, Umakishore Ramachandran, and Jessica K. Hodgins. "Temporal Notions of Synchronization and Consistency in Beehive". In: *SPAA.* 1997, pp. 211–220. DOI: 10.1145/258492.258513.

[SW13] Michael Stonebraker and Ariel Weisberg. "The VoltDB Main Memory DBMS". In: *IEEE Data Eng. Bull.* 36.2 (2013), pp. 21–27. URL: http://sites.computer.org/debull/A13june/VoltDB1.pdf.

[TAR99] Francisco J. Torres-Rojas, Mustaque Ahamad, and Michel Raynal. "Timed Consistency for Shared Distributed Objects". In: *Proceedings of the Eighteenth Annual ACM Symposium on Principles of Distributed Computing, PODC, '99Atlanta, Georgia, USA, May 3–6, 1999*. Ed. by Brian A. Coan and Jennifer L. Welch. ACM, 1999, pp. 163–172. DOI: 10.1145/301308.301350.

[Ter+13] Douglas B. Terry et al. "Consistency-based service level agreements for cloud storage". In: *ACM SIGOPS 24th Symposium on Operating Systems Principles, SOSP '13, Farmington, PA, USA, November 3–6, 2013*. Ed. by Michael Kaminsky and Mike Dahlin. ACM, 2013, pp. 309–324. DOI: 10.1145/2517349.2522731.

[Tho+12] Alexander Thomson et al. "Calvin: fast distributed transactions for partitioned database systems". In: *Proceedings of the 2012 ACM SIGMOD International Conference on Management of Data*. ACM. 2012, pp. 1–12.

[TM05] Francisco J. Torres-Rojas and Esteban Meneses. "Convergence Through a Weak Consistency Model: Timed Causal Consistency".In: *CLEI Electron. J.* 8.2 (2005). URL: http://www.clei.org/cleiej/paper.php?id=110.

[Tor+17] Alexandre Torres et al. "Twenty years of object-relational mapping: A survey on patterns, solutions, and their implications on application design". In: *Information and Software Technology* 82 (2017), pp. 1–18.

[TS07] Andrew S. Tanenbaum and Maarten van Steen. *Distributed systems - principles and paradigms, 2nd Edition*. Pearson Education, 2007. ISBN: 978-0-13-239227-3.

[Use] *Apache Usergrid*. https://usergrid.apache.org/. (Accessed on 07/16/2017). 2017. URL: https://usergrid.apache.org/ (visited on 02/19/2017).

[Vog09] Werner Vogels. "Eventually consistent". In: *Communications of the ACM* 52.1 (2009), pp. 40–44.

[VV16] Paolo Viotti and Marko VukoliÄ. "Consistency in Non-Transactional Distributed Storage Systems". en. In: *ACM Computing Surveys* 49.1 (June 2016), pp. 1–34. ISSN: 03600300. DOI: 10.1145/2926965. URL: http://dl.acm.org/citation.cfm?doid=2911992.2926965 (visited on 11/25/2016).

[Wad+11] Hiroshi Wada et al. "Data Consistency Properties and the Trade-offs in Commercial Cloud Storage: the Consumers' Perspective". In: *CIDR 2011, Fifth Biennial Conference on Innovative Data Systems Research, Asilomar, CA, USA, January 9–12, 2011, Online Proceedings*. www.cidrdb.org, 2011, pp. 134–143. URL: http://www.cidrdb.org/cidr2011/Papers/CIDR11_Paper15.pdf.

[WB09] Craig D. Weissman and Steve Bobrowski. "The design of the force.com multitenant internet application development platform". In: *Proceedings of the ACM SIGMOD International Conference on Management of Data, SIGMOD 2009, Providence, Rhode Island, USA, June 29 - July 2, 2009*. Ed. by Ugur Çetintemel et al. ACM, 2009, pp. 889–896. DOI: 10.1145/1559845.1559942.

[WGR+18] Wolfram Wingerath, Felix Gessert, Norbert Ritter et al. "Real-Time Data Management for Big Data". In: *Proceedings of the 21th International Conference on Extending Database Technology, EDBT 2018, Vienna, Austria, March 26–29, 2018*. OpenProceedings.org, 2018.

[WGR19] Wolfram Wingerath, Felix Gessert, and Norbert Ritter. "NoSQL & Real-Time Data Management in Research & Practice". In: *Datenbanksysteme für Business, Technologie und Web (BTW 2019), 18. Fachtagung des GI-Fachbereichs „Datenbanken und Informationssysteme" (DBIS), 4.–8. März 2019, Rostock, Germany, Workshopband*. 2019, pp. 267–270. URL: https://dl.gi.de/20.500.12116/21595.

[WGR20] Wolfram Wingerath, Felix Gessert, and Norbert Ritter. "InvaliDB: Scalable Push-Based Real-Time Queries on Top of Pull-Based Databases". In: *36th IEEE International Conference on Data Engineering, ICDE 2020, Dallas, Texas, April 20–24, 2020*. 2020.

[WGW+20] Wolfram Wingerath, Felix Gessert, Erik Witt, et al. "Speed Kit: A Polyglot & GDPR-Compliant Approach For Caching Personalized Content". In: *36th IEEE International Conference on Data Engineering, ICDE 2020, Dallas, Texas, April 20–24, 2020*. 2020.

[Win+15] Wolfram Wingerath et al. "Who Watches the Watchmen? On the Lack of Validation in NoSQL Benchmarking". In: *Datenbanksysteme fÃijr Business, Technologie und Web (BTW), 16. Fachtagung des GI-Fachbereichs "Datenbanken und Informationssysteme"*. 2015.

[Win19] Wolfram Wingerath. "Scalable Push-Based Real-Time Queries on Top of Pull-Based Databases". PhD thesis. University of Hamburg, 2019. URL: https://invalidb.info/thesis.

[WRG19] Wolfram Wingerath, Norbert Ritter, and Felix Gessert. *Real-Time & Stream Data Management: Push-Based Data in Research & Practice*. Ed. by Susan Evans. Springer International Publishing, 2019. ISBN: 978-3-030-10554-9. DOI: 10.1007/978-3-030-10555-6.

[WV02] G. Weikum and G. Vossen. *Transactional information systems*. Series in Data Management Systems. Morgan Kaufmann Pub, 2002. ISBN: 9781558605084. URL: http://books.google.de/books?hl=de&lr=&id=wV5Ran71zNoC&oi=fnd&pg=PP2&dq=transactional+information+systems&ots=PgJAaN7R5X&sig=Iya4r9DiFhmb_wWgOI5QMuxm6zU (visited on 06/28/2012).

[Xio+11] P. Xiong et al. "ActiveSLA: A profit-oriented admission control frame-work for database-as-a-service providers". In: *Proceedings of the 2nd ACM Symposium on Cloud Computing*. 00019. ACM, 2011, p. 15. URL: http://dl.acm.org/citation.cfm?id=2038931 (visited on 11/15/2012).

[Zha+14] Liang Zhao et al. *Cloud Data Management*. Englisch. Auflage: 2014. Springer, 2014.

[ZS17] Albert Y. Zomaya and Sherif Sakr, eds. *Handbook of Big Data Technologies*. Springer, 2017. ISBN: 978-3-319-49339-8. DOI: 10.1007/978-3-319-49340-4.

Chapter 5
Caching in Research and Industry

Caching technology can be categorized by several dimensions as illustrated in Fig. 5.1. The first dimension is the *location* of the cache. In this book, we focus on caches relevant for cloud and database applications, particularly server-side and database caching, reverse and forward proxy caching (mid-tier), and client caching [Lab+09]. The second dimension is the *granularity* of cached data. Examples are files, database records and pages, query results, and page fragments [Ami+03a, Ami+03b, Ant+02, Can+01a, CZB99, CRS99, Dat+04, LC99, LN01]. The third dimension is the *update* strategy that determines the provided level of consistency [Cat92, GS96, NWO88, LC97, CL98, Bor+03, Bor+04].

Besides these major dimensions, there are smaller distinctions. The cache replacement strategy defines how the limited amount of storage is best allocated to cached data [PB03, Dar+96]. The initialization strategy determines whether the cache is filled on-demand or proactively[1] [Alt+03, LGZ04, Luo+02, Bor+03, LR00, LR01a]. The update processing strategy indicates whether changes to cached data are replacements, incremental changes, or based on recomputation [Han87, BCL89, AGK95, LR01a, IC98, BLT86].

Table 5.1 summarizes current research on caching according to the dimensions *location* and *updates*. In the following, we will first discuss server-side and client-side application caching as well as database caching and contrast both to web caching approaches. After that, we will show the different methods for cache coherence that can be grouped into expiration-based and invalidation-based approaches. Finally, we will review work on caching query and search results and discuss summary data structures for caching.

---

[1]Proactive filling of the cache is also referred to as *materialization* [LR00].

© Springer Nature Switzerland AG 2020
F. Gessert et al., *Fast and Scalable Cloud Data Management*,
https://doi.org/10.1007/978-3-030-43506-6_5

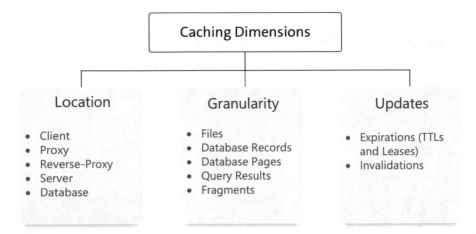

Fig. 5.1 The three central dimensions of caching

Table 5.1 Selected related work on caching classified by location and update strategy

	Expiration-based	Invalidation-based	Hybrid
Client	Browser cache [IET15], ORMs [Rus03, Ady+07, Che+16], ODMs [Stö15], User Profiles [BR02], Alex Protocol [GS96], CSI [Rab+03], Service Workers [Ama16]	Avoidance-based Algorithms [ÖV11, FCL97, WN90]	Client-Server Databases [KK94, ÖDV92, Cas+97], Oracle Result Cache [Ora], Speed Kit [WGW+20]
Mid-Tier	HTTP proxies [IET15], PCV [KW97], ESI [Tsi+01]	PSI [KW98], CDNs [PB08, FFM04, Fre10]	Leases [Vak06], Volume Leases [Yin+99, Yin+98], TTR [Bhi+02], Orestes/Baqend [Ges19]
Server and DB	Incremental TTLs [Ali+12],	CachePortal[Can+01b], DCCP [KLM97], Reverse Proxies [Kam17], Ferdinand [Gar+08], Facebook Tao [Bro+13], Cache Hierarchies [Wor94], DBProxy [Ami+03a], DBCache [Bor+04], MTCache [LGZ04], WebView [LR01a]	Memcache [Fit04, Nis+13, Xu+14], Redis [Car13], IMDGs [ERR11, Lwe10], CIP [Bla+10], Materialized Views [Lab+09]

5.1 Reducing Latency: Replication, Caching and Edge Computing

There are three primary backend-focused technologies that are concerned with lowering latency. Replication, caching, and edge computing follow the idea of distributing data storage and processing for better scalability and reduced latency towards dispersed clients.

5.1.1 Eager and Lazy Geo-Replication

To improve scalability and latency of reads, **geo-replication** distributes copies of the primary database over different geographical sites. *Eager geo-replication* (e.g., in Google's Megastore [Bak+11], Spanner [Cor+13, Cor+12], F1 [Shu+13], MDCC [Kra+13], and Mencius [MJM08]) has the goal of achieving strong consistency combined with geo-redundancy for failover. However, it comes at the cost of higher write latencies that are usually between 100 ms [Cor+12] and 600 ms [Bak+11]. The second problem of eager geo-replication is that it requires extensive, database-specific infrastructure which introduces system-specific trade-offs that cannot be adapted at runtime. For example, it is not possible to relax consistency on a per-operation basis, as the guarantee is tied to the system-wide replication protocol (typically variants of Paxos [Lam01]). Also, while some eagerly geo-replicated systems support transactions, these suffer from high abort rates, as cross-site latency in commit protocols increases the probability of deadlocks and conflicts [Shu+13].

Lazy geo-replication (e.g., in Dynamo [DeC+07], BigTable/HBase [Cha+08, Hba], Cassandra [LM10], MongoDB [CD13], CouchDB [ALS10], Couchbase [Lak+16], Espresso [Qia+13], PNUTS [Coo+08], Walter [Sov+11], Eiger [Llo+13], and COPS [Llo+11]) on the other hand aims for high availability and low latency at the expense of consistency. Typically, replicas are only allowed to serve reads, in order to simplify the processing of concurrent updates. The problem of lazy geo-replication is that consistency guarantees are lowered to a minimum (eventual consistency) or cause a prohibitive overhead (e.g., causal consistency [Llo+11, Llo+13]). Similar to eager geo-replication, system-specific infrastructure is required to scale the database and lower latency. Therefore, providing low end-to-end latency for web applications through a network of different replica sites is often both financially and technically infeasible. Furthermore, geo-replication requires the application tier to be co-located with each replica to make use of the distribution for latency reduction. Geo-replication is nonetheless an indispensable technique for providing resilience against disaster scenarios.

5.1.2   Caching

Caching has been studied in various fields for many years. It can be applied at different *locations* (e.g., clients, proxies, servers, databases), *granularities* (e.g., files, records, pages, query results) and with different *update strategies* (e.g., expirations, leases, invalidations). Client-side caching approaches are usually designed for application servers and therefore not compatible with REST/HTTP, browsers and mobile devices [ÖV11, FCL97, WN90, KK94, ÖV11, Cas+97, Ora, Tor+17]. Mid-tier (proxy) caches provide weak guarantees in order not to create synchronous dependencies on server-side queries and updates or only cache very specific types of data [KW97, Tsi+01, KW98, PB08, FFM04, Fre10, Vak06, Yin+99, Yin+98, Bhi+02]. The various approaches for server-side caching have the primary goal of minimizing query latency by offloading the database for repeated queries [Ali+12, Can+01b, KLM97, Kam17, Gar+08, Bro+13, Ami+03a, Bor+04, LGZ04, LR01a, Bla+10, Lab+09].

Combining expiration-based and invalidation-based cache maintenance is an open problem, as both mechanisms provide different consistency guarantees and therefore would degrade to the weaker model when combined. In practice, most caching approaches rely on the application to maintain cache coherence instead of using declarative models that map consistency requirements to cache coherence protocols [Rus03, Ady+07, Che+16, Stö+15, Ama16, Fit04, Nis+13, Xu+14]. Very few caching approaches tackle end-to-end latency for the web at all or consider the distributed nature of cloud services. Caching and replication approaches bear many similarities, as caching is a form of lazy, on-demand replication [RS03].

5.1.3   Edge Computing

A **cloudlet** is a "data center in a box" [AG17, p. 7] that can be deployed in proximity to mobile devices for reduced latency. The underlying idea is to enhance the computing capacities of mobile devices by offloading computationally expensive operations to cloudlets [Sat+09]. Typical applications for the concept of cloudlets are virtual and augmented reality that require powerful resources for rendering and low latency for interactivity. For data management, cloudlets are less useful as they would have to replicate or cache data from the main data center and would therefore have to act as a geo-replica.

Fog computing takes the idea of highly distributed cloud resources further and suggests provisioning storage, compute, and network resources for Internet of Things (IoT) applications in a large amount of interconnected "fog nodes" [Bon+12]. By deploying fog nodes close to end users and IoT devices, better quality of service for latency and bandwidth can potentially be achieved. Fog computing targets applications such as smart grids, sensor networks, and autonomous driving and is therefore orthogonal to web and mobile applications [SW14].

Edge computing refers to services and computations provided at the network edge. Edge computing in CDNs has already been practiced for years through reverse proxy caches that support restricted processing of incoming and outgoing requests [Kam17, PB08]. *Mobile edge computing* enhances 3G, 4G, and 5G base stations to provide services close to mobile devices (e.g., video transcoding) [AR17].

The problem of cloudlets, fog computing, and edge computing regarding low latency for web applications is that they do not provide integration into data management and shared application data but instead expose independent resources. Therefore, data shipping is required to execute business logic on the edge which shifts the latency problem to the communication path between edge nodes and cloud data storage. To minimize end-to-end latency in edge computing, it is necessary to perform data management operations on cached data, in particular authentication and authorization [Ges19].

5.1.4   Challenges

In summary, the open challenges of replication, caching, and edge computing for low latency cloud data management are:

- Eager geo-replication introduces high **write and commit latency**, while lazy geo-replication does not allow fine-grained **consistency choices**.
- Replication requires extensive, database-specific infrastructure and cannot be employed for **polyglot persistence**.
- Geo-replicated database systems assume the co-distribution of **application logic** and do not have the abstractions and interfaces for direct DBaaS/BaaS access by clients.
- Common caching approaches only improve **backend performance** instead of end-to-end latency or suffer from the same limitations as geo-replication.
- **Expiration-based caching** is considered irreconcilable with non-trivial consistency requirements.
- Edge computing does not solve the **distribution of data** and hence does not improve latency for stateful computations and business logic.

5.2   Server-Side, Client-Side and Web Caching

5.2.1   Server-Side Caching

Caching is often a primary concern in distributed backend applications. Numerous caching systems have been developed to allow application-controlled storage and queries of volatile data. Typically, they are employed as **look-aside** caches storing hot data of the underlying database system, with the application being responsible for keeping the data up-to-date. Among the most popular of these systems is Memcache, an open-source, in-memory hash table with a binary access protocol introduced by Fitzpatrick in 2004 [Fit04]. Memcache does not have any native support for sharding, but there are client-side libraries for distribution of records over instances using consistent hashing. Facebook, for example, uses this approach for their high fan-out reads of pages [Nis+13, Xu+14] and their social media graph [Bro+13]. The key-value store Redis is used for similar caching scenarios, enabling more advanced access patterns with its support for data structures (e.g., hashes, lists, sorted sets) instead of opaque data values [Car13]. In contrast to Memcache, Redis additionally supports different levels of persistence and an optimistic batch transaction model. Considerable research went into the optimization of these caches in terms of hashing performance [FAK13], fair cache resource sharing between clients [Pu+16], and optimal memory allocation [Cid16]. For the Java programming language, a standard caching API has been defined and implemented by various open-source and commercial caching projects [Luc14]. For server-side caching with higher persistence guarantees, key-value stores such as Riak [Ria], Voldemort [Aur+12], Aerospike [Aer], HyperDex [EWS12], and DynamoDB [Dyn] are suitable.

In-memory data grids (IMDGs) [Raj+15, p. 247] are distributed object stores used for state management and caching in Java and .Net applications. Industry products include Oracle Coherence, VMware Gemfire, Alachisoft NCache, Gigaspaces XAP, Hazelcast, Scaleout StateServer, Terracotta, JBoss Infinispan, and IBM eXtreme Scale [ERR11, Lwe10]. Compared to key-value caches, IMDGs offer the advantage of tightly integrating into the application's programming language and its class and object models. In this respect, IMDGs are similar to object-oriented database management systems (OODBMSs), as they expose native data types (e.g., maps and lists). Additionally, distributed coordination abstractions such as semaphores, locks, and atomic references as well execution of MapReduce jobs are typically supported. IMDGs are also used in related research projects (e.g., CloudSim [KV14]), due to the simple abstractions for shared distributed state.

Server-side caching with key-value stores and IMDGs is a proven technique for reducing backend processing latency by offloading persistent data stores in I/O-bound applications. This comes at a cost, however: the application has to maintain the caches using domain-specific logic. The complexities of maintaining consistency and retrieving cached data are thus left to application developers.

5.2.2   Client-Side Database Caching

Client-side database caching has been discussed for decades in the database community [Lab+09, Bor+03, Luo+02, LGZ04]. In this case, the term "client" does not refer to a browser or mobile device, but to a server node of a backend application. In the context of distributed object databases, object-based, page-based, and hybrid approaches have been studied [KK94, ÖV11, Cas+97]. Object-based buffer management has the advantage of a lower granularity, allowing for higher concurrency in the client for transactional workloads. Page-based buffers are more efficient when queries tend to access all objects within a page and imposes less messaging overhead. This caching model is fundamentally different from web caching, as the client buffer has to support the transaction model of the database system. As the cache is retained across transaction boundaries (inter-transaction caching), the problem of transactional isolation is closely tied to that of cache consistency [Car+91, BP95]: neither transactions from the same client nor transactions from different clients are allowed to exhibit anomalies caused by stale reads and concurrent buffer updates.

Cache consistency algorithms from the literature can be classified as *avoidance-based* or *detection-based* [ÖV11, FCL97, WN90]. The idea of avoidance-based cache consistency is to prevent clients from reading stale data. This can be achieved by having writing clients ensure that any updated objects are not concurrently cached by any other client. Detection-based algorithms allow reading stale data, but perform a validation at commit time to check for violations of consistency. The second dimension of cache consistency algorithms is their approach to handling writes. Writes can be *synchronous*, meaning that at the time a client issues a write, the write request is sent to the server. The server can then, for example, propagate a write lock to all clients holding a cached copy of the written object (Callback-Read Locking [FC92]). With *asynchronous* writes, clients still inform the server about each write, but optimistically continue processing until informed by the server. This can lead to higher abort rates [ÖVU98]. In the *deferred* scheme, clients batch write requests and send them at the end of each transaction, thus reducing the write message overhead. Avoidance-based deferred algorithms typically suffer from high abort rates as well [FC92].

There are commercial relational database systems that offer client-side caching, for example, Oracle implements a client- and server-side result cache [Ora]. The protocols and algorithms for client-side caching in databases serve the purpose of reducing the load on the database system, thereby decreasing backend processing latency. However, they are not applicable to end-to-end latency reduction in cloud data management, as web and mobile clients cannot exploit this form of caching. The overhead of locks distributed over potentially hundreds of thousands of clients and the complexity of client-specific state in the database server impose a prohibitive overhead.

Özsu et al. [ÖDV92] employ invalidations to minimize the probability of stale reads. In their model, though, expiration-based caches can neither execute custom consistency logic nor receive server-side invalidations. To resolve this issue, Orestes [Ges19] and its commercial derivative Baqend[2] introduce the Cache Sketch approach [Ges+15] for informing clients about stale entries in their local caches. A list of all stale cache entries is maintained at the server side and periodically retrieved by clients in fixed intervals of Δ, thus providing a Δ-atomicity guarantee

---

[2]Baqend: https://www.baqend.com/.

by default while allowing tighter staleness bounds as an opt-in feature: For strong consistency, the client simply has to retrieve the current Cache Sketch before every read. By enabling clients to avoid stale cache entries that have not yet expired, the Cache Sketch approach effectively enables invalidation even in combination with purely expiration-based caches. Orestes uses an optimistic transaction protocol for distributed catch-aware transactions (DCAT) [Ges19, Sec. 4.8.2] which performs conflict checks at commit time, making it a *detection-based deferred consistency scheme*. Adya et al. [Ady+95] have proposed a similar scheme called Adaptive Optimistic Concurrency Control (AOCC). It also relies on a backward-oriented validation step [Agr+86, CO82, LW84], but serializes transactions in timestamp order of the committing server. Effectively, AOCC performs timestamp ordering [SS94] with a two-phase commit protocol [Lec09] and thus accepts a smaller class of schedules than DCAT which is based on BOCC+ [KR81, Rah88]. Moreover, instead of relying on version numbers like DCAT, AOCC servers maintain a set of metadata items for each of the client's cached data. Unlike DCAT, AOCC was designed for the case of very few clients: the metadata maintained in each server increases with both the number of cached records and the number of clients, making it unable to scale for web scenarios with many clients.

5.2.3 Caching in Object-Relational and Object-Document Mappers

Due to the reasons laid out above, most persistence frameworks today rely on programmatic control of object-based caches with no support from the database system. With the increasing adoption of scalable NoSQL systems, the landscape of mappers bridging the **impedance mismatch** between the data model of the database system and the application has grown [Stö+15]. In fact, many applications do not use any native database system API, but instead rely on the convenience of object mappers such as Hibernate, DataNucleus, Kundera, EclipseLink, Doctrine, and Morphia [Tor+17]. In case of Java, the Java Persistence API (JPA) standard [DeM09] is considered state-of-art superseding the older Java Data Objects API (JDO) [Rus03].

Both JPA and JDO and the equivalent technology from Microsoft called Entity Framework [Ady+07], support the notion of a first-level (L1) and a second-level (L2) cache. The L1 cache is exclusive to a persistence context and ensures that queries and lookups always resolve to the same object instances. The L2 is shared across contexts to leverage access locality between different contexts, processes, or even machines. The L2 interface is pluggable, so various options from in-process storage to Memcache- or IMDG-backed distributed implementations are available. Both L1 and L2 caches are write-through caches that directly reflect any updates passing through them. However, if data is changed from different contexts or even different clients, the L1 and L2 caches suffer from stale reads. The application has to explicitly flush or bypass these caches in order to prevent violations of consistency.

5.2.4   Web Caching

In literature, web caches are either treated as a storage tier for immutable content or as a means of content distribution for media that do not require freshness guarantees [Hua+13, Fre10]. Web caches are further defined by their implementation of the HTTP caching standards [IET15]. They can be employed in every location on the end-to-end path from clients to server. The granularity is typically files, though this is up to the application. Updates are purely expiration-based.

The applicability of web caching schemes is closely tied to web workloads and their properties. Breslau et al. were the first to systematically analyze how Zipf-distributed access patterns lend themselves for limited storage capacities of web caches [Bre+99, HL08, WF11]. Across six different traces, they found a steep average exponent of 0.85. Zipf-distributed popularity is closely related to our proposed capacity management scheme: even if only a small subset of "hot" queries can be actively matched against update operations, this is sufficient to achieve high cache hit rates.

The literature on workload characterization presents mixed conclusions. Based on an analysis of school logs, Gewertzman et al. [GS96], and Besavros [Bes95] found that most popular files tend to remain unchanged. Labrindis et al. [LR01b] and Douglis et al. [Dou+97], however, concluded that there is a strong correlation between update frequency and popularity of files. In another analysis of a more diverse set of university and industry traces conducted by Breslau et al. [Bre+99], the correlation between popularity and update rate was found to be present, but weak.

Another question particularly important for simulations is, how the arrival processes of reads, writes, and queries can be modeled stochastically. Poisson processes with exponentially distributed inter-reference times are most widely used [Tot09, Wil+05, VM14]. However, homogeneous Poisson processes do not capture any rate changes (e.g., increased popularity) or seasonality (e.g., massive frequent changes upon deployments). Session-based models describe web traffic as a combination of individual user sessions. Session inter-arrival times typically follow a Poisson process, while inter-click times follow heavy-tailed distributions like Weibull, LogNormal, and Pareto distributions [Den96, Gel00]. For all Poisson-like workloads, TTL estimators will exhibit high error rates due to the high variance of the exponential distribution.

Many optimizations of web caches have been studied. This includes cache replacement schemes [CI97], cooperative caching [RL04, RLZ06, TC03], and bandwidth-efficient updates [Mog+97]. In the past twenty years, numerous cache prefetching schemes have been proposed for browser, proxy, and CDN caches [PM96, Bes96, KLM97, MC+98]. Today, these schemes are not widely used in practice due to the overhead in the cache and excess network usage caused by wrong prefetching decisions. For the Cache Sketch approach [Ges+15], the concrete work-load and estimation accuracy only affect the false positive and cache hit rates, so that correctness is guaranteed regardless of estimation errors. This is in stark contrast to pure TTL-based cache coherence schemes [GS96, Lab+09, BR02, RS03, KR01] which will exhibit high staleness rates, if workloads are inherently unpredictable.

5.3 Cache Coherence: Expiration-Based vs. Invalidation-Based Caching

Cache coherence is a major concern for any caching approach. Similar to distributed databases, there is an inherent trade-off in caching approaches between throughput and latency on the one side and ease-of-use and provided correctness guarantees on the other. Often in practice, developers even have to bypass caching manually in order to achieve the desired consistency level [Nis+13, Ajo+15].

5.3.1 Expiration-Based Caching

In the literature, the idea of using an expiration-based caching model has previously been explored in the context of file and search result caching [Dar+96, Ami+03a, LGZ04, Bor+04, KFD00, KB96, How+88, Mog94]. Expiration-based caching (also referred to as pull-based caching [Lab+09]) can be categorized into *TTL-based*, *lease-based*, and *piggybacking* strategies. Expiration-based caching usually involves *asynchronous* validation of cached entries, i.e., the freshness is validated when cached data is expired. *Synchronous* validation (polling-every-time [Lab+09]) only reduces bandwidth, but not latency, which makes it inapplicable for the goal of this work.

5.3.2 Leases

The lease model is a concept from the distributed file systems literature [How+88, Mog94] originally proposed by Gray et al. [GC89]. A lease grants access to a local copy of an object until a defined expiration time [Vak06]. It is therefore similar to a lock, however combined with a limited validity to mitigate the problem of client failures and deadlocks. For the duration of the lease, the holder has to acknowledge each server-side invalidation in order to maintain strong consistency. A lease combines the concepts of expiration-based and invalidation-based cache coherence: while the lease is still active, the client will receive invalidations, afterwards the client has to acquire a new lease which is accompanied by a renewed expiration time [Vak06].

A central problem of leases is that long leases may incur high waiting times for updates, if a client does not respond, whereas short leases imply a large control message overhead and increase latency. A major refinement of the basic lease scheme addressing this problem are volume leases proposed by Yin et al. [Yin+99, Yin+98]. A volume groups related objects together and introduces a coarser level of granularity. Clients need to have both an active volume and object lease in order to perform an object read. By giving volume leases short expiration times and object leases longer expiration times, writes experience shorter delays and the message overhead for object lease renewals is reduced. By additionally incorporating access metrics, adaptive leases introduced by Duvuri et al. [DST03] can further optimize the read-versus-write latency trade-off by dynamically calculating lease durations.

The lease model is not well-suited for client caches in the web. Especially with mobile devices and high-traffic websites, leases on objects will usually expire, as client connectivity is intermittent and potentially thousands of clients will hold leases on the same object. The effect would therefore be similar to a TTL-based model, where the server has to delay writes until the respective TTL is expired.

5.3.3 Piggybacking

Piggybacking schemes batch together validations or invalidations and transfer them in bulk. Krishnamurthy et al. [KW97] proposed Piggyback Cache Validation (PCV). PCV is designed for proxy caches to decrease staleness by proactively renewing cached data. Each time a proxy cache processes a request for an origin server, the local cache is checked for objects from that origin that are either expired or will be expired soon. The revalidation requests for these objects are then batched and attached (piggybacked) with the original request to the origin server. With sufficient traffic to frequently piggyback revalidations, this can reduce latency and staleness as cached data is refreshed before it is requested by a client. Piggyback Server Invalidation (PSI) [KW98] follows a similar idea: when the server receives a revalidation request based on the version, the server additionally piggybacks a list of resources that have been invalidated since that modification, too. PCV and PSI can be combined in a hybrid approach [KW99, CKR98]. The idea is to use PSI, if little time has passed since the last revalidation, and PSV otherwise as the overhead of invalidation messages is smaller, if few objects have changed. As a major problem, However, these piggybacking schemes only work for shared caches (proxy caches, ISP caches, reverse proxy caches) and require modifications of the caching logic of HTTP [FR14].

5.3.4   Time-to-Live (TTL)

TTLs are usually assumed to be implicit, i.e., they are not explicitly defined by the application as they are not known in advance [Lab+09]. HTTP adopted the TTL model as it is the most scalable and simple approach to distribute cached data in the web [Fie+99, IET15]. The core of every TTL scheme is the **latency-recency trade-off**. Cao et al. [BR02] propose to employ user profiles for browsers that express the preference towards either higher recency or lower latency. Fixed TTL schemes that neither vary in time nor between requested objects/queries lead to a high level of staleness [Wor94]. This approach is often considered to be incompatible with the modern web, since users expect maximum performance without noticeable staleness. It therefore becomes the task of the application and the cloud services to minimize and hide any occurring staleness.

A popular and widely used TTL estimation strategy is the Alex protocol [GS96] (also referred to as Adaptive TTL [RS03, Wan99, KW97, CL98]) that originates from the Alex FTP server [Cat92]. It calculates the TTL as a percentage (e.g., 20%) of the time since the last modification, capped by an upper TTL bound. Simulations have shown that for certain workloads this scheme can contain the staleness rate to roughly 5% [GS96]. In an AT&T trace analyzed by Feldmann et al. [Fel+99] for a low percentage of 20%, the overall staleness for the Alex protocol was 0.22%. On the other hand, 58.5% of all requests were revalidations on unchanged resources. The Alex protocol has the downside of neither converging to the actual TTL nor being able to give estimates for new queries.

Alici et al. proposed an adaptive TTL computation scheme for search results on the web [Ali+12]. In their incremental TTL model, expired queries are compared with their latest cached version. If the result has changed, the TTL is reset to a minimum TTL, otherwise the TTL is augmented by an increment function (linear, polynomial, exponential) that can either be configured manually or trained from logs. Though the model is adaptive, it requires offline learning and assumes a central cache co-located with the search index. If the time of an invalidation is known (e.g., in a database setting instead of a search engine application), TTLs can potentially be computed more precisely than in their scheme, which only relies on subsequent reads to detect staleness and freshness. With the notable exception of the Cache Sketch that only performs less efficient when over- or underestimating expiration times, current TTL-based approaches exhibit potentially high levels of staleness in the presence of unpredictable invalidations that are only bounded by the maximum permissible TTLs.

5.3.5   Invalidation-Based Caching

Arguably, invalidations are the most intuitive mechanism to deal with updates of cached data. In this case, the server is responsible for detecting changes and distributing invalidation messages to all caches that might have cached that data. Invalidation-based caching can either be invalidation-only or update-based [Lab+09]. In the invalidation-only scheme, stale content is only evicted from the cache and reloaded upon the next cache miss. With the update-based approach, new versions are proactively pushed to caches. Almost every CDN works with the invalidation-only scheme in order to limit network overhead [PB08]. A notable exception is the academic Coral CDN, which is mainly designed for static, non-changing content and hence supports the update-based model [FFM04, Fre10].

Candan et al. [Can+01b] first explored automated invalidation-based web caching with the CachePortal system that detects changes of HTML pages by analyzing corresponding SQL queries. CachePortal is a reverse proxy cache with two major components. The *sniffer* is responsible for logging incoming HTTP requests and relating them to SQL queries detected at the JDBC database driver level to produce a query-to-URL mapping. The *invalidator* monitors update operations and detects which queries are affected to purge the respective URLs. The authors find the overhead of triggers or materialized views prohibitive and hence rely on a different approach. For each incoming update, a polling query is constructed. The polling query is either issued against the underlying relational database or an index structure maintained by the invalidator itself. If a non-empty result is returned, the update changes the result set of a query and a URL invalidation is triggered. The number of polling queries is proportional to both the number of updates and the number of cached queries. CachePortal therefore incurs a very high overhead for caching on the database and the invalidator. Since the load on the invalidator cannot be scaled horizontally, CachePortal is not suitable for large-scale web applications with potentially many users and high write throughput. Furthermore, the approach is strictly specific to a fixed set of technologies (JDBC, Oracle RDBMS, BEA Weblogic application server) and only covers reverse proxy caching. Furthermore, the mapping from HTTP requests to queries breaks under concurrent access, as it is based on observing queries within a time window. If multiple users request different resources at the same time, the mapping is flawed.

The Quaestor architecture [Ges+17] exploits the existing infrastructure of the web to accelerate delivery of dynamic content, specifically query results. To make this feasible, it registers all cached query results in the distributed real-time query engine InvaliDB [Win19, WGR20] which matches all incoming database writes to all currently cached queries in order to discover result changes with minimal latency. As soon as an invalidating change to one of the cached query results is detected, InvaliDB notifies one of the Quaestor application servers which in turn sends out invalidations to all affected invalidation-based caches (specifically the CDN). To prevent clients from reading stale query results from expiration-based caches (e.g. the browser cache within the user device), the Quaestor architecture relies on the Cache Sketch approach [Ges+15]: Through this mechanism, clients are periodically informed about stale expiration-based caches which can thus be avoided (and thereby effectively be invalidated). Since InvaliDB is scalable with both the number of concurrently registered queries and also with write throughput, the Quaestor architecture is feasible for large-scale web applications with many users and high data volumes. Baqend is the only commercial implementation at the time of writing.

Dilley et al. [KLM97] proposed the invalidation-based protocol DOCP (Distributed Object Consistency Protocol). The protocol extends HTTP to let caches subscribe to invalidations. DOCP therefore presents an effort to standardize invalidation messages, which are provided through custom and vendor-specific approaches in practice (e.g., the HTTP PURGE method [Kam17]). The authors call the provided consistency level *delta-consistency* which is similar Δ-atomicity, i.e., all subscribed caches will have received an invalidation of a written data item at most *delta* seconds after the update has been processed. DOCP's invalidation-only approach is less powerful than InvaliDB's update-based query subscription mechanism as InvaliDB allows subscriptions to an arbitrary number of conditions and queries multiplexed over a single Websocket connection to the origin.

Worrel [Wor94] studied hierarchical web caches to derive more efficient cache coherence schemes. He designed an invalidation protocol specifically suited for hierarchical topologies and compared it to fixed TTL schemes w.r.t. server load, bandwidth usage, and staleness. He found the scheme to be superior in terms of staleness and competitive to TTLs in server load and bandwidth usage. A particular problem of deep hierarchies is the *age penalty* problem studied by Cohen et al. [CK01]: older content in the upper levels of the hierarchy propagates downstream and negatively impacts dependent caches.

An alternative to cache invalidation was proposed by the Akamai founders Leighton and Lewin [LL00]. The idea is to include a hash value of the content in the URL, so that upon changes the old version does not get invalidated, but instead is superseded by a new URL containing the new fingerprint (*cache busting*). This approach is widely used in practice through build tools such as Grunt, Gulp, and Webpack. The downside is that this scheme only works for embedded content that does not require stable URLs (e.g., images and scripts). In particular, it cannot be applied to database objects, query results, and HTML pages. Furthermore, it only allows for invalidation at application deployment time and not at runtime.

Edge Side Includes (ESI) [Tsi+01] take the approach of Leighton and Lewon a step further by shifting template-based page assembly to the edge, i.e., CDN caches. ESI is a simple markup language that allows to describe HTML pages using inclusion of referenced fragments that can be cached individually. Rabinovich et al. [Rab+03] proposed to move ESI assembly to the client arguing that the rendering of ESI on the edge adds to the presumed main bottleneck of last-mile latency [Nag04]. While ESI has not gained relevance for the browser, the underlying idea is now widely used in practice [BPV08]. Every single-page application based on Ajax and MVC-frameworks for rendering employs the idea of assembling as website from individual fragments usually consumed from cloud-based REST APIs.

Bhide et al. [Bhi+02] also proposed a scheme to combine invalidation- and expiration-based caching in proxies. They argue that web workloads are inherently unpredictable for the server and therefore propose a **Time-to-Refresh** (TTR) computed in the proxy to replace TTLs. TTRs are computed for each data item based on previous changes and take a user-provided *temporal coherency requirement* into account that expresses the tolerable staleness based on data values (e.g., the stock price should never diverge by more than one dollar). TTRs therefore dynamically reflect both the rate of change (as expressed in TTLs) and the desired level of coherence. Bhide et al. present algorithms to mix the communication-intensive expiration-based revalidations through TTRs with invalidations.

5.3.6   Browser Caching

Traditionally, browsers only supported transparent caching at the level of HTTP, as specified in the standard [Fie+99]. The only recent additions to the original caching model are means to specify that stale content may be served during revalidation or unavailability of the backend [Not10], as well as an immutability flag to prevent the browser from revalidating upon user-initiated page refreshes [McM17]. For workloads of static content, Facebook reported that the browser cache served by far the highest portion of traffic (65.5%) compared to the CDN (20.0%) and reverse proxy caches (4.6%) [Hua+13].

Two extensions have been added to browsers in order to facilitate offline website usage and application-level caching beyond HTTP caching. *AppCache* was the attempt to let the server specify a list of cacheable resources in the cache manifest. The approach suffered from various problems, the most severe being that no resource-level cache coherence mechanism was included and displaying non-stale data required refreshing the manifest [Ama16]. To address these problems, *Service Workers* were proposed. They introduce a JavaScript-based proxy interface to intercept requests and programmatically define appropriate caching decisions [Ama16]. While cache coherence is not in the scope of Service Workers and has to rely on application-specific heuristics, there already are approaches for transparent website acceleration based on Service workers (e.g. Speed Kit[3] [Win18] [WGW+20]). A set of best practices for developing with Service Workers was published by Google and termed *Progressive Web Apps* [Mal16].

To structure client-side data beyond a hash table from URLs to cached data and enable processing of the data, three techniques have been proposed and partly standardized [Cam16] (cf. Sect. 3.4.2). *LocalStorage* provides a simple key-value interface to replace the use of inefficient cookies. *Web SQL Database* is an API that exposes access to an embedded relational database, typically SQLite. The specification is losing traction and will likely be dropped [Cam16, p. 63]. *IndexedDB* is also based on an embedded relational database system. Data is grouped into databases and object stores that present unordered collections of JSON documents. By defining indexes on object stores, range queries and point lookups are possible via an asynchronous API.

---

[3] Speed Kit: https://speed-kit.com.

5.3.7   Web Performance

A central finding of performance in modern web applications is that perceived speed
and page load times (cf. Sect. 3.4.1) are a direct result of physical **network latency**
[Gri13]. The HTTP/1.1 protocol that currently forms the basis of the web and REST
APIs suffers from inefficiencies that have partly been addressed by *HTTP/2* [IET15].

Wang et al. [WKW16] explored the idea of offloading the client by preprocessing
data in proxies with higher processing power. Their system Shandian evaluates
websites in the proxy and returns them as a combination of HTML, CSS, and
JavaScript including the heap to continue the evaluation. For slow Android devices,
this scheme yielded a page load time improvement of about 50%. Shandian does,
however, require a modified browser which makes it inapplicable for broad usability
in the web. The usefulness of the offloading is also highly dependent on the
processing power of the mobile device, as the proxy-side evaluation blocks delivery
and introduces a trade-off between increased latency and reduced processing time.

Netravali et al. proposed Polaris [Net+16] as an approach to improve page load
times. The idea is to inject information about dependencies between resources into
HTML pages, as well as JavaScript-based scheduling logic that loads resources
according to the dependency graph. This optimization works well in practice,
because browsers rely on heuristics to prioritize fetching of resources. By an offline
analysis of a specific server-generated website, the server can determine actual
read/write and write/write dependencies between JavaScript and CSS ahead of time
and express them as a dependency graph. This allows parallelism where normally
the browser would block to guarantee side-effect free execution. Depending on
the client-server round-trip time and bandwidth, Polaris yields a page load time
improvement of roughly 30%. The limitations of the approach are that it does not
allow non-determinism and that dependency graphs have to be generated for every
client view. For personalized websites, this overhead can be prohibitive. Contra-
dicting the current trend in web development towards single-page applications, the
approach furthermore assumes server-side rendering.

5.4   Query Caching

Query caching has been tackled from different angles in the context of distributed
database systems [Dar+96, Ami+03a, LGZ04, Bor+04, KFD00, KB96], mediators
[LC99, CRS99, Ada+96], data warehouses [Des+98, KP01, Lou+01], peer-to-
peer systems [Gar+08, PH03, Kal+02], and web search results [BLV11, Cam+10,
Bla+10, Ali+11]. Most of this work is focused on the details of answering queries
based on previously cached results, while only few approaches also cover cache
coherence.

5.4.1   Peer-to-Peer Query Caching

Garrod et al. have proposed Ferdinand, a proxy-based caching architecture forming
a peer-to-peer distributed hash table (DHT) [Gar+08]. When clients query data,
the proxy checks a local, disk-based map from query strings to result sets. If the
result is not present, a lookup in another proxy is performed according to the DHT
scheme. The consistency management is based on a publish/subscribe invalidation
architecture. Each proxy subscribes to multicast groups corresponding to the locally
cached queries. A limiting assumption of Ferdinand is that updates and queries
follow a small set of fixed templates defined by the application. This is required to
map updates and queries to the same publish/subscribe topics, so that only relevant
updates will be received in each caching proxy. Peer-to-peer query caching has
also been employed for reducing traffic in file sharing protocols [PH03], as well
as to distributed OLAP queries [Kal+02]. IPFS [Ben14] also employs a peer-to-peer
approach with DHTs to cache file chunks across many users. Since the overhead of
metadata lookups is prohibitive for low latency, though, this scheme cannot be used
to accelerate the delivery of web content.

5.4.2   Mediators

In contrast to reverse proxies that can serve any web application, mediators are
typically designed to handle one specific use case, type of data, or class of data
sources. Work in this area is mostly concerned with constructing query plans using
semantic techniques to leverage both locally cached data from the mediator as well
as distributed data sources [LC99, CRS99, Ada+96].

5.4.3   Query Caching Proxies and Middlewares

DBProxy, DBCache, and MTCache [Ami+03a, LGZ04, Bor+04] rely on dedicated
database proxies to generate distributed query plans that can efficiently combine
cached data with the original database. However, these systems need built-in tools of
the database system for consistency management and are less motivated by latency
reduction than by reducing query processing overhead in the database similar to
materialized views [Shi11].

   DBProxy [Ami+03a] is designed to cache SQL queries in a proxy, similar to a
reverse proxy cache or a CDN. DBProxy adapts the schema as new queries come
in and learns query templates by comparing queries to each other. When a query
is executed in the database, results are stored in DBProxy. To reuse cached data,
DBProxy performs a containment check that leverages the simplicity of templates
to lower the complexity of traditional query containment algorithms [Ami+03b].

DBProxy receives asynchronous updates from the database system and hence offers Δ-atomicity by default. The authors describe monotonic reads and strong consistency as two potential options for reducing staleness in DBProxy, but do not evaluate or elaborate on the implications. DBProxy assumes that the application runs as a Java-based program in the proxy and enhances the JDBC driver to inject the caching logic. The authors do not discuss the impact of transactional queries on correctness when they are invisible to the database system.

DBCache [Bor+04, Luo+02, Bor+03] and *MTCache* [LGZ04] are similar approaches that employ nodes of relational database systems for caching (IBM DB2 and Microsoft SQL Server, respectively). Both systems rewrite query plans to exploit both local and remote data. In DBCache, the query plan is called a *Janus* plan and consists of a probe query and a regular query. The probe query performs an existence check to determine whether the local tables can be used for the query. Afterwards, a regular query containing a clause for both local and remote data is executed. Cache coherence is based on the DB2 replication interface that asynchronously propagates all updates of a transaction. MTCache uses the corresponding asynchronous replication mechanism from Microsoft SQL Server. It maintains the cache as a set of materialized views and performs cost-based optimization on query templates to decide between local and remote execution. Due to their strong relation to database replication protocols, DBCache and MTCache are effectively lazily populated read replicas.

Labrinidis et al. proposed *WebViews* as a technique of caching website fragments [LR01a, LR00]. A WebView refers to HTML fragments generated by database queries, e.g., a styled table of stock prices. Through a cost-based model, WebViews are either materialized in the web servers, in the database, or not at all. The authors found that materialization in the web servers is generally more effective than materialization in the database by at least a factor of 10, since it incurs fewer round-trips to the database.

5.4.4 Search Result Caching

According to Bortnikov et al. [BLV11], caching approaches for search results can be classified into coupled and decoupled design. In a *decoupled design* (e.g., [Cam+10]), the caches are independent from the search index (i.e., the database), while a *coupled design* is more sophisticated and actively uses the index to ensure cache coherence. Blanco et al. investigated query caching in the context of incremental search indices at Yahoo and proposed a coupled design [Bla+10]. To achieve cache coherence, their cache invalidation predictor (CIP) generates a synopsis of invalidated documents in the document ingestion pipeline. This summary is checked before returning a cached search query to bypass the cache when new indexed document versions are available. Unlike evolving summary data structures like the Cache Sketch [Ges+15], the synopses are immutable, created in batch, and only used to predict likely invalidations of server-side caches.

Bortnikov et al. [BLV11] improved the basic CIP architecture using realistic workloads, more efficient cache replacement algorithms and optimizations to deal with less popular documents. Alici et al. [Ali+11] were able to achieve comparable invalidation accuracy using a timestamp-based approach where an invalidation is detected by having the cache distribute the timestamp metadata of a cached query to all responsible search servers. These confirm freshness, if they did not index updated document versions, nor new documents that also match the search term, based on the respective timestamps. The broadcast is less expensive than reevaluating the query, but not suitable for latency reduction in a web caching scenario.

5.4.5   Summary Data Structures for Caching

5.4.5.1   Bloom Filters for Caching

Summary Cache proposed by Fan et al. [Fan+00] is a system for web caching that employs Bloom filters as metadata digests in cooperative web caches. As such, it bears some resemblance to Orestes [Ges19] which uses the Cache Sketch as a Bloom filter-based data structure for informing clients of possibly outdated caches. Summary Cache, however, is fundamentally different as its summaries ("cache digests") are generated in intervals to communicate the set of locally available cached data to cooperating web caches. In the context of Summary Cache, Counting Bloom filters were introduced in the literature for the first time. Since each server has to delete URLs from the Bloom filter when they are replaced from the cache, a removal operation is necessary. In this setting, considerations about the optimal Bloom filter size and invalidations are not required as the Bloom filter only serves as a means of bandwidth reduction.

Recently, cache fingerprinting has been proposed for improving HTTP/2 push [ON16]. The idea is to construct a digest of the browser cache's contents—similar to Summary Cache—to efficiently identify resources that are already available in the client and therefore do not have to be pushed by the server. Instead of Bloom filters, Golomb-compressed sets (GCS) [PSS09] are used. GCS exploit the fact that in a Bloom filter with only one hash function, the differences between values follow a geometrical distribution [MU05]. This pattern can be optimally compressed using Golomb-coding, yielding a smaller size than Bloom filters. The fingerprinting scheme has not been standardized, yet, but an experimental implementation is available in the H2O web server [Hev].

In NoSQL systems, Bloom filters are frequently used to accelerate storage engines based on log-structured merge-trees (LSMs). Google's BigTable [Cha+08] pioneered the approach that has been adopted in various systems (e.g., Cassandra, LevelDB, HyperDex, WiredTiger, RocksDB, TokuDB) [LM10, EWS12, GD11]. In BigTable, data is stored in immutable SSTables located on disk. In order to avoid disk I/O for the lookup of a key for each SSTable, a Bloom filter is loaded into memory. Only when the check is positive, the SSTable is queried on disk. In contrast to the Cache Sketch in Orestes, the Bloom filters in BigTable only need to be constructed once, as BigTable's on-disk data is immutable.

5.4.5.2 Alternatives to Bloom Filters

Space-efficient alternatives to Bloom filters have been proposed. While Golomb-coded sets [PSS09] achieve slightly smaller sizes, they are not suited for Orestes, as fast $O(1)$ lookups are not possible. Mitzenmacher [Mit02] proposed Compressed Bloom Filters. They are based on the observation that a very sparse Bloom filter can be efficiently compressed by an entropy encoding like Huffman and arithmetic codes [Rom97]. However, due to the size of the uncompressed filter, memory consumption is infeasible for the client. Using several Blocked Bloom filters with additional compression would mitigate this problem, but increase the complexity and latency of lookups [PSS09]. Cuckoo filters have been proposed by Fan et al. [Fan+14] as a more space-efficient alternative to Counting Bloom filters. In contrast to a Counting Bloom filter, however, the number of duplicate entries in a Cuckoo filter is strictly bounded. Matrix filters proposed by Porat et al. [PPR05, Por09] achieve the lower limit of required space for a given false positive rate. This advantage is contrasted by linear lookup time and a complex initial construction of the data structure. The original Bloom filters are already within a factor of 1.44 of the theoretical lower bound of required space [BM03] and offer $O(1)$ inserts and lookups. Kirsch et al. [KM06] showed that the use of a linear combination of two independent hash functions reduces the amount of costly hash computations without loss of uniformity. An overview of other Bloom filter variants and applications is given by Broder and Mitzenmacher [BM03] and Tarkoma et al. [TRL12].

Bloom filters, Golomb-compressed sets, and other summary data structures are popular means for optimization in both networking and data management. But as is often the case for optimizations, the application scenario and workload determine which approach is considered the right one. For example, the choice between using Golomb-compressed sets or original Bloom filters may depend on whether the superior space-efficiency of the former is valued over the constant-time lookups of the latter.

5.5   Eager vs. Lazy Geo Replication

5.5.1   Replication and Caching

The goal of replication is to increase read scalability and to decouple reads from writes to offload the database and reduce latency. Replication can protect the system against data loss. In case of geographically distributed replicas (geo-replication), read latency for distributed access from clients is improved, too [Bak+11, Shu+13,

Kra+13, Llo+13, Cor+12, Cor+13, Sov+11, Cha+08, DeC+07, Coo+08, Ter+13]. In this setting, a central constraint is that intra-data center latencies are small (<5 ms), while inter-data center communication is expensive (50–150 ms) [Agr+13]. Caching can be viewed as an alternative to replication. With caching, data is fetched and stored on-demand, while with geo-replication the complete data set is synchronized between multiple replica sites, incurring higher management overhead. However, two different kinds of caches can be distinguished: caches that require expensive updates (invalidation-based caches) and passive caches that do not incur any overhead to the server (expiration-based caches). If replicas are allowed to accept writes (multi-master), considerable coordination is required to guarantee consistency.

Charron-Bost et al. [CBPS10, Chapter 12] and Öszu and Valduriez [ÖV11, Chapter 13] provide a comprehensive review of replication techniques. We will focus on a discussion of exemplary, influential geo-replicated systems and an outline of how their trade-offs differ from one another.

5.5.2 Eager Geo-Replication

Through eager geo-replication as implemented in Megastore [Bak+11], Spanner [Cor+13, Cor+12], and F1 [Shu+13] as well as in MDCC [Kra+13] and Mencius [MJM08], applications achieve strong consistency at the cost of higher write latencies (typically 100 ms [Cor+12] to 600 ms [Bak+11]).

5.5.2.1 Megastore

Baker et al. [Bak+11] came to the conclusion, that the cost of strong consistency and ACID transactions in highly distributed systems is often acceptable in order to empower developers. Megastore's data model is based on entity groups, that represent fine-grained, application-defined data partitions (e.g., a user's message inbox). Transactions are supported per co-located entity group, each of which is mapped to a single row in BigTable that offers row-level atomicity. Transactions spanning multiple entity groups are possible, but not encouraged, as they require expensive 2PC [Lec09].

Megastore (also available as a DBaaS called Google Cloud Datastore) uses synchronous wide-area replication. The replication protocol is based on Paxos consensus [Lam98] over positions in a shared write-ahead log. Megastore uses the Multi-Paxos [Lam01] optimization to achieve best-case performance of one wide-area round-trip per write as opposed to two round-trips with regular Paxos. This replication protocol has been improved by Kraska et al. [Kra+13] in MDCC (Multi-Data Center Consistency). They include two additional Paxos optimizations (fast and generalized Paxos) and reduce conflicts by leveraging commutativity of certain updates.

To allow consistent local read operations, Megastore tracks the replication status of each entity group in a per-site coordinator. In order for the coordinator to reflect the latest state of each entity group, the Paxos replication not only has to contact a quorum as in the original protocol, but has to wait for acknowledgments from each replica site. This implies that lower latency for consistent reads is achieved at the expense of slower writes.

The authors report average read latencies of 100 ms and write latencies of 600 ms. These numbers illustrate the considerable cost of employing synchronous wide-area replication. The high latency of writes is critical, as Megastore employs a form of optimistic concurrency for writes on the same entity group: if two writes happen concurrently during replication, only one will succeed. This limits the throughput to $1/l_w$, where l_w is the write latency, i.e., about ten writes per second in the best case. Megastore is also available as a DBaaS called Google Cloud Datastore in the Google App Engine PaaS.

5.5.2.2   Spanner and F1

Spanner [Cor+13, Cor+12] evolved from the observation that Megastore's guarantees—though useful—come at performance penalty that is prohibitive for some applications. Spanner is a multi-version database system that unlike Megastore provides efficient cross-shard ACID transactions. The authors argue: "We believe it is better to have application programmers deal with performance problems due to overuse of transactions as bottlenecks arise, rather than always coding around the lack of transactions" [Cor+12, p. 4]. Spanner automatically groups data into partitions (tablets) that are synchronously replicated across sites via Paxos and stored in Colossus, the successor of GFS [GGL03]. Transactions in Spanner are based on two-phase locking and 2PC executed over the leaders for each partition involved in the transaction. Spanner serializes transactions according to their global commit times.[4] To make this feasible, Spanner introduces TrueTime, an API for high precision timestamps with uncertainty bounds implemented using atomic clocks and GPS. Each transaction is assigned a commit timestamp from TrueTime. Using the uncertainty bounds, the leader can wait until the transaction is guaranteed to be visible at all sites before releasing locks. This also enables efficient read-only transactions that can read a consistent snapshot for a certain timestamp across all data centers without any locking.

Mahmoud et al. [Mah+13] proposed an optimization for faster commits that integrates local 2PC in data centers with a Paxos consensus as to whether the transaction should commit (*replicated commit* protocol). This reduces commit latency, but comes at the cost of high read latency, since every read needs to contact a majority of data centers to only read committed data.

---

[4]This is termed *external consistency* by the Spanner authors and known in the literature as *strict serializability* or *commit order-preserving conflict serializable (COCSR)* [WV02].

F1 [Shu+13] and its commercial version Cloud Spanner [Bre17] build on Spanner to support SQL-based access for Google's advertising business. To this end, F1 introduces a hierarchical schema based on Protobuf, a rich data encoding format similar to Avro and Thrift [Kle17]. To support both OLTP and OLAP queries, it uses Spanner's abstractions to provide consistent indexing. A lazy protocol for schema changes allows non-blocking schema evolution [Rae+13]. Besides pessimistic Spanner transactions, F1 supports optimistic transactions. Each row bears a version timestamp that is used at commit time to perform a short-lived pessimistic transaction to validate a transaction's read set. Optimistic transactions in F1 suffer from the abort rate problem [Gra+81], as the read phase is latency-bound and the commit requires slow, distributed Spanner transactions.

According to the CAP theorem [Bre00], Spanner and F1 cannot be highly available systems. Brewer [Bre17] argues that in practice, however, they behave as highly available systems through engineering best practices. For example, Cloud Spanner does not rely on the public Internet to perform geo-replication, but instead transfers data over private, redundant networks owned and operated by Google.

CockroachDB [Coc] is an open-source, geo-replicated, relational database system based on the design of Spanner and F1. To support commodity hardware, CockroachDB does not use TrueTime, but instead uses NTP synchronization with hybrid logical clocks[5] [Kul+14]. As a consequence, CockroachDB cannot provide strict serializability for transactions, only serializability.[6] The transaction protocol is based on an underlying key-value store that is replicated using Raft consensus [OO13] for groups of keys. Atomicity is achieved through a locking protocol on per-record metadata, similar to Percolator [PD10]. Isolation is implemented as multi-version timestamp ordering[WV02] per consensus group and 2PC across groups. Read-write and write-write conflicts therefore cause transaction aborts, if the operations are not ordered according to the transaction begin timestamps. Like Spanner and F1, CockroachDB is prone to high read, write, and transaction latency due to synchronous geo-replication and 2PC.

Summing up, strict serializability is an important property for applications. Without this guarantee, blind writes (e.g., inserting a comment record) can be delayed arbitrarily and may never become visible. Spanner and F1 achieve strict serializability by delaying transaction commits and using high-precision clocks, while CockroachDB sacrifices the guarantee for performance reasons.

---

[5]Hybrid logical clocks combine the benefits of logical clocks [Lam78] for simple tracking of causality with physical clocks that are within a defined drift from real time by merging both.

[6]In particular for individual operations (transactions with a single read or write), the lack of strict serializability implies that linearizability is not guaranteed in CockroachDB.

5.5.3 *Lazy Geo-Replication*

With lazy geo-replication as in Dynamo [DeC+07], BigTable/HBase [Cha+08, Hba], Cassandra [LM10], MongoDB [CD13], CouchDB [ALS10], Couchbase [Lak+16], Espresso [Qia+13], PNUTS [Coo+08], Walter [Sov+11], Eiger [Llo+13], and COPS [Llo+11] stale reads are allowed, but the system performs better and remains available during partitions.

5.5.3.1 Eventually Consistent Geo-Replication

Most asynchronously replicated NoSQL systems support using their intra-data center replication protocol for cross-data center replication. In contrast to systems with transparent geo-replication, the application needs to be explicitly configured to route read and write requests to the correct data center. MongoDB [CD13] allows tagging shards with a zone parameter to allocate data to regions based on properties (e.g., an "address" field in user documents). It also supports distributing replicas within a replica set over multiple locations. However, this comes at a cost, as replicas from another data center can be elected to masters upon network partitions and transient failures. Couchbase [Lak+16] uses the asynchronous Memcache replication protocol for geo-replication. Most RDBMSs include only limited support for geo-distributed deployments, mostly directly based on their asynchronous intra-data center replication protocols (e.g., in MySQL, MySQL Cluster, and PostgresSQL [Pos]).

CouchDB [ALS10] has a multi-master replication protocol that was designed for heavily geo-distributed setups from device-embedded instances to multiple data centers. As writes are allowed on each slave, conflicts are tracked using hash histories [Agr+13], an alternative to vector clocks [DeC+07] for causality tracking. Quorum systems such as Dynamo, Cassandra, and Riak [LM10, DeC+07] require location-awareness for each key's preference list, i.e., the information on whether the responsible database nodes are local to the data center or connected through wide-area networks. Cassandra, for example, supports configuring remote site behavior through topology strategies and per operation quorums. These quorums define whether data is replicated purely asynchronously (e.g., for analytics) or whether a remote cluster has to participate in the overall quorum ("EACH_QUORUM") [CH16]. Riak distinguishes between a source cluster for operational workloads and sink clusters that do not participate in quorums and only asynchronously receive writes from the source cluster.

BigTable and HBase [Cha+08, Hba] are synchronously replicated within a data center at the file system level (GFS and HDFS [GGL03], respectively), but offer asynchronous wide-area replication, mainly for purposes of disaster recovery. LinkedIn's Espresso is a document store that uses asynchronous master-slave replication within a data center built on top of a change data capturing system called Databus [Das+12]. Subscribers to this replication bus can be placed in remote data centers.

5.5.3.2 PNUTS

Causal consistency is the strongest level of consistency achievable without inter-data center coordination [Llo+11]. Yahoo's PNUTS system [Coo+08] was influential in this respect, as it combines stronger consistency with a geo-replicated design. PNUTS leverages the observation that updates for a particular record tend to originate from the same region. Therefore, the primary is chosen per record ("record-level mastering"). Updates are propagated through an asynchronous pub-/sub message broker that enforces a serial order for updates on the same key which guarantees causal consistency per key (termed "timeline consistency"). Reads can be directed to any replica, if timeline consistency is sufficient ("read-any"), or explicitly request monotonic reads ("read-critical") or strong consistency ("read-latest") else. In each region, records are range-sharded and stored in MySQL. The design of PNUTS presents a compromise between multi-master and master-slave replication. It decouples failures of primaries for different records and achieves low latency, if the primary only receives writes from nearby clients.

5.5.3.3 Eiger, COPS, and Walter

Eiger [Llo+13] and COPS [Llo+11] are two approaches for providing full causal consistency for asynchronous replication. Eiger and COPS have strong similarities, their major difference is that causality tracking in COPS is based on per-record metadata, while Eiger tracks dependencies between operations. COPS introduces the notion of *causal+ consistency* that combines causal consistency with guaranteed convergence of writes. While COPS is not the first system to provide causal+ consistency for geo-replication, it is the first that is not based on unscalable use of the database log like Bayou [Dem+94] and PRACTI [Bel+06]. The key idea of COPS is to have clients attach metadata of causally relevant read operations to each write operation. During replication at a remote site, a write is only applied if all causal dependencies have also been applied already. To ensure convergence, conflicting writes are resolved using a commutative and associative handler (e.g., last-writer-wins). COPS also introduces a two-phase commit algorithm for read-only transactions that only see causally consistent records.

Walter [Sov+11] extends the COPS approach for causality tracking to transactions, by introducing *Parallel Snapshot Isolation* as an isolation level that relaxes snapshot isolation to allow different transaction orderings on different sites. Bailis et al. have proposed *bolt-on causal consistency* [Bai+13a] that provides causal consistency at the client side. The idea is similar to the concept behind COPS:

writes are only made visible for reads, once their casual dependencies are available. However, as this safety guarantee is not paired with a liveness guarantee, clients can end up reading very stale data.

The main problem of all geo-replication schemes for causal consistency is that either potential causality is tracked which imposes a large overhead or that developers are faced with the burden of explicitly declaring causal relationships.

5.5.3.4   Pileus

Pileus [Ter+13] proposed by Terry et al. from Microsoft Research achieves low latency, single round-trip writes, and bounded staleness. It is based on an SLA concept, in which developers can annotate consistency levels and latency bounds with utility values. For example, an application could specify that up to 5 min of staleness are tolerable and then define the monetary value of requests that return in 200 ms, 400 ms, or 600 ms. Pileus has a key-value data model with CRUD-based access. It employs a primary site for updates and all geo-replicated secondary sites are asynchronously replicated.

Clients are responsible for selecting a replica by evaluating the SLA and returning the sub-SLA (a combination of a consistency and latency requirement with a utility) that has the highest utility multiplied by the probability of meeting the consistency and latency requirement. Data is then read from the replica that maximizes the selected sub-SLA. The decision whether a replica can satisfy a consistency requirement is based on computing a minimum acceptable read timestamp that indicates how far a replica is allowed to lag behind the primary without violating the consistency level. To make this feasible, clients need to frequently collect information about network latency and replication lag from all replicas. Different consistency levels are supported (e.g. monotonic reads, eventual/causal/strong consistency, Δ-atomicity). For Δ-atomicity, however Pileus assumes a relatively high Δ (typically minutes [Ter+13, p. 316]), as otherwise polling from replicas becomes inefficient and strict clock synchronization would be required.

In a follow-up work, Pileus was extended by the ability for dynamic primary/secondary reconfiguration in order to maximize global utility of SLAs in a system called Tuba [AT14]. Here, a configuration service periodically collects observed latencies and SLA violations from clients and selects a new configuration with the best utility-to-cost ratio. Potential reconfigurations include adding or switching a primary site and changing the replication factor and replica locations. Clients need to always be aware of configuration changes in order not to perform strongly consistent reads and writes on non-primaries. Compared to Pileus, Tuba increases the probability of strongly consistent reads from 33% to 55%.

5.5.3.5 Tao

Tao is an example of a system that combines geo-replication with caching. Bronson et al. [Bro+13] describe the system that stores Facebook's multi-petabyte social graph. The data is held in a sharded MySQL which is asynchronously replicated across data centers. Caching is performed at two levels of cache tiers. The *leader cache tier* is located in front of MySQL and is allowed to perform writes on it. Multiple *follower cache tiers* service requests to their nearest application servers and forward requests to the leader if necessary. Each tier consists of many modified Memcache [Fit04] servers with custom memory allocation and LRU cache eviction schemes [Xu+14, Nis+13]. Tiers are sharded through consistent hashing to avoid reshuffling of data in case of failures. To mitigate popularity-induced hotspots, each shard inside a tier can be master-slave replicated. The tiers behave like synchronous write-through caches, i.e., when a write request arrives at a follower tier's Memcache shard, it is forwarded to the respective leader shard. If the current data center is the master for that data item, the write is performed on the corresponding MySQL shard. Otherwise, it is forwarded to the leader tier of the master data center. When the write is complete, invalidation messages are issued to every cache holding that data item. Cache coherence is thus asynchronous, i.e., there are no consistency guarantees, but anecdotally the lag is in the order of one second [Bro+13]. Tao handles roughly one billion reads per second with a read-heavy workload (over 99% reads).

Lu et al. [Lu+15] performed extensive consistency checking for Tao's two-level caching architecture by sampling requests. They analyzed violations of linearizability, read-your-writes consistency, and per-object sequential consistency. For Facebook's workload, the violation are reported to be very rare (e.g., 0.00151% in case of linearizability). The authors attribute this to the fact that writes are very rare and only 10–25% of all objects experience both reads and writes. The effects on transactional isolation were not measured, as the distributed nature of transactions made a tracing and checking approach impossible.

5.5.3.6 Tunable Consistency and the Latency-Consistency Trade-Off

The idea of exposing tunable consistency to developers is found in other systems. In many applications some operations need to be performed with strong consistency (e.g., password checking), while eventual consistency is acceptable for others (e.g., adding a product to the shopping cart). Both Twitter and Facebook have sub-systems providing strong consistency for operations on critical data [Sch16, Lu+15]. In Google's Megastore [Bak+11], weakly consistent reads are allowed for performance reasons despite strongly consistent updates. In Gemini [Li+12], red (strongly consistent) and blue (weakly consistent) operations are distinguished for geo-replicated storage. Gemini maximizes the use of fast, locally executed blue operations by determining when an operation is commutative to every potentially concurrent operation.

Kraska et al. [Kra+09] proposed to attach SLAs to objects in order to include the cost as an optimization factor for cloud-based storage systems (*consistency rationing*). The two SLA classes A and C reflect data that is always handled with strong or weak consistency, respectively, while class B is continuously optimized according to a cost function. Florescu and Kossmann [FK09] argue that most cloud-based applications are not concerned with the concrete level of consistency, but the overall cost of the application.

Application complexity is usually increased by different consistency choices [Li+14]. Guerraoui et al. [GPS16] proposed *Correctables* as a new programming model that abstracts different consistency levels. The main idea is to provide a Promise-based [LS88b] interface that can either directly execute an operation at the desired consistency level or return multiple results with increasing consistency and delay. For example, in a ticket checkout process, a potentially stale stock counter could be returned first to proceed, when it is sufficiently high, with the option to abort shortly afterwards, if the actual stock value is already zero. A similar scheme is used in Meteor [HS16], to hide potentially slow write operations from users (*latency compensation*).

5.5.3.7 Geo-Replica Placement

In contrast to caching, the decision *where* to best replicate data involves intimate knowledge of workloads and access patterns. Web caching is inherently more adaptive than replication, as data is materialized on demand and as near to the client as possible. Wu et al. [Wu+13] have proposed SPANStore to address replica-placement in multi-cloud environments. SPANStore minimizes the cost of a data storage deployment based on application requirements such as latency SLOs and desired consistency levels. For each access set of an application's workload, a placement manager decides where to store data and from where to serve reads and writes. To provide transparency to the application, a client library proxies access to the different cloud data centers.

The problem of geo-replication was also studied for transactional workloads by Sharov et al. [Sha+15]. They proposed a replication framework for transactional, highly distributed workloads that minimizes latency through appropriate primary and replica placement. Zakhary et al. [Zak+16] described a similar approach for majority-based replication. They employ a cache-like "optimistic read" optimization: instead of always reading from a majority of replicas, a passive replica (effectively a client cache) can be used and reads can be validated before transaction commit.

5.5.3.8 Consistency

Consistency in replicated storage systems has been studied in both theory [GLS11] and practice [Bai+12, Lu+15, Ber14]. An up-to-date and in-depth discussion of consistency in distributed systems and databases is provided by Viotti and Vukolic [VV16]. Their two main observations are that there is a complex relationship between different consistency levels and that similar guarantees are often named differently across research communities.

Lee et al. [Lee+15] proposed to decouple the problem of consistency from database system design through a system called RIFL (Reusable Infrastructure for Linearizability). RIFL builds on remote procedure calls (RPCs) with at-least-once semantics (i.e., invocations with retries) and enhances them to exactly-once semantics which are sufficient to guarantee linearizability. To this end, each request is assigned a unique identifier and a persistent log guarantees that completed requests will not be re-executed.[7] The authors report a write overhead of their implementation in RAMCloud [Ous+11] of only 4% compared to the base system without RIFL. The exactly-once semantics also simplify the implementation of transactions. Their approach builds on Sinfonia [Agu+07], an in-memory service infrastructure that provides a mini-transaction primitive for atomic cross-node memory access. A central limitation of RIFL is its assumption that clients are reliable and do not lose their state upon crashes. In the web this assumption does not hold.

5.6 Summary

Web caching and geo-replication are both widely used for increasing scalability and achieving low latency in globally distributed applications.

Invalidation-based caching can be used to provide rigorous consistency guarantees for accessing clients, but requires continuous change monitoring for all cached resources and is therefore typically considered infeasible for complex access patterns (e.g. for query caching). Expiration-based caching is often used instead, but here staleness is only bounded by TTLs, so that high efficiency (large TTLs) has to be weighed against data freshness (low TTLs). The advantage of geo-replication is that consistency and transactional isolation levels can be chosen through the replication protocol and be tuned for the respective database system. It is more powerful to provide protection against disaster scenarios and can reduce latency for strongly consistent reads. As a major downside, however, geo-replication either has to perform multiple synchronous wide-area round-trips for consistent updates or it can only provide eventual consistency without recency guarantees.

---

[7]The idea of building distributed transactions on a shared log is also found in Calvin [Tho+12] (cf. p. 141).

References

[Ada+96] Sibel Adali et al. "Query Caching and Optimization in Distributed Mediator Systems". In: *Proceedings of the 1996 ACM SIGMOD International Conference on Management of Data, Montreal, Quebec, Canada, June 4–6, 1996*. Ed. by H. V. Jagadish and Inderpal Singh Mumick. ACM Press, 1996, pp. 137–148. https://doi.org/10.1145/233269.233327.

[Ady+07] Atul Adya et al. "Anatomy of the ado. net entity framework". In: *Proceedings of the 2007 ACM SIGMOD international conference on Management of data*. ACM. 2007, pp. 877–888.

[Ady+95] Atul Adya et al. "Efficient Optimistic Concurrency Control Using Loosely Synchronized Clocks". In: *Proceedings of the 1995 ACM SIGMOD International Conference on Management of Data, San Jose, California, May 22–25, 1995*. Ed. by Michael J. Carey and Donovan A. Schneider. ACM Press, 1995, pp. 23–34. https://doi.org/10.1145/223784.223787.

[Aer]   *Aerospike*. http://www.aerospike.com/. (Accessed on 05/11/2018). 2018. URL: http://www.aerospike.com/ (visited on 01/13/2017).

[AG17]   Nick Antonopoulos and Lee Gillam, eds. *Cloud Computing: Principles, Systems and Applications (Computer Communications and Networks)*. 2nd ed. 2017. Springer, July 2017. ISBN: 9783319546445. URL: http://amazon.com/o/ASIN/3319546449/.

[AGK95]   Brad Adelberg, Hector Garcia-Molina, and Ben Kao. "Applying Update Streams in a Soft Real-Time Database System". In: *Proceedings of the 1995 ACM SIGMOD International Conference on Management of Data, San Jose, California, May 22–25, 1995*. Ed. by Michael J. Carey and Donovan A. Schneider. ACM Press, 1995, pp. 245–256. https://doi.org/10.1145/223784.223842.

[Agr+13] Divyakant Agrawal et al. "Managing Geo-replicated Data in Multi-datacenters". In: *Databases in Networked Information Systems - 8th International Workshop, DNIS 2013, Aizu-Wakamatsu, Japan, March 25–27, 2013. Proceedings*. Ed. by Aastha Madaan, Shinji Kikuchi, and Subhash Bhalla. Vol. 7813. Lecture Notes in Computer Science. Springer, 2013, pp. 23–43. https://doi.org/10.1007/978-3-642-37134-9_2.

[Agr+86] Divyakant Agrawal et al. "Distributed Multi-Version Optimistic Concurrency Control for Relational Databases". In: *Spring COMPCON'86, Digest of Papers, Thirty-First IEEE Computer Society International Conference, San Francisco, California, USA, March 3–6, 1986*. IEEE Computer Society, 1986, pp. 416–421.

[Agu+07] Marcos K. Aguilera et al. "Sinfonia: a new paradigm for building scalable distributed systems". In: *ACM SIGOPS Operating Systems Review*. ACM, 2007, pp. 159–174. URL: http://dl.acm.org/citation.cfm?id=1294278 (visited on 01/03/2015).

[Ajo+15] Phillipe Ajoux et al. "Challenges to adopting stronger consistency at scale". In: *15th Workshop on Hot Topics in Operating Systems (HotOS XV)*. 2015. URL: https://www.usenix.org/conference/hotos15/workshop-program/presentation/ajoux (visited on 11/28/2016).

[Ali+11] Sadiye Alici et al. "Timestamp-based result cache invalidation for web search engines". In: *Proceedings of the 34th international ACM SIGIR conference on Research and development in Information Retrieval*. ACM, 2011, pp. 973–982. URL: http://dl.acm.org/citation.cfm?id=2010046 (visited on 04/24/2015).

[Ali+12] Sadiye Alici et al. "Adaptive time-to-live strategies for query result caching in web search engines". In: *European Conference on Information Retrieval*. Springer, 2012, pp. 401–412. URL: http://link.springer.com/chapter/10.1007/978-3-642-28997-2_34 (visited on 11/26/2016).

[ALS10]   J. Chris Anderson, Jan Lehnardt, and Noah Slater. *CouchDB - The Definitive Guide: Time to Relax.* O'Reilly, 2010. ISBN: 978-0-596-15589-6. URL: http://www.oreilly.de/catalog/9780596155896/index.html.

[Alt+03]   Mehmet Altinel et al. "Cache Tables: Paving the Way for an Adaptive Database Cache". In: *VLDB.* 2003, pp. 718–729. URL: http://www.vldb.org/conf/2003/papers/S22P01.pdf.

[Ama16]   Sean Amarasinghe. *Service worker development cookbook.* English. OCLC: 958120287. 2016. ISBN: 978-1-78646-952-6. URL: http://lib.myilibrary.com?id=952152 (visited on 01/28/2017).

[Ami+03a] K. Amiri et al. "DBProxy: A dynamic data cache for Web applications". In: *Proceedings of the ICDE.* 2003, pp. 821–831. URL: http://www-2.cs.cmu.edu/~amiri/icde-indus.pdf (visited on 06/28/2012).

[Ami+03b] Khalil Amiri et al. "Scalable template-based query containment checking for web semantic caches". In: *Proceedings of the 19th International Conference on Data Engineering, March 5–8, 2003, Bangalore, India.* Ed. by Umeshwar Dayal, Krithi Ramamritham, and T. M. Vijayaraman. IEEE Computer Society, 2003, pp. 493–504. https://doi.org/10.1109/ICDE.2003.1260816.

[Ant+02]   Jesse Anton et al. "Web caching for database applications with Oracle Web Cache". In: *Proceedings of the 2002 ACM SIGMOD International Conference on Management of Data, Madison, Wisconsin, June 3–6, 2002.* Ed. by Michael J. Franklin, Bongki Moon, and Anastassia Ailamaki. ACM, 2002, pp. 594–599. https://doi.org/10.1145/564691.564762.

[AR17]   Ejaz Ahmed and Mubashir Husain Rehmani. "Mobile Edge Computing: Opportunities, solutions, and challenges". In: *Future Generation Comp. Syst.*, 70 (2017), pp. 59–63. https://doi.org/10.1016/j.future.2016.09.015.

[AT14]   Masoud Saeida Ardekani and Douglas B. Terry. "A Self-Configurable Geo-Replicated Cloud Storage System". In: *11th USENIX Symposium on Operating Systems Design and Implementation, OSDI '14, Broomfield, CO, USA, October 6–8, 2014.* Ed. by Jason Flinn and Hank Levy. USENIX Association, 2014, pp. 367–381. URL: https://www.usenix.org/conference/osdi14/technical-sessions/presentation/ardekani.

[Aur+12]   Aditya Auradkar et al. "Data Infrastructure at LinkedIn". In: *IEEE 28th International Conference on Data Engineering (ICDE 2012), Washington, DC, USA (Arlington, Virginia), 1–5 April, 2012.* Ed. by Anastasios Kementsietsidis and Marcos Antonio Vaz Salles. IEEE Computer Society, 2012, pp. 1370–1381. https://doi.org/10.1109/ICDE.2012.147.

[Bai+12]   Peter Bailis et al. *Probabilistically bounded staleness for practical partial quorums.* Tech. rep. 8. 2012, pp. 776–787. URL: http://dl.acm.org/citation.cfm?id=2212359 (visited on 07/16/2014).

[Bai+13a] Peter Bailis et al. "Bolt-on Causal Consistency". In: *Proceedings of the 2013 ACM SIGMOD International Conference on Management of Data.* SIGMOD'13. New York, New York, USA: ACM, 2013, pp. 761–772.

[Bak+11]   J. Baker et al. "Megastore: Providing scalable, highly available storage for interactive services". In: *Proc. of CIDR.* Vol. 11. 2011, pp. 223–234.

[BCL89]   José A. Blakeley, Neil Coburn, and Per-Åke Larson. "Updating Derived Relations: Detecting Irrelevant and Autonomously Computable Updates". *ACM Trans. Database Syst.*, 14.3 (1989), pp. 369–400. https://doi.org/10.1145/68012.68015.

[Bel+06]   Nalini Moti Belaramani et al. "PRACTI Replication". In: *3rd Symposium on Networked Systems Design and Implementation (NSDI 2006), May 8–10, 2007, San Jose, California, USA, Proceedings.* Ed. by Larry L. Peterson and Timothy Roscoe. USENIX, 2006. URL: http://www.usenix.org/events/nsdi06/tech/belaramani.html.

[Ben14]   Juan Benet. "IPFS - content addressed, versioned, P2P file system". In: *CoRR*, abs/1407.3561 (2014). arXiv: 1407.3561. URL: http://arxiv.org/abs/1407.3561.

[Ber14]   David Bermbach. *Benchmarking Eventually Consistent Distributed Storage Systems*. eng. Karlsruhe, Baden: KIT Scientific Publishing, 2014. ISBN: 978-3-7315-0186-2 3-7315-0186-4 978-3-7315-0186-2.

[Bes95]   Azer Bestavros. "Demand-based document dissemination to reduce traffic and balance load in distributed information systems". In: *Proceedings of the Seventh IEEE Symposium on Parallel and Distributed Processing, SPDP 1995, San Antonio, Texas, USA, October 25–28, 1995*, IEEE, 1995, pp. 338–345. https://doi.org/10.1109/SPDP.1995.530703.

[Bes96]   A. Bestavros. "Speculative data dissemination and service to reduce server load, network traffic and service time in distributed information systems". In: *Proc. Twelfth Int. Conf. Data Engineering*. Feb. 1996, pp. 180–187. https://doi.org/10.1109/ICDE.1996.492104.

[Bhi+02] Manish Bhide et al. "Adaptive push-pull: Disseminating dynamic web data". In: *IEEE Transactions on Computers* 51.6 (2002), pp. 652–668.

[Bla+10] Roi Blanco et al. "Caching search engine results over incremental indices". In: *Proceedings of the 33rd international ACM SIGIR conference on Research and development in information retrieval*. ACM, 2010, pp. 82–89. URL: http://dl.acm.org/citation.cfm?id=1835466 (visited on 04/24/2015).

[BLT86]   José A. Blakeley, Per-Åke Larson, and Frank Wm. Tompa. "Efficiently Updating Materialized Views". In: *Proceedings of the 1986 ACM SIGMOD International Conference on Management of Data, Washington, D.C., May 28–30, 1986*. Ed. by Carlo Zaniolo. ACM Press, 1986, pp. 61–71. https://doi.org/10.1145/16894.16861.

[BLV11]   Edward Bortnikov, Ronny Lempel, and Kolman Vornovitsky. "Caching for Realtime Search". In: *Advances in Information Retrieval - 33rd European Conference on IR Research, ECIR 2011, Dublin, Ireland, April 18–21, 2011. Proceedings*. Ed. by Paul D. Clough et al. Vol. 6611. Lecture Notes in Computer Science. Springer, 2011, pp. 104–116. https://doi.org/10.1007/978-3-642-20161-5_12.

[BM03]   Andrei Broder and Michael Mitzenmacher. "Network Applications of Bloom Filters: A Survey". In: *Internet Mathematics* 1.4 (2003), pp. 485–509. URL: http://projecteuclid.org/euclid.im/1109191032 (visited on 01/03/2015).

[Bon+12] Flavio Bonomi et al. "Fog computing and its role in the internet of things". In: *Proceedings of the first edition of the MCC workshop on Mobile cloud computing, MCC@SIGCOMM 2012, Helsinki, Finland, August 17, 2012*. Ed. by Mario Gerla and Dijiang Huang. ACM, 2012, pp. 13–16. https://doi.org/10.1145/2342509.2342513.

[Bor+03] Christof Bornhövd et al. "DBCache: Middle-tier Database Caching for Highly Scalable e-Business Architectures". In: *Proceedings of the 2003 ACM SIGMOD International Conference on Management of Data, San Diego, California, USA, June 9–12, 2003*. Ed. by Alon Y. Halevy, Zachary G. Ives, and AnHai Doan. ACM, 2003, p. 662. https://doi.org/10.1145/872757.872849.

[Bor+04] C. Bornhövd et al. "Adaptive database caching with DBCache". In: *Data Engineering* 27.2 (2004), pp. 11–18. URL: http://sipew.org/staff/bornhoevd/IEEEBull'04.pdf (visited on 06/28/2012).

[BP95]   Alexandros Biliris and Euthimios Panagos. "A High Performance Configurable Storage Manager". In: *Proceedings of the Eleventh International Conference on Data Engineering, March 6–10, 1995, Taipei, Taiwan*. Ed. by Philip S. Yu and Arbee L. P. Chen. IEEE Computer Society, 1995, pp. 35–43. https://doi.org/10.1109/ICDE.1995.380412.

[BPV08]   Rajkumar Buyya, Mukaddim Pathan, and Athena Vakali, eds. *Content Delivery Networks (Lecture Notes in Electrical Engineering)*. 2008th ed. Springer, Sept. 2008. ISBN: 9783540778868. URL: http://amazon.com/o/ASIN/3540778861/.

[BR02]   Laura Bright and Louiqa Raschid. "Using Latency-Recency Profiles for Data Delivery on the Web". In: *VLDB 2002, Proceedings of 28th International Conference on Very Large Data Bases, August 20–23, 2002, Hong Kong, China*. Morgan Kaufmann, 2002, pp. 550–561. URL: http://www.vldb.org/conf/2002/ S16P01.pdf.

[Bre+99] Lee Breslau et al. "Web caching and Zipf-like distributions: Evidence and implications". In: *INFOCOM'99. Eighteenth Annual Joint Conference of the IEEE Computer and Communications Societies. Proceedings. IEEE.* Vol. 1, IEEE, IEEE, 1999, pp. 126–134. URL: http://ieeexplore.ieee.org/xpls/abs_all. jsp?arnumber=749260 (visited on 01/03/2015).

[Bre00]   Eric A. Brewer. *Towards Robust Distributed Systems*. 2000.

[Bre17]   Eric Brewer. *Spanner, TrueTime and the CAP Theorem*. Tech. rep. 2017.

[Bro+13] Nathan Bronson et al. "TAO: Facebook's Distributed Data Store for the Social Graph." In: *USENIX Annual Technical Conference.* 2013, pp. 49–60. URL: http://dl.frz.ir/FREE/papers-we-love/datastores/tao-facebook-distributed-datastore.pdf (visited on 09/28/2014).

[Cam+10] Berkant Barla Cambazoglu et al. "A refreshing perspective of search engine caching". In: *Proceedings of the 19th International Conference on World Wide Web, WWW 2010, Raleigh, North Carolina, USA, April 26–30, 2010.* Ed. by Michael Rappa et al. ACM, 2010, pp. 181–190. https://doi.org/10.1145/ 1772690.1772710.

[Cam16]   Raymond Camden. *Client-side data storage: keeping it local*. First edition. OCLC: ocn935079139. Beijing: O'Reilly, 2016. ISBN: 978-1-4919-3511-8.

[Can+01a] K. Selçuk Candan et al. "Enabling Dynamic Content Caching for Database-Driven Web Sites". In" *Proceedings of the 2001 ACM SIGMOD international conference on Management of data, Santa Barbara, CA, USA, May 21–24, 2001.* Ed. by Sharad Mehrotra and Timos K. Sellis. ACM, 2001, pp. 532–543. https://doi.org/10.1145/375663.375736.

[Can+01b] K. Selçuk Candan et al. "Enabling Dynamic Content Caching for Database-driven Web Sites". In: *SIGMOD*. New York, NY, USA: ACM, 2001, pp. 532– 543. ISBN: 1-58113-332-4. https://doi.org/10.1145/375663.375736. URL: http:// doi.acm.org/10.1145/375663.375736 (visited on 10/04/2014).

[Car+91] Michael J. Carey et al. "Data caching tradeoffs in client-server DBMS architectures". In: *Proceedings of the 1991 ACM SIGMOD International Conference on Management of Data, Denver, Colorado, May 29–31, 1991.* Ed. by James Clifford and Roger King, ACM Press, 1991, pp. 357–366. https://doi. org/10.1145/115790.115854.

[Car13]   Josiah L. Carlson. *Redis in Action*. Greenwich, CT, USA: Manning Publications Co., 2013. ISBN: 1617290858, 9781617290855.

[Cas+97] Miguel Castro et al. "HAC: hybrid adaptive caching for distributed storage systems". In: *Proceedings of the Sixteenth ACM Symposium on Operating System Principles, SOSP 1997, St. Malo, France, October 5–8, 1997.* Ed. by Michel Banâtre, Henry M. Levy, and William M. Waite. ACM, 1997, pp. 102– 115. https://doi.org/10.1145/268998.266666.

[Cat92]   Vincent Cate. "Alex-a global filesystem". In: *Proceedings of the 1992 USENIX File System Workshop*. Citeseer, 1992, pp. 1–12.

[CBPS10] Bernadette Charron-Bost, Fernando Pedone, and André Schiper, eds. *Replication: Theory and Practice*. Vol. 5959. Lecture Notes in Computer Science. Springer, 2010.

[CD13]   Kristina Chodorow and Michael Dirolf. *MongoDB - The Definitive Guide*. O'Reilly, 2013. ISBN: 978-1-449-38156-1. URL: http://www.oreilly.de/catalog/ 9781449381561/index.html.

[CH16]   Jeff Carpenter and Eben Hewitt. *Cassandra: The Definitive Guide*. "O'Reilly Media, Inc.", 2016.

[Cha+08]   Fay Chang et al. "Bigtable: A distributed storage system for structured data".
           In: *ACM Transactions on Computer Systems (TOCS)* 26.2 (2008), p. 4.
[Che+16]   Tse-Hsun Chen et al. "CacheOptimizer: helping developers configure caching
           frameworks for hibernate-based database-centric web applications". In: *Pro-
           ceedings of the 24th ACM SIGSOFT International Symposium on Foundations
           of Software Engineering, FSE 2016, Seattle, WA, USA, November 13–18, 2016.*
           Ed. by Thomas Zimmermann, Jane Cleland-Huang, and Zhendong Su, ACM,
           2016, pp. 666–677. https://doi.org/10.1145/2950290.2950303.
[CI97]   Pei Cao and Sandy Irani. "Cost-aware WWW Proxy Caching Algorithms".
           In: *1st USENIX Symposium on Internet Technologies and Systems, USITS'97,
           Monterey, California, USA, December 8–11, 1997.* USENIX, 1997. URL: http://
           www.usenix.org/publications/library/proceedings/usits97/cao.html.
[Cid16]   Asaf Cidon et al. "Cliffhanger: scaling performance cliffs in web memory
           caches". In: *13th USENIX Symposium on Networked Systems Design and
           Implementation (NSDI 16).* 2016, pp. 379–392.
[CK01]   Edith Cohen and Haim Kaplan. "The Age Penalty and Its Effect on Cache
           Performance". In: *3rd USENIX Symposium on Internet Technologies and
           Systems, USITS'01, San Francisco, California, USA, March 26–28, 2001.* Ed.
           by Tom Anderson. USENIX, 2001, pp. 73–84. URL: http://www.usenix.org/
           events/usits01/cohen.html.
[CKR98]   Edith Cohen, Balachander Krishnamurthy, and Jennifer Rexford. "Improving
           End-to-End Performance of the Web Using Server Volumes and Proxy Filters".
           In: *SIGCOMM.* 1998, pp. 241–253. https://doi.org/10.1145/285237.285286.
[CL98]   Pei Cao and Chengjie Liu. "Maintaining Strong Cache Consistency in the World
           Wide Web". In: *IEEE Trans. Computers* 47.4 (1998), pp. 445–457. https://doi.
           org/10.1109/12.675713.
[CO82]   Stefano Ceri and Susan S. Owicki. "On the Use of Optimistic Methods for
           Concurrency Control in Distributed Databases". In: *Berkeley Workshop.* 1982,
           pp. 117–129.
[Coc]   *CockroachDB - the scalable, survivable, strongly-consistent SQL database.*
           https://github.com/cockroachdb/cockroach. 2017.   URL: https://github.com/
           cockroachdb/cockroach (visited on 02/17/2017).
[Coo+08]   B. F. Cooper et al. "PNUTS: Yahoo!'s hosted data serving platform". In:
           PVLDB 1.2 (2008), pp. 1277–1288. URL: http://dl.acm.org/citation.cfm?id=
           1454167 (visited on 09/12/2012).
[Cor+12]   James C. Corbett et al.   "Spanner: Google's Globally-Distributed
           Database". In: *10th USENIX Symposium on Operating Systems Design
           and Implementation, OSDI 2012, Hollywood, CA, USA, October 8–10,
           2012.* Ed. by Chandu Thekkath and Amin Vahdat. USENIX Association,
           2012, pp. 261–264. URL: https://www.usenix.org/conference/osdi12/technical-
           sessions/presentation/corbett.
[Cor+13]   James C. Corbett et al. "Spanner: Google's Globally Distributed Database".
           In: *ACM Trans. Comput. Syst.* 31.3 (2013), 8:1–8:22, 2013. https://doi.org/10.
           1145/2491245.
[CRS99]   Boris Chidlovskii, Claudia Roncancio, and Marie-Luise Schneider. "Seman-
           tic Cache Mechanism for Heterogeneous Web Querying". In: *Computer
           Networks,* 31(11–16) (1999), pp. 1347–1360. https://doi.org/10.1016/S1389-
           1286(99)00035-3.
[CZB99]   Pei Cao, Jin Zhang, and Kevin Beach. "Active Cache: caching dynamic contents
           on the Web". In: *Distributed Systems Engineering* 6.1 (1999), pp. 43–50. https://
           doi.org/10.1088/0967-1846/6/1/305.
[Dar+96]   Shaul Dar et al. "Semantic Data Caching and Replacement". In: *VLDB'96,
           Proceedings of 22th International Conference on Very Large Data Bases,
           September 3–6, 1996, Mumbai (Bombay), India.* Ed. by T. M. Vijayaraman

et al. Morgan Kaufmann, 1996, pp. 330–341. URL: http://www.vldb.org/conf/1996/P330.PDF.

[Das+12] Shirshanka Das et al. "All aboard the Databus!: Linkedin's scalable consistent change data capture platform". In: *Proceedings of the Third ACM Symposium on Cloud Computing*. ACM, 2012, p. 18. URL: http://dl.acm.org/citation.cfm?id=2391247 (visited on 11/26/2016).

[Dat+04] Anindya Datta et al. "Proxy-based acceleration of dynamically generated content on the world wide web: An approach and implementation". In: *ACM Trans. Database Syst.* 29.2 (2004), pp. 403–443. https://doi.org/10.1145/1005566.1005571.

[DeC+07] G. DeCandia et al. "Dynamo: amazon's highly available key-value store". In: *ACM SOSP*. Vol. 14. 17. ACM. 2007, pp. 205–220. URL: http://dl.acm.org/citation.cfm?id=1294281 (visited on 09/12/2012).

[Dem+94] Alan J. Demers et al. "The Bayou Architecture: Support for Data Sharing Among Mobile Users". In: *First Workshop on Mobile Computing Systems and Applications, WMCSA 1994, Santa Cruz, CA, USA, December 8–9, 1994*. IEEE Computer Society, 1994, pp. 2–7. https://doi.org/10.1109/WMCSA.1994.37.

[DeM09] Linda DeMichiel. "JSR 317: Java Persistence 2.0". In: *Java Community Process, Tech. Rep* (2009).

[Den96] Shuang Deng. "Empirical model of WWW document arrivals at access link". In: *Communications, 1996. ICC'96, Conference Record, Converging Technologies for Tomorrow's Applications. 1996 IEEE International Conference on.* Vol. 3. IEEE. 1996, pp. 1797–1802.

[Des+98] Prasad Deshpande et al. "Caching Multidimensional Queries Using Chunks". In: *SIGMOD 1998, Proceedings ACM SIGMOD International Conference on Management of Data, June 2–4, 1998, Seattle, Washington, USA*. Ed. by Laura M. Haas and Ashutosh Tiwary. ACM Press, 1998, pp. 259–270. https://doi.org/10.1145/276304.276328.

[Dou+97] Fred Douglis et al. "Rate of Change and other Metrics: a Live Study of the World Wide Web". In: *1st USENIX Symposium on Internet Technologies and Systems, USITS'97, Monterey, California, USA, December 8–11, 1997*. USENIX, 1997. URL: http://www.usenix.org/publications/library/proceedings/usits97/douglis_rate.html.

[DST03] Venkata Duvvuri, Prashant J. Shenoy, and Renu Tewari. "Adaptive Leases: A Strong Consistency Mechanism for the World Wide Web". In: *IEEE Trans. Knowl. Data Eng.* 15.5 (2003), pp. 1266–1276. https://doi.org/10.1109/TKDE.2003.1232277.

[Dyn] DynamoDB. http://docs.aws.amazon.com/amazondynamodb/latest/developerguide/Introduction.html. (Accessed on 05/20/2017). 2017. URL: http://docs.aws.amazon.com/amazondynamodb/latest/developerguide/Introduction.html (visited on 01/13/2017).

[ERR11] Mohamed El-Refaey and Bhaskar Prasad Rimal. "Grid, soa and cloud computing: On-demand computing models". In: *Computational and Data Grids: Principles, Applications and Design: Principles, Applications and Design* (2011), p. 45.

[EWS12] Robert Escriva, Bernard Wong, and Emin GÃijn Sirer. "HyperDex: A distributed, searchable key-value store". In: *ACM SIGCOMM Computer Communication Review* 42.4 (2012), pp. 25–36. URL: http://dl.acm.org/citation.cfm?id=2377681 (visited on 01/03/2015).

[FAK13] Bin Fan, David G. Andersen, and Michael Kaminsky. "MemC3: Compact and Concurrent MemCache with Dumber Caching and Smarter Hashing". In: *Proceedings of the 10th USENIX Symposium on Networked Systems Design and Implementation, NSDI 2013, Lombard, IL, USA, April 2–5, 2013*. Ed. by Nick Feamster and Jeffrey C. Mogul. USENIX Association, 2013, pp. 371–384. URL: https://www.usenix.org/conference/nsdi13/technical-sessions/presentation/fan.

[Fan+00] Li Fan et al.   "Summary cache: a scalable wide-area web cache sharing protocol". In: *IEEE/ACM TON* 8.3 (2000), pp. 281–293. URL: http://dl.acm. org/citation.cfm?id=343572 (visited on 10/04/2014).

[Fan+14] Bin Fan et al.   "Cuckoo Filter: Practically Better Than Bloom".   en. In: ACM Press, 2014, pp. 75–88. ISBN: 978-1-4503-3279-8. https://doi.org/10. 1145/2674005.2674994.   URL: http://dl.acm.org/citation.cfm?doid=2674005. 2674994 (visited on 01/03/2015).

[FC92]   Michael J. Franklin and Michael J. Carey. "Client-Server Caching Revisited". In: *Distributed Object Management, Papers from the International Workshop on Distributed Object Management (IWDOM), Edmonton, Alberta, Canada, August 19–21, 1992*. Ed. by M. Tamer Özsu, Umeshwar Dayal, and Patrick Valduriez. Morgan Kaufmann, 1992, pp. 57–78.

[FCL97]   Michael J. Franklin, Michael J. Carey, and Miron Livny. "Transactional Client-Server Cache Consistency: Alternatives and Performance".   In: *ACM Trans. Database Syst.* 22.3 (1997), pp. 315–363. https://doi.org/10.1145/261124. 261125.

[Fel+99] Anja Feldmann et al. "Performance of Web Proxy Caching in Heterogeneous Bandwidth Environments". In: *Proceedings IEEE INFOCOM '99, The Conference on Computer Communications, Eighteenth Annual Joint Conference of the IEEE Computer and Communications Societies, The Future Is Now, New York, NY, USA, March 21–25, 1999*. IEEE, 1999, pp. 107–116.

[FFM04]   Michael J. Freedman, Eric Freudenthal, and David Mazieres. "Democratizing Content Publication with Coral." In: *NSDI*. Vol. 4. 2004, pp. 18–18. URL: https://www.usenix.org/legacy/events/nsdi04/tech/full_papers/freedman/ freedman_html/ (visited on 09/28/2014).

[Fie+99] R. Fielding et al. "RFC 2616: Hypertext Transfer ProtocolâHTTP/1.1, 1999". In: *URL* http://www.rfc.net/rfc2616.html (1999).

[Fit04]   Brad Fitzpatrick. "Distributed caching with Memcached". In: *Linux journal* 2004.124 (2004), p. 5.

[FK09]   Daniela Florescu and Donald Kossmann. "Rethinking cost and performance of database systems". In: *SIGMOD Record* 38.1 (2009), pp. 43–48. https://doi. org/10.1145/1558334.1558339.

[FR14]   Roy Fielding and J Reschke.   RFC 7234: Hypertext Transfer Protocol (HTTP/1.1): Caching. Tech. rep. IETF, 2014.

[Fre10]   Michael J. Freedman. "Experiences with CoralCDN: A Five-Year Operational View." In: *NSDI*. 2010, pp. 95–110. URL: http://static.usenix.org/legacy/events/ nsdi10/tech/full_papers/freedman.pdf (visited on 01/03/2015).

[Gar+08] Charles Garrod et al. "Scalable query result caching for web applications". In: *Proceedings of the VLDB Endowment* 1.1 (2008), pp. 550–561. URL: http://dl. acm.org/citation.cfm?id=1453917 (visited on 04/24/2015).

[GC89]   Cary G. Gray and David R. Cheriton.   "Leases: An Efficient Fault-Tolerant Mechanism for Distributed File Cache Consistency".   In: *Proceedings of the Twelfth ACM Symposium on Operating System Principles, SOSP 1989, The Wigwam, Litchfield Park, Arizona, USA, December 3–6, 1989*. Ed. by Gregory R. Andrews. ACM, 1989, pp. 202–210. https://doi.org/10.1145/74850. 74870.

[GD11]   Sanjay Ghemawat and Jeff Dean. *LevelDB*. http://leveldb.org, 2011. URL: http:// leveldb.org.

[Gel00]   Erol Gelenbe. *System performance evaluation: methodologies and applications*. CRC press, 2000.

[Ges+15] Felix Gessert et al. "The Cache Sketch: Revisiting Expiration-based Caching in the Age of Cloud Data Management". In: *Datenbanksysteme fÃijr Business, Technologie und Web (BTW), 16. Fachtagung des GI-Fachbereichs "Datenbanken und Informationssysteme"*. GI, 2015.

[Ges+17] Felix Gessert et al. "Quaestor: Query Web Caching for Database-as-a-Service Providers". In: *Proceedings of the VLDB Endowment* (2017).

[Ges19] Felix Gessert. "*Low Latency for Cloud Data Management*". PhD thesis. University of Hamburg, Germany, 2019. URL: http://ediss.sub.uni-hamburg.de/volltexte/2019/9541/.

[GGL03] S. Ghemawat, H. Gobioff, and S. T. Leung. "The Google file system". In: *ACM SIGOPS Operating Systems Review*. Vol. 37. 2003, pp. 29–43. URL: http://dl.acm.org/citation.cfm?id=945450 (visited on 09/12/2012).

[GLS11] Wojciech Golab, Xiaozhou Li, and Mehul A. Shah. "Analyzing consistency properties for fun and profit". In: *ACM PODC*. ACM, 2011, pp. 197–206. URL: http://dl.acm.org/citation.cfm?id=1993834 (visited on 09/28/2014).

[GPS16] Rachid Guerraoui, Matej Pavlovic, and Dragos-Adrian Seredinschi. "Incremental Consistency Guarantees for Replicated Objects". In: *12th USENIX Symposium on Operating Systems Design and Implementation, OSDI 2016, Savannah, GA, USA, November 2–4, 2016*. Ed. by Kimberly Keeton and Timothy Roscoe. USENIX Association, 2016, pp. 169–184. URL: https://www.usenix.org/conference/osdi16/technical-sessions/presentation/guerraoui.

[Gra+81] Jim Gray et al. "A Straw Man Analysis of the Probability of Waiting and Deadlock in a Database System". In: *Berkeley Workshop*. 1981, p. 125.

[Gri13] Ilya Grigorik. *High performance browser networking*. English. [S.l.]: O'Reilly Media, 2013. ISBN: 1-4493-4476-3 978-1-4493-4476-4. URL: https://books.google.de/books?id=tf-AAAAQBAJ.

[GS96] James Gwertzman and Margo I Seltzer. "World Wide Web Cache Consistency." In: *USENIX ATC*. 1996, pp. 141–152.

[Han87] Eric N. Hanson. "A Performance Analysis of View Materialization Strategies". In: *Proceedings of the Association for Computing Machinery Special Interest Group on Management of Data 1987 Annual Conference, San Francisco, California, May 27–29, 1987*. Ed. by Umeshwar Dayal and Irving L. Traiger. ACM Press, 1987, pp. 440–453. https://doi.org/10.1145/38713.38759.

[Hba] *HBase*. http://hbase.apache.org/. (Accessed on 05/25/2017). 2017. URL: http://hbase.apache.org/ (visited on 07/16/2014).

[Hev] *H2O Server*. https://h2o.example.net/configure/http2_directives.html. (Accessed on 05/26/2017). 2016. URL: https://h2o.example.net/configure/http2_directives.html (visited on 01/20/2017).

[HL08] R. T. Hurley and B. Y. Li. "A Performance Investigation of Web Caching Architectures". In: *Proceedings of the 2008 C3S2E Conference*. C3S2E '08. Montreal, Quebec, Canada: ACM, 2008, pp. 205–213. ISBN: 978-1-60558-101-9. https://doi.org/10.1145/1370256.1370291. URL: http://doi.acm.org/10.1145/1370256.1370291.

[How+88] John H. Howard et al. "Scale and Performance in a Distributed File System". In: *ACM Trans. Comput. Syst.* 6.1 (1988), pp. 51–81. https://doi.org/10.1145/35037.35059.

[HS16] Stephan Hochhaus and Manuel Schoebel. *Meteor in action*. Manning Publ., 2016.

[Hua+13] Qi Huang et al. "An analysis of Facebook photo caching". In: *SOSP*. 2013, pp. 167–181. URL: http://dl.acm.org/citation.cfm?id=2522722 (visited on 09/28/2014).

[IC98] Arun Iyengar and Jim Challenger. *Data Update Propagation: A Method for Determining How Changes to Underlying Data Affect Cached Objects on the Web*. Tech. rep. Technical Report RC 21093 (94368), IBM Research Division, Yorktown Heights, NY, 1998.

[Kal+02] Panos Kalnis et al. "An adaptive peer-to-peer network for distributed caching of OLAP results". In: *Proceedings of the 2002 ACM SIGMOD International Conference on Management of Data, Madison, Wisconsin, June 3–6, 2002*. Ed.

by Michael J. Franklin, Bongki Moon, and Anastassia Ailamaki. ACM, 2002, pp. 25–36. https://doi.org/10.1145/564691.564695.

[Kam17] Poul-Henning Kamp.   *Varnish HTTP Cache.*   https://varnish-cache.org/. (Accessed on 04/30/2017). 2017. URL: https://varnish-cache.org/ (visited on 01/26/2017).

[KB96] Arthur M. Keller and Julie Basu. "A Predicate-based Caching Scheme for Client-Server Database Architectures". In: *VLDB J.* 5.1 (1996), pp. 35–47. https://doi.org/10.1007/s007780050014.

[KFD00] Donald Kossmann, Michael J. Franklin, and Gerhard Drasch. "Cache investment: integrating query optimization and distributed data placement". In: *ACM Trans. Database Syst.* 25.4 (2000), pp. 517–558. URL: http://portal.acm.org/citation.cfm?id=377674.377677.

[KK94] Alfons Kemper and Donald Kossmann. "Dual-Buffering Strategies in Object Bases". In: *VLDB'94, Proceedings of 20th International Conference on Very Large Data Bases, September 12–15, 1994, Santiago de Chile, Chile.* Ed. by Jorge B. Bocca, Matthias Jarke, and Carlo Zaniolo. Morgan Kaufmann, 1994, pp. 427–438. URL: http://www.vldb.org/conf/1994/P427.PDF.

[Kle17] Martin Kleppmann. *Designing Data-Intensive Applications.* English. 1 edition. O'Reilly Media, Jan. 2017. ISBN: 978-1-4493-7332-0.

[KLM97] Tom M. Kroeger, Darrell D. E. Long, and Jeffrey C. Mogul. "Exploring the Bounds of Web Latency Reduction from Caching and Prefetching". In: *1st USENIX Symposium on Internet Technologies and Systems, USITS'97, Monterey, California, USA, December 8–11, 1997.* USENIX, 1997. URL: http://www.usenix.org/publications/library/proceedings/usits97/kroeger.html.

[KM06] Adam Kirsch and Michael Mitzenmacher. "Less hashing, same performance: Building a better Bloom filter". In: *AlgorithmsâESA 2006.* Springer, 2006, pp. 456–467. URL: http://link.springer.com/chapter/10.1007/11841036_42 (visited on 01/03/2015).

[KP01] Panos Kalnis and Dimitris Papadias. "Proxy-Server Architectures for OLAP". In: *Proceedings of the 2001 ACM SIGMOD international conference on Management of data, Santa Barbara, CA, USA, May 21–24, 2001.* Ed. by Sharad Mehrotra and Timos K. Sellis. ACM, 2001, pp. 367–378. https://doi.org/10.1145/375663.375712.

[KR01] B. Krishnamurthy and J. Rexford.   "Web Protocols and Practice, HTTP/1.1, Networking Protocols, Caching, and Traffic Measurement". In: *Recherche* 67 (2001), p. 02. URL: http://www.lavoisier.fr/livre/notice.asp?id=O3OWRLAROSSOWB (visited on 06/30/2012).

[KR81] H. T. Kung and J. T. Robinson. "On optimistic methods for concurrency control". In: *ACM Transactions on Database Systems (TODS)* 6.2 (1981), pp. 213–226. URL: http://dl.acm.org/citation.cfm?id=319567 (visited on 11/19/2012).

[Kra+09] Tim Kraska et al. "Consistency rationing in the cloud: pay only when it matters". In: *Proceedings of the VLDB Endowment* 2.1 (2009), pp. 253–264. URL: http://dl.acm.org/citation.cfm?id=1687657 (visited on 11/28/2016).

[Kra+13] Tim Kraska et al. "MDCC: Multi-data center consistency". In: *EuroSys.* ACM, 2013, pp. 113–126. URL: http://dl.acm.org/citation.cfm?id=2465363 (visited on 04/15/2014).

[Kul+14] S Kulkarni et al. *Logical physical clocks and consistent snapshots in globally distributed databases.* 2014.

[KV14] Pradeeban Kathiravelu and Luís Veiga. "An Adaptive Distributed Simulator for Cloud and MapReduce Algorithms and Architectures". In: *Proceedings of the 7th IEEE/ACM International Conference on Utility and Cloud Computing, UCC 2014, London, United Kingdom, December 8–11, 2014.* IEEE Computer Society, 2014, pp. 79–88. https://doi.org/10.1109/UCC.2014.16.

[KW97]   Balachander Krishnamurthy and Craig E. Wills. "Study of Piggyback Cache
          Validation for Proxy Caches in the World Wide Web". In: *1st USENIX
          Symposium on Internet Technologies and Systems, USITS'97, Monterey, Cal-
          ifornia, USA, December 8–11, 1997*. USENIX, 1997. URL: http://www.usenix.
          org/publications/library/proceedings/usits97/krishnamurthy.html.

[KW98]   Balachander Krishnamurthy and Craig E. Wills. "Piggyback Server Invalidation
          for Proxy Cache Coherency". In: *Computer Networks* 30.1-7 (1998), pp. 185–
          193. https://doi.org/10.1016/S0169-7552(98)00033-6.

[KW99]   Balachander Krishnamurthy and Craig E. Wills. "Proxy Cache Coherency and
          Replacement - Towards a More Complete Picture". In: *Proceedings of the 19th
          International Conference on Distributed Computing Systems, Austin, TX, USA,
          May 31 - June 4, 1999*. IEEE Computer Society, 1999, pp. 332–339. https://doi.
          org/10.1109/ICDCS.1999.776535.

[Lab+09] Alexandros Labrinidis et al. "Caching and Materialization for Web Databases".
          In: *Foundations and Trends in Databases* 2.3 (2009), pp. 169–266. https://doi.
          org/10.1561/1900000005.

[Lak+16] Sarath Lakshman et al. "Nitro: A fast, scalable in-memory storage engine for
          nosql global secondary index". In: *PVLDB* 9.13 (2016), pp. 1413–1424. URL:
          http://www.vldb.org/pvldb/vol9/p1413-lakshman.pdf.

[Lam01]   Leslie Lamport. "Paxos made simple". In: *ACM Sigact News* 32.4 (2001),
          pp. 18–25. URL: http://www.cs.utexas.edu/users/lorenzo/corsi/cs380d/past/03F/
          notes/paxos-simple.pdf (visited on 07/16/2014).

[Lam78]   Leslie Lamport. "Time, Clocks, and the Ordering of Events in a Distributed
          System". In: *Commun. ACM* 21.7 (1978), pp. 558–565. https://doi.org/10.1145/
          359545.359563.

[Lam98]   Leslie Lamport. "The part-time parliament". In: *ACM Transactions on
          Computer Systems (TOCS)* 16.2 (1998), pp. 133–169.

[LC97]   Chengjie Liu and Pei Cao. "Maintaining Strong Cache Consistency in the
          World-Wide Web". In: *Proceedings of the 17th International Conference
          on Distributed Computing Systems, Baltimore, MD, USA, May 27–30, 1997*.
          IEEE Computer Society, 1997, pp. 12–21. https://doi.org/10.1109/ICDCS.1997.
          597804.

[LC99]   Dongwon Lee and Wesley W. Chu. "Semantic Caching via Query Matching for
          Web Sources". In: *Proceedings of the 1999 ACM CIKM International Confer-
          ence on Information and Knowledge Management, Kansas City, Missouri, USA,
          November 2–6, 1999*. ACM, 1999, pp. 77–85. https://doi.org/10.1145/319950.
          319960.

[Lec09]   Jens LechtenbÃůrger. "Two-Phase Commit Protocol". English. In: *Encyclope-
          dia of Database Systems*. Ed. by LING LIU and M.TAMER ÃZSU. Springer
          US, 2009, pp. 3209–3213. ISBN: 978-0-387-35544-3. https://doi.org/10.1007/
          978-0-387-39940-9_2.

[Lee+15] Collin Lee et al. "Implementing linearizability at large scale and low latency".
          In: *Proceedings of the 25th Symposium on Operating Systems Principles, SOSP
          2015, Monterey, CA, USA, October 4–7, 2015*. ACM, 2015, pp. 71–86. https://
          doi.org/10.1145/2815400.2815416.

[LGZ04]   Per-Åke Larson, Jonathan Goldstein, and Jingren Zhou. "MTCache: Trans-
          parent Mid-Tier Database Caching in SQL Server". In: *Proceedings of the
          20th International Conference on Data Engineering, ICDE 2004, 30 March -
          2 April 2004, Boston, MA, USA*. Ed. by Z. Meral Özsoyoglu and Stanley B.
          Zdonik. IEEE Computer Society, 2004, pp. 177–188. https://doi.org/10.1109/
          ICDE.2004.1319994.

[Li+12]   Cheng Li et al. "Making Geo-Replicated Systems Fast as Possible, Consis-
          tent when Necessary". In: *10th USENIX Symposium on Operating Systems
          Design and Implementation, OSDI 2012, Hollywood, CA, USA, October 8–*

10, 2012. Ed. by Chandu Thekkath and Amin Vahdat. USENIX Association, 2012, pp. 265–278. URL: https://www.usenix.org/conference/osdi12/technical-sessions/presentation/li.

[Li+14] Cheng Li et al. "Automating the Choice of Consistency Levels in Replicated Systems". In: *2014 USENIX Annual Technical Conference, USENIX ATC '14, Philadelphia, PA, USA, June 19–20, 2014*. Ed. by Garth Gibson and Nickolai Zeldovich. USENIX Association, 2014, pp. 281–292. URL: https://www.usenix.org/conference/atc14/technical-sessions/presentation/li_cheng_2.

[LL00]   F Thomson Leighton and Daniel M Lewin. *Global hosting system*. US Patent 6,108,703. 2000

[Llo+11] Wyatt Lloyd et al. "Don't settle for eventual: scalable causal consistency for wide-area storage with COPS". In: *Proceedings of the Twenty-Third ACM Symposium on Operating Systems Principles*. ACM, 2011, pp. 401–416. URL: http://dl.acm.org/citation.cfm?id=2043593 (visited on 01/03/2015).

[Llo+13] Wyatt Lloyd et al. "Stronger semantics for low-latency geo-replicated storage". In: *Presented as part of the 10th USENIX Symposium on Networked Systems Design and Implementation (NSDI 13)*. 2013, pp. 313–328.

[LM10]   Avinash Lakshman and Prashant Malik. "Cassandra: a decentralized structured storage system". In: *ACM SIGOPS Operating Systems Review* 44.2 (2010), pp. 35–40. URL: http://dl.acm.org/citation.cfm?id=1773922 (visited on 04/15/2014).

[LN01]   Qiong Luo and Jeffrey F. Naughton. "Form-Based Proxy Caching for Database-Backed Web Sites". In: *VLDB 2001, Proceedings of 27th International Conference on Very Large Data Bases, September 11–14, 2001, Roma, Italy*. Ed. by Peter M. G. Apers et al. Morgan Kaufmann, 2001, pp. 191–200. URL: http://www.vldb.org/conf/2001/P191.pdf.

[Lou+01] Thanasis Loukopoulos et al. "Active Caching of On-Line-Analytical-Processing Queries in WWW proxies". In: *Proceedings of the 2001 International Conference on Parallel Processing, ICPP 2002, 3–7 September 2001, Valencia, Spain*. Ed. by Lionel M. Ni and Mateo Valero. IEEE Computer Society, 2001, pp. 419–426. https://doi.org/10.1109/ICPP.2001.952088.

[LR00]   Alexandros Labrinidis and Nick Roussopoulos. "WebView Materialization". In: *Proceedings of the 2000 ACM SIGMOD International Conference on Management of Data, May 16–18, 2000, Dallas, Texas, USA*. Ed. by Weidong Chen, Jeffrey F. Naughton, and Philip A. Bernstein. ACM, 2000, pp. 367–378. https://doi.org/10.1145/342009.335430.

[LR01a] Alexandros Labrinidis and Nick Roussopoulos. "Adaptive WebView Materialization". In: *WebDB*. 2001, pp. 85–90.

[LR01b] Alexandros Labrinidis and Nick Roussopoulos. "Update Propagation Strategies for Improving the Quality of Data on the Web". In: *VLDB 2001, Proceedings of 27th International Conference on Very Large Data Bases, September 11–14, 2001, Roma, Italy*. Ed. by Peter M. G. Apers et al. Morgan Kaufmann, 2001, pp. 391–400. URL: http://www.vldb.org/conf/2001/P391.pdf.

[LS88b] Barbara Liskov and Liuba Shrira. "Promises: Linguistic Support for Efficient Asynchronous Procedure Calls in Distributed Systems". In: *Proceedings of the ACM SIGPLAN'88 Conference on Programming Language Design and Implementation (PLDI), Atlanta, Georgia, USA, June 22–24, 1988*. Ed. by Richard L. Wexelblat. ACM, 1988, pp. 260–267. https://doi.org/10.1145/53990.54016.

[Lu+15] Haonan Lu et al. "Existential consistency: measuring and understanding consistency at Facebook". In: *Proceedings of the 25th Symposium on Operating Systems Principles, SOSP 2015, Monterey, CA, USA, October 4–7, 2015*. Ed. by Ethan L. Miller and Steven Hand. ACM, 2015, pp. 295–310. https://doi.org/10.1145/2815400.2815426.

[Luc14]   Gregory Robert Luck. The Java Community Process(SM) Program - JSRs: Java
          Specification Requests - detail JSR# 107. https://www.jcp.org/en/jsr/detail?id=
          107, 2014. (Accessed on 04/30/2017).

[Luo+02] Qiong Luo et al. "Middle-tier database caching for e-business". In: *Proceedings
          of the 2002 ACM SIGMOD International Conference on Management of Data,
          Madison, Wisconsin, June 3–6, 2002*. Ed. by Michael J. Franklin, Bongki Moon,
          and Anastassia Ailamaki. ACM, 2002, pp. 600–611.

[LW84]   Ming-Yee Lai and W. Kevin Wilkinson. "Distributed Transaction Management
          in Jasmin". In: *Tenth International Conference on Very Large Data Bases,
          August 27–31, 1984, Singapore, Proceedings*. Ed. by Umeshwar Dayal, Gunter
          Schlageter, and Lim Huat Seng. Morgan Kaufmann, 1984, pp. 466–470. URL:
          http://www.vldb.org/conf/1984/P466.PDF.

[Lwe10]   Bernhard Lwenstein.   *Benchmarking of Middleware Systems: Evaluating
          and Comparing the Performance and Scalability of XVSM (MozartSpaces),
          JavaSpaces (GigaSpaces XAP) and J2EE (JBoss AS)*. VDM Verlag, 2010.

[Mah+13] Hatem A. Mahmoud et al. "Low-Latency Multi-Datacenter Databases using
          Replicated Commit". In: *PVLDB* 6.9 (2013), pp. 661–672. URL: http://www.
          vldb.org/pvldb/vol6/p661-mahmoud.pdf.

[Mal16]   Ivano Malavolta.   "Beyond native apps: web technologies to the res-
          cue!(keynote)". In: *Proceedings of the 1st International Workshop on Mobile
          Development*. ACM, 2016, pp. 1–2.

[MC+98]   Evangelos P Markatos, Catherine E Chronaki, et al. "A top-10 approach to
          prefetching on the web". In: *Proceedings of INET*. Vol. 98. 1998, pp. 276–290.

[McM17]   Patrick McManus. *Using Immutable Caching To Speed Up The Web*. https://
          hacks.mozilla.org/2017/01/using-immutable-caching-to-speed-up-the-web/.
          (Accessed on 04/30/2017). 2017. URL: https://hacks.mozilla.org/2017/01/
          using-immutable-caching-to-speed-upthe-web/ (visited on 01/28/2017).

[Mit02]   M. Mitzenmacher. "Compressed bloom filters". In: *IEEE/ACM Transactions on
          Networking (TON)* 10.5 (2002), pp. 604–612. URL: http://dl.acm.org/citation.
          cfm?id=581878 (visited on 11/15/2012).

[MJM08]   Yanhua Mao, Flavio Paiva Junqueira, and Keith Marzullo. "Mencius: Building
          Efficient Replicated State Machine for WANs". In: *8th USENIX Symposium
          on Operating Systems Design and Implementation, OSDI 2008, December 8–
          10, 2008, San Diego, California, USA, Proceedings*. Ed. by Richard Draves and
          Robbert van Renesse. USENIX Association, 2008, pp. 369–384. URL: http://
          www.usenix.org/events/osdi08/tech/full_papers/mao/mao.pdf.

[Mog+97] Jeffrey C. Mogul et al. "Potential benefits of delta encoding and data compres-
          sion for HTTP". In: *Proceedings of the ACM SIGCOMM 1997 Conference
          on Applications, Technologies, Architectures, and Protocols for Computer
          Communication, September 14–18, 1997, Cannes, France*. Ed. by Christophe
          Diot et al. ACM, 1997, pp. 181–194. https://doi.org/10.1145/263105.263162.

[Mog94]   Jeffrey C. Mogul. "Recovery in spritely NFS". In: *Computing Systems* 7.2
          (1994), pp. 201–262. URL: http://www.usenix.org/publications/compsystems/
          1994/spr_mogul.pdf.

[MU05]   Michael Mitzenmacher and Eli Upfal. *Probability and computing - randomized
          algorithms and probabilistic analysis*. Cambridge University Press, 2005. ISBN:
          978-0-521-83540-4.

[Nag04]   S. V. Nagaraj. *Web caching and its applications*. Vol. 772. Springer, 2004.
          URL: http://books.google.de/books?hl=de&lr=&id=UgFhOl2lF0oC&oi=fnd&
          pg=PR11&dq=web+caching+and+its+applications&ots=X0Ow-cvXMH&
          sig=eNu7MDyfbGLKMGxwv6MZpZlyo6c (visited on 06/28/2012).

[Net+16] Ravi Netravali et al. "Polaris: Faster page loads using fine-grained dependency
          tracking". In: *13th USENIX Symposium on Networked Systems Design and
          Implementation (NSDI 16)*. USENIX Association, 2016.

[Nis+13] Rajesh Nishtala et al. "Scaling Memcache at Facebook". In: *NSDI*. USENIX Association, 2013, pp. 385–398.

[Not10] Mark Nottingham. "RFC 5861 - HTTP Cache-Control Extensions for Stale Content". In: (2010).

[NWO88] Michael N. Nelson, Brent B. Welch, and John K. Ousterhout. "Caching in the Sprite Network File System". In: *ACM Trans. Comput. Syst.* 6.1 (1988), pp. 134–154. https://doi.org/10.1145/35037.42183.

[ON16] Kazuho Oku and Mark Nottingham. *Cache Digests for HTTP/2*. https://tools. ietf.org/html/draft-ietf-httpbis-cache-digest-01. (Accessed on 06/05/2017). 2016. URL: https://tools.ietf.org/html/draft-ietf-httpbis-cache-digest-01 (visited on 01/20/2017).

[OO13] Diego Ongaro and John Ousterhout. "In search of an understandable consensus algorithm". In: *Draft of October* 7 (2013). URL: http://bestfuturepractice.org/ mirror/https/ramcloud.stanford.edu/wiki/download/attachments/11370504/raft. pdf (visited on 07/16/2014).

[Ora] *Oracle Result Cache*. https://docs.oracle.com/database/121/TGDBA/tune_ result_cache.htm#TGDBA616. (Accessed on 06/05/2017). 2017. URL: https:// docs.oracle.com/database/121/TGDBA/tune_result_cache.htm#TGDBA616 (visited on 01/20/2017).

[Ous+11] John K. Ousterhout et al. "The case for RAMCloud". In: *Commun. ACM* 54.7 (2011), pp. 121–130. https://doi.org/10.1145/1965724.1965751.

[PB03] Stefan Podlipnig and László Böszörményi. "A survey of Web cache replacement strategies". In: *ACM Comput. Surv.* 35.4 (2003), pp. 374–398. https://doi. org/10.1145/954339.954341.

[PB08] Mukaddim Pathan and Rajkumar Buyya. "A Taxonomy of CDNs". English. In: *Content Delivery Networks*. Ed. by Rajkumar Buyya, Mukaddim Pathan, and Athena Vakali. Vol. 9. Lecture Notes Electrical Engineering. Springer Berlin Heidelberg, 2008, pp. 33–77. ISBN: 978-3-540-77886-8. http://dx.doi.org/10. 1007/978-3-540-77887-5_2.

[PD10] Daniel Peng and Frank Dabek. "Large-scale Incremental Processing Using Distributed Transactions and Notifications". In: *OSDI*. Vol. 10. 2010, pp. 1– 15. URL: https://www.usenix.org/legacy/events/osdi10/tech/full_papers/Peng. pdf?origin=publication_detail (visited on 01/03/2015).

[PH03] Sunil Patro and Y. Charlie Hu. "Transparent Query Caching in Peer-to-Peer Overlay Networks". In: *17th International Parallel and Distributed Processing Symposium (IPDPS 2003), 22–26 April 2003, Nice, France, CD-ROM/Abstracts Proceedings*. IEEE Computer Society, 2003, p. 32. https://doi.org/10.1109/ IPDPS.2003.1213112.

[PM96] Venkata N. Padmanabhan and Jeffrey C. Mogul. "Using predictive prefetching to improve World Wide Web latency". In: *Computer Communication Review* 26.3 (1996), pp. 22–36. https://doi.org/10.1145/235160.235164.

[Por09] Ely Porat. "An Optimal Bloom Filter Replacement Based on Matrix Solving". In: *Computer Science - Theory and Applications, Fourth International Computer Science Symposium in Russia, CSR 2009, Novosibirsk, Russia, August 18–23, 2009. Proceedings*. Ed. by Anna E. Frid et al. Vol. 5675. Lecture Notes in Computer Science. Springer, 2009, pp. 263–273. https://doi.org/10.1007/ 978-3-642-03351-3_25.

[Pos] *PostgreSQL: Documentation: 9.6: High Availability, Load Balancing, and Replication*. https://www.postgresql.org/docs/9.6/static/high-availability.html. (Accessed on 07/28/2017). 2017. URL: https://www.postgresql.org/docs/9.6/ static/high-availability.html (visited on 02/04/2017).

[PPR05] Anna Pagh, Rasmus Pagh, and S. Srinivasa Rao. "An optimal Bloom filter replacement". In: *Proceedings of the Sixteenth Annual ACM-SIAM Symposium on Discrete Algorithms, SODA 2005, Vancouver, British Columbia, Canada,*

           January 23–25, 2005. SIAM, 2005, pp. 823–829. URL: http://dl.acm.org/citation.cfm?id=1070432.1070548.

[PSS09] Felix Putze, Peter Sanders, and Johannes Singler. "Cache-, hash-, and space-efficient bloom filters". In: *ACM Journal of Experimental Algorithmics* 14 (2009). https://doi.org/10.1145/1498698.1594230.

[Pu+16] Qifan Pu et al. "FairRide: near-optimal, fair cache sharing". In: *13th USENIX Symposium on Networked Systems Design and Implementation (NSDI 16)*. 2016, pp. 393–406.

[Qia+13] Lin Qiao et al. "On brewing fresh espresso: LinkedIn's distributed data serving platform". In: *Proceedings of the 2013 international conference on Management of data*. ACM, 2013, pp. 1135–1146. URL: http://dl.acm.org/citation.cfm?id=2465298 (visited on 09/28/2014).

[Rab+03] Michael Rabinovich et al. "Moving Edge-Side Includes to the Real Edge - the Clients". In: *4th USENIX Symposium on Internet Technologies and Systems, USITS'03, Seattle, Washington, USA, March 26–28, 2003*. Ed. by Steven D. Gribble. USENIX, 2003. URL: http://www.usenix.org/events/usits03/tech/rabinovich.html.

[Rae+13] Ian Rae et al. "Online, asynchronous schema change in F1". In: *Proceedings of the VLDB Endowment* 6.11 (2013), pp. 1045–1056. URL: http://dl.acm.org/citation.cfm?id=2536230 (visited on 01/03/2015).

[Rah88] Erhard Rahm. "Optimistische Synchronisationskonzepte in zentralisierten und verteilten Datenbanksystemen/Concepts for optimistic concurrency control in centralized and distributed database systems". In: *it-Information Technology* 30.1 (1988), pp. 28–47.

[Raj+15] Pethuru Raj et al. *High-Performance Big-Data Analytics - Computing Systems and Approaches*. Computer Communications and Networks. Springer, 2015. ISBN: 978-3-319-20743-8. https://doi.org/10.1007/978-3-319-20744-5.

[Ria] Riak. http://basho.com/products/. (Accessed on 05/25/2017). 2017. URL: http://basho.com/products/ (visited on 01/13/2017).

[RL04] Lakshmish Ramaswamy and Ling Liu. "An Expiration Age-Based Document Placement Scheme for Cooperative Web Caching". In: *IEEE Trans. Knowl. Data Eng.* 16.5 (2004), pp. 585–600. https://doi.org/10.1109/TKDE.2004.1277819.

[RLZ06] Lakshmish Ramaswamy, Ling Liu, and Jianjun Zhang. "Efficient Formation of Edge Cache Groups for Dynamic Content Delivery". In: *26th IEEE International Conference on Distributed Computing Systems (ICDCS 2006), 4–7 July 2006, Lisboa, Portugal*. IEEE Computer Society, 2006, p. 43. https://doi.org/10.1109/ICDCS.2006.33.

[Rom97] Steven Roman. *Introduction to coding and information theory*. Undergraduate texts in mathematics. Springer, 1997. ISBN: 978-0-387-94704-4.

[RS03] M. Rabinovich and O. Spatscheck. "Web caching and replication". In: *SIGMOD Record* 32.4 (2003), p. 107. URL: http://www.sigmod.org/publications/sigmod-record/0312/20.WebCachingReplication2.pdf (visited on 06/28/2012).

[Rus03] C Russell. "Java data objects (jdo) specification jsr-12". In: *Sun Microsystems* (2003).

[Sat+09] Mahadev Satyanarayanan et al. "The Case for VM-Based Cloudlets in Mobile Computing". In: *IEEE Pervasive Computing* 8.4 (2009), pp. 14–23. https://doi.org/10.1109/MPRV.2009.82.

[Sch16] Peter Schuller. "Manhattan, our real-time, multi-tenant distributed database for Twitter scale". In: *Twitter Blog* (2016).

[Sha+15] Artyom Sharov et al. "Take me to your leader! Online Optimization of Distributed Storage Configurations". In: *PVLDB* 8.12 (2015), pp. 1490–1501. URL: http://www.vldb.org/pvldb/vol8/p1490-shraer.pdf.

[Shi11] Rada Shirkova. "Materialized Views". In: *Foundations and TrendsẤő in Databases* 4.4 (2011), pp. 295–405. ISSN: 1931-7883, 1931-7891. https://doi.

           org/10.1561/1900000020. URL: http://www.nowpublishers.com/product.aspx?
product=DBS&doi=1900000020 (visited on 01/03/2015).

[Shu+13]   Jeff Shute et al. "F1: A distributed SQL database that scales". In: *Proceedings of the VLDB Endowment* 6.11 (2013). 00004, pp. 1068–1079.

[Sov+11]   Yair Sovran et al. "Transactional storage for geo-replicated systems". In: *Proceedings of the Twenty-Third ACM Symposium on Operating Systems Principles*. ACM, 2011, pp. 385–400.

[SS94]   Mukesh Singhal and Niranjan G Shivaratri. *Advanced concepts in operating systems*. McGraw-Hill, Inc., 1994.

[Stö+15]   Uta Störl et al. "Schemaless NoSQL Data Stores - Object-NoSQL Mappers to the Rescue?" In: *Datenbanksysteme für Business, Technologie und Web (BTW), 16. Fachtagung des GI-Fachbereichs "Datenbanken und Informationssysteme" (DBIS), 4.-6.3.2015 in Hamburg, Germany. Proceedings*. Ed. by Thomas Seidl et al. Vol. 241. LNI. GI, 2015, pp. 579–599. URL: http://subs.emis.de/LNI/Proceedings/Proceedings241/article13.html (visited on 03/10/2015).

[SW14]   Ivan Stojmenovic and Sheng Wen. "The Fog Computing Paradigm: Scenarios and Security Issues". In: *Proceedings of the 2014 Federated Conference on Computer Science and Information Systems, Warsaw, Poland, September 7–10, 2014*. Ed. by Maria Ganzha, Leszek A. Maciaszek, and Marcin Paprzycki. 2014, pp. 1–8. https://doi.org/10.15439/2014F503.

[TC03]   Xueyan Tang and Samuel T. Chanson. "Coordinated Management of Cascaded Caches for Efficient Content Distribution". In: *Proceedings of the 19th International Conference on Data Engineering, March 5–8, 2003, Bangalore, India*. Ed. by Umeshwar Dayal, Krithi Ramamritham, and T. M. Vijayaraman. IEEE Computer Society, 2003, pp. 37–48. https://doi.org/10.1109/ICDE.2003.1260780.

[Ter+13]   Douglas B. Terry et al. "Consistency-based service level agreements for cloud storage". In: *ACM SIGOPS 24th Symposium on Operating Systems Principles, SOSP '13, Farmington, PA, USA, November 3–6, 2013*. Ed. by Michael Kaminsky and Mike Dahlin. ACM, 2013, pp. 309–324. https://doi.org/10.1145/2517349.2522731.

[Tho+12]   Alexander Thomson et al. "Calvin: fast distributed transactions for partitioned database systems". In: *Proceedings of the 2012 ACM SIGMOD International Conference on Management of Data*. ACM, 2012, pp. 1–12.

[Tor+17]   Alexandre Torres et al. "Twenty years of object-relational mapping: A survey on patterns, solutions, and their implications on application design". In: *Information and Software Technology* 82 (2017), pp. 1–18.

[Tot09]   Alexander Totok. *Modern Internet Services*. Alexander Totok, 2009.

[TRL12]   Sasu Tarkoma, Christian Esteve Rothenberg, and Eemil Lagerspetz. "Theory and Practice of Bloom Filters for Distributed Systems". In: *IEEE Communications Surveys & Tutorials* 14.1 (2012), pp. 131–155. ISSN: 1553-877X. https://doi.org/10.1109/SURV.2011.031611.00024. URL: http://ieeexplore.ieee.org/document/5751342/ (visited on 11/25/2016).

[Tsi+01]   Mark Tsimelzon et al. "ESI language specification 1.0". In: *Akamai Technologies, Inc. Cambridge, MA, USA, Oracle Corporation, Redwood City, CA, USA* (2001), pp. 1–0.

[Vak06]   Athena Vakali. *Web Data Management Practices: Emerging Techniques and Technologies: Emerging Techniques and Technologies*. IGI Global, 2006.

[VM14]   Piet Van Mieghem. *Performance analysis of complex networks and systems*. Cambridge University Press, 2014. URL: http://books.google.de/books?hl=de&lr=&id=lc3aWG0rL_MC&oi=fnd&pg=PR11&dq=mieghem+performance&ots=ohyJ3Qz2Lz&sig=1MOrNY0vHG-D4pDsf_DygD_3vDY (visited on 10/03/2014).

[VV16] Paolo Viotti and Marko VukoliÄ. "Consistency in Non-Transactional Distributed Storage Systems". en. In: *ACM Computing Surveys* 49.1 (June 2016), pp. 1–34. ISSN: 03600300. https://doi.org/10.1145/2926965. URL: http://dl.acm.org/citation.cfm?doid=2911992.2926965 (visited on 11/25/2016).

[Wan99] J. Wang. "A survey of web caching schemes for the internet". In: *ACM SIGCOMM Computer Communication Review* 29.5 (1999), pp. 36–46. URL: http://dl.acm.org/citation.cfm?id=505701 (visited on 06/28/2012).

[WF11] Patrick Wendell and Michael J. Freedman. "Going viral: flash crowds in an open CDN". In: *Proceedings of the 2011 ACM SIGCOMM conference on Internet measurement conference*. ACM, 2011, pp. 549–558. URL: http://dl.acm.org/citation.cfm?id=2068867 (visited on 01/03/2015).

[WGR20] Wolfram Wingerath, Felix Gessert, and Norbert Ritter. "InvaliDB: Scalable Push-Based Real-Time Queries on Top of Pull-Based Databases". In: *36th IEEE International Conference on Data Engineering, ICDE 2020, Dallas, Texas, April 20–24, 2020*, 2020.

[WGW+20] Wolfram Wingerath, Felix Gessert, Erik Witt, et al. "Speed Kit: A Polyglot & GDPR-Compliant Approach For Caching Personalized Content". In: *36th IEEE International Conference on Data Engineering, ICDE 2020, Dallas, Texas, April 20–24, 2020*, 2020.

[Wil+05] Adepele Williams et al. "Web workload characterization: Ten years later". In: *Web content delivery*. Springer, 2005, pp. 3–21.

[Win18] Wolfram Wingerath. "Rethinking Web Performance with Service Workers: 30 Man-Years of Research in a 30-Minute Read". In: *Baqend Tech Blog* (2018). URL: https://medium.com/p/2638196fa60a.

[Win19] Wolfram Wingerath. "Scalable Push-Based Real-Time Queries on Top of Pull-Based Databases". PhD thesis. University of Hamburg, 2019. URL: https://invalidb.info/thesis.

[WKW16] Xiao Sophia Wang, Arvind Krishnamurthy, and David Wetherall. "Speeding up web page loads with Shandian". In: *13th USENIX Symposium on Networked Systems Design and Implementation (NSDI 16)*. 2016, pp. 109–122. URL: https://www.usenix.org/conference/nsdi16/technical-sessions/presentation/wang (visited on 11/25/2016).

[WN90] W. Kevin Wilkinson and Marie-Anne Neimat. "Maintaining Consistency of Client-Cached Data". In: *16th International Conference on Very Large Data Bases, August 13–16, 1990, Brisbane, Queensland, Australia, Proceedings*. Ed. by Dennis McLeod, Ron Sacks-Davis, and Hans-Jörg Schek. Morgan Kaufmann, 1990, pp. 122–133. URL: http://www.vldb.org/conf/1990/P122.PDF.

[Wor94] Kurt Jeffery Worrell. "Invalidation in Large Scale Network Object Caches". In: (1994).

[Wu+13] Zhe Wu et al. "*SPANStore*: cost-effective geo-replicated storage spanning multiple cloud services". In: *ACM SIGOPS 24th Symposium on Operating Systems Principles, SOSP '13, Farmington, PA, USA, November 3–6, 2013*. Ed. by Michael Kaminsky and Mike Dahlin. ACM, 2013, pp. 292–308. https://doi.org/10.1145/2517349.2522730.

[WV02] G. Weikum and G. Vossen. *Transactional information systems*. Series in Data Management Systems. Morgan Kaufmann Pub, 2002. ISBN: 9781558605084. URL: http://books.google.de/books?hl=de&lr=&id=wV5Ran71zNoC&oi=fnd&pg=PP2&dq=transactional+information+systems&ots=PgJAaN7R5X&sig=Iya4r9DiFhmb_wWgOI5QMuxm6zU (visited on 06/28/2012).

[Xu+14] Yuehai Xu et al. "Characterizing Facebook's Memcached Workload". In: *IEEE Internet Computing* 18.2 (2014), pp. 41–49.

[Yin+98] Jian Yin et al. "Using Leases to Support Server-Driven Consistency in Large-Scale Systems". In: *Proceedings of the 18th International Conference on Distributed Computing Systems, Amsterdam, The Netherlands, May 26–29, 1998*. IEEE Computer Society, 1998, pp. 285–294. https://doi.org/10.1109/ICDCS.1998.679726.

[Yin+99] Jian Yin et al. "Volume Leases for Consistency in Large-Scale Systems". In: *IEEE Trans. Knowl. Data Eng.* 11.4 (1999), pp. 563–576. https://doi.org/10.1109/69.790806.

[Zak+16] Victor Zakhary et al. "DB-Risk: The Game of Global Database Placement". In: *Proceedings of the 2016 International Conference on Management of Data, SIGMOD Conference 2016, San Francisco, CA, USA, June 26 - July 01, 2016*. Ed. by Fatma Özcan, Georgia Koutrika, and Sam Madden. ACM, 2016, pp. 2185–2188. https://doi.org/10.1145/2882903.2899405.

[IET15]   IETF. "RFC 7540 - Hypertext Transfer Protocol Version 2 (HTTP/2)". In: (2015).

[ÖV11]   M.T. Özsu and P. Valduriez.   *Principles of distributed database systems.* Springer, 2011.

[ÖVU98]   M Tamer Özsu, Kaladhar Voruganti, and Ronald C Unrau. "An Asynchronous Avoidance-Based Cache Consistency Algorithm for Client Caching DBMSs." In: *VLDB*. Vol. 98. Citeseer. 1998, pp. 440–451.

[ÖDV92]   M. Tamer Özsu, Umeshwar Dayal, and Patrick Valduriez. "An Introduction to Distributed Object Management". In: *Distributed Object Management, Papers from the International Workshop on Distributed Object Management (IWDOM), Edmonton, Alberta, Canada, August 19–21, 1992*. Ed. by M. Tamer Özsu, Umeshwar Dayal, and Patrick Valduriez. Morgan Kaufmann, 1992, pp. 1–24.

Chapter 6
Transactional Semantics for Globally Distributed Applications

In this chapter, we will review both concepts and systems on transaction processing for cloud data management and NoSQL databases. We will give a short discussion of each approach and summarize the differences among them.

6.1 Latency vs. Distributed Transaction Processing

Transactions are one of the central concepts in data management, as they solve the problem of keeping data correct and consistent under highly concurrent access. While the adoption of distributed NoSQL databases first lead to a decline in the support of transactions, numerous systems have started to support transactions again, often with relaxed guarantees (e.g., Megastore [Bak+11], G-Store [DAEA10], Elas-Tras [DAEA13], Cloud SQL Server [Ber+11], Spanner [Cor+12], F1 [Shu+13], Percolator [PD10], Baqend [Ges19], MDCC [Kra+13], TAPIR [Zha+15b], CloudTPS [WPC12], Cherry Garcia [DFR15a], FaRMville [Dra+15], Omid [GÃ+14], RAMP [Bai+14c], Walter [Sov+11], Calvin [Tho+12], H-Store/VoltDB [Kal+08]). The core challenge is that serializability—like strong consistency—enforces a difficult trade-off between high availability and correctness in distributed systems [Bai+13c].

The gold standard for transactions is ACID [WV02, HR83]:

Atomicity. A transaction must either commit or abort as a complete unit. Atomicity is implemented through recovery, rollbacks, and atomic commitment protocols.

Consistency. A transaction takes the database from one consistent state to another. Consistency is implemented through constraint checking and requires transactions to be logically consistent in themselves.

Isolation. The concurrent and interleaved execution of operations leaves transactions isolated, so that they do not affect each other. Isolation is implemented through concurrency control algorithms.

© Springer Nature Switzerland AG 2020
F. Gessert et al., *Fast and Scalable Cloud Data Management*,
https://doi.org/10.1007/978-3-030-43506-6_6

Durability.   The effects of committed transactions are persistent even in the face of failures. Durability is implemented through logging, recovery, and replication.

A comprehensive overview of centralized and distributed transactions is given by Agrawal et al. [ADE12], Weikum and Vossen [WV02], Öszu and Valduriez [ÖV11], Bernstein and Newcomer [BN09], and Sippu and Soisalon-Soininen [SSS15].

6.1.1   Distributed Transaction Architectures

A *transaction* is a finite sequence of read and write operations. The interleaved operations of a set of transactions is called a *history* and any prefix of it is a *schedule* [WV02]. To provide isolation, concurrency control algorithms only allow schedules that do not violate isolation. The strongest level of isolation is serializability. However, many concurrency control protocols allow certain update anomalies for performance reasons, forming different isolation levels of relaxed transaction isolation.

Update anomalies describe undesired behavior caused by transaction interleaving [ALO00, Ady99]. A *dirty write* overwrites data from an uncommitted transaction. With a *dirty read*, stale data is exposed. A *lost update* describes a write that does not become visible, due to two transactions reading the same object version for a subsequent write. A *non-repeatable read* occurs if data read by an in-flight transaction was concurrently overwritten. A *phantom read* describes a predicate-based read that becomes invalid due to concurrent transactions writing data that matches the query predicate. *Read and Write Skew* are two anomalies caused by transactions operating on different, isolated database snapshots.

The strongest **isolation level** of serializability can also be refined into different classes of histories, depending on defined correctness criteria [WV02, p. 109]. In practice, the most relevant class is conflict-serializability (CSR), and its subclass commit order-preserving conflict serializability (COCSR). CSR and COCSR are efficiently decidable and easy to reason about from a developer's perspective. Figure 6.1 gives an overview of typical distributed transaction architectures as originally described by Gray [GL06] and Liskov [Lis+99] and still used in most systems [Bak+11, Cor+13, EWS13]. Distributed databases are partitioned into shards, with each shard being replicated for fault tolerance. Therefore, an atomic commitment protocol is required to enforce an all-or-nothing decision across all shards. Common protocols such as two-phase commit (2PC) [Lec09], three-phase commit (3PC) [SS83], and Paxos Commit [GL06] have to make a trade-off between availability and correctness: any correct atomic commitment protocol blocks under some network partitions. The replication protocol is required to keep replicas in sync, so that staleness does not interfere with the concurrency control algorithm. Traditionally, the replication protocol has to ensure linearizability (e.g., through Paxos [Lam98], Virtual Synchrony [BJ87], and Viewstamped Replication [OL88]) but it has been shown that an appropriate concurrency control scheme

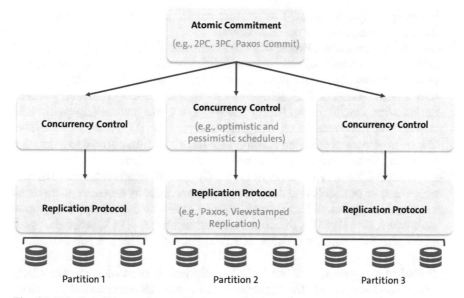

Fig. 6.1 Distributed transaction architecture consisting of an atomic commitment protocol, concurrency control and a replication protocol

can potentially tolerate weaker consistency of the underlying replication protocol without compromising isolation [Zha+15b].

6.1.1.1 Concurrency Control

Concurrency control schemes can be grouped into **pessimistic** and **optimistic** approaches. Pessimistic schemes proactively prevent isolation violations during transaction execution. Optimistic schemes do not interfere with the transaction execution and validate the absence of violations at commit time. The major concurrency control algorithms are:

Lock-based protocols.   For operations that would create cyclic conflicts, mutual exclusion can be achieved through locking. According to the two-phase locking (2PL) theorem, any execution of transactions that use 2PL is serializable [Esw+76]. The granularity and types of locks vary in different protocols, as well as the specifics of 2PL [WV02, ÖV11, BN09]. All 2PL-based protocols without preclaiming (acquiring locks at transaction begin) suffer from potential deadlocks or external aborts[1] [Gra+81, Gra+76]. Preclaiming on the other hand

---

[1]Follwing the terminology of Bailis et al. [Bai+13c] we refer to *external aborts* as transaction rollbacks caused by a system's implementation (e.g., for deadlock prevention) whereas *internal aborts* are triggered by the transaction itself (e.g., as a rollback operation).

is not applicable if accessed objects are unknown in advance but determined through queries, reads, or user interactions.

Non-Locking Pessimistic Protocols. Timestamp Ordering (TO) [Ber99] enforces serializability by ordering conflicting operations by the begin timestamp of transactions. The main downside of TO schedulers is that they produce only a small subset of CSR schedules and therefore cause unnecessary aborts. Serialization Graph Testing (SGT) [Cas81] is another non-locking pessimistic scheme that constructs the conflict graph and prevents it from becoming cyclic. The internal state of SGT can become very large as it is non-trivial to determine when old transactions' information can be safely discarded.

Multi-version Concurrency Control (MVCC).   A straightforward improvement of pessimistic protocols is to decouple concurrent reads by executing them on an immutable snapshot. TO, SGT, and 2PL can easily be extended to incorporate multi-versioning [WV02]. Due to reduced conflict rates, MVCC schedulers such as Serializable Snapshot Isolation [CRF08, Fek+05, PG12] are popular among RDBMSs.

Optimistic Concurrency Control (OCC).   Optimistic schedulers operate across three transaction phases. The principle idea is to allow all transactional operations and to apply rollbacks at commit time when serializability would be violated [KR81].

1. **Read Phase.** In the read phase, the transaction performs its operations, including reads, writes, and queries. Writes are not applied to the database but buffered until commit, typically in the client.
2. **Validation Phase.** The validation phase is executed as a critical section and ensures that the transaction can safely commit. The type of validation depends on the optimistic protocol. In Forward-Oriented Optimistic Concurrency Control (**FOCC**) the committing transaction's write set is validated against the read set of all parallel transactions that are still in the read phase [Här84]. In Backward-Oriented Optimistic Concurrency (**BOCC**), the committing transaction's read set is validated against the write set of all transactions that completed while the committing transaction was in the read phase. To resolve a conflict, two strategies are possible:

   - **Kill/Broadcast-OCC**: transactions that are running and preventing the committing transaction from completing are aborted.
   - **Die**: the committing transaction aborts.

   In BOCC, only the *Die* strategy is applicable, as conflicting transactions are already committed. FOCC permits both resolution strategies. However, FOCC has two important drawbacks. First, it needs to consider reads of active transactions, which prevents serving them from caches or replicas. Second, the FOCC validation has to block concurrent reads and thus strongly limits concurrency and performance.

3. **Write Phase.** If validation was successful, the transaction's changes are persisted to the database and made visible. Usually, this also includes writing recovery information into logs to ensure durability.

The problem of pessimistic concurrency control is that preventing violations of serializability requires transactional reads and writes to be forwarded to the scheduler. In replicated or cached systems, this defeats the purpose of **data distribution**. This also applies to MVCC as it requires local tracking of transaction-specific versions which cannot be offloaded to replicas or caches without including them in the concurrency control algorithm. Therefore, in highly distributed systems, optimistic transactions are advantageous, as they allow to combine client-local processing of reads and writes with a global commit decision [Bak+11, DAEA10, DAEA13, Cor+12, Shu+13, DFR15a, Dra+15]. Stonebraker et al. [Sto+07] identify "locking-based concurrency control mechanisms" as a substantial performance bottleneck and one of the relics of System R that hinder the progress of database systems.

6.1.1.2   Impact of Latency On Transaction Success

Compared to pessimistic mechanisms, optimistic concurrency control offers the advantage of never blocking running transactions due to lock conflicts. The downside of optimistic transactions is that they can lead to transaction aborts since this is the only way of handling cyclic read/write conflicts [KR81].

Locking strategies suffer from deadlocks. Let A be a random variable that describes the outcome of a transaction. Gray et al. [Gra+81] showed that the probability of aborts $P(A = 1)$ increases with the second power of the number T of parallel transactions and with the fourth power of transaction duration D [BN09]:

$$A(w) = \begin{cases} 0 & \text{if w = commit} \\ 1 & \text{if w = abort} \end{cases} \tag{6.1}$$

$$P(A = 1) \sim D^4 \quad and \quad P(A = 1) \sim T^2 \tag{6.2}$$

Deadlocks are resolved by rollbacks. Thus, the more high-latency reads are involved in a pessimistic transaction, the higher the abort probability. In general, optimistic transactions are superior for read-intensive workloads while pessimistic transactions are more appropriate for write-intensive workloads [WV02].

In a simplified model, Franaszek et al. [FRT92] showed the **quadratic effect** of optimistic transactions that states that the abort probability is k^2/N, where k is the number of objects accessed in transactions and N the size of the database [Tho98]. This model assumes preclaiming, an even access probability across all objects, and that every read object is also written. In that case, if the first transaction accesses n objects and the second m, the probability of accessing at least one object in both transactions is:

$$P(n, m) = 1 - \frac{\binom{N-n}{m}}{\binom{N}{m}} \approx 1 - (1 - \frac{n}{N})^m \approx \frac{nm}{N} \tag{6.3}$$

Thus, if all transactions read and write k objects, the abort probability for two concurrent transactions is $P(k, k) = \frac{k^2}{N}$, the quadratic effect. However, this model has many limitations, most importantly the assumption of preclaiming, the missing distinction between reads and writes, and the discarded influence of latency.

6.1.1.3 Example of High-Latency Transactions

To illustrate the role of latency in transaction processing, we briefly discuss an example application use case. In the web, high latency is ubiquitous, especially for applications employing the DBaaS and BaaS model. Transactions requiring client-server round-trips are therefore usually avoided through heuristics, compensations, and other non-transactional workarounds.

As an example consider a checkout process in a booking system, e.g., for an airline or a theatre. A transaction would proceed in two steps:

1. The available seats are read from the database and shipped over a high-latency network to the end user.
2. The end user performs a selection of seats in the frontend and sends a booking or reservation request (i.e., a write) to the system, back over the high-latency network.

This use case is difficult to implement with lock-based concurrency control, as applying read locks in step 1 would cause very high deadlock probabilities and block resources in the database system. In practice, this use case is solved by decoupling step 1 and step 2 into two unrelated transactions [SF12]. If step 2 cannot be applied due to a violation of isolation (i.e., seats were concurrently booked) the transaction is rolled back, and the user is presented with an error. This solution is effectively an optimistic transaction implemented in the application layer. Even a database system with native optimistic concurrency control could not prevent these errors. Furthermore, for security reasons, a database transaction API cannot be exposed to end users, but only to the server-side business logic tier.

6.1.1.4 Challenges

In summary, high-latency environments have a detrimental effect on transaction abort rates in both pessimistic and optimistic concurrency control algorithms. Providing the transaction logic in an application-independent and client-accessible way would be preferable for modern web applications, but transaction APIs are traditionally designed for three-tier applications and do not support end users directly executing transactions. However, this type of access simplifies the development of data-driven web applications and is required for Backend-as-a-Service (BaaS) BaaS architectures.

6.2 Entity Group Transactions

Approaches for distributed transactions can be distinguished by their scope and the degree to which they exploit data locality. Megastore [Bak+11] made the concept of *entity groups* popular that define a set of records that can be accessed in the same transactional context. Megastore's transaction protocol suffers from low throughput per entity group as discussed in the previous chapter.

In G-Store [DAEA10], entity groups (termed key groups) are created dynamically by the system as opposed to statically through schema-based definitions as in Megastore. Each group has a dedicated master that runs the transactions in order to avoid cross-node coordination. Ownership of a group can be transferred to a different master using a protocol similar to 2PC. G-Store assumes a stable mapping of records to groups, as otherwise many migrations are required to run transactions. The master uses optimistic concurrency to run transactions locally on a single group.

Microsoft's Cloud SQL Server [Ber+11] is also based on entity groups, which are defined through a partition key. Unlike the primary key, a partition key is not unique and identifies a group of records that can be updated in single transactions. A similar concept is employed in Cassandra, Twitter's Manhattan, Amazon DynamoDB, and Microsoft Azure Table Services [Cal+11, LM10] to enable local sorting or multi-record atomic updates. By introducing the partition key, the concurrency control protocol of Microsoft SQL Server can remain unchanged and still serve multi-tenant workloads, as long as the data per partition key does not exceed the limits of a single database node.

ElasTras [DAEA13] is a DBaaS architecture that builds on entity groups and optimistic concurrency per group managed by an *owning transaction manager*. The central assumption is that either each tenant is so small that data fits into a single partition or that larger databases can be split into independent entity groups. ElasTras employs the *mini-transactions* concept by Aguilera et al. [Agu+07] to support transactions across nodes for management operations like schema changes. ElasTras supports elasticity through a live-migration protocol (Albatross [Das+11]) that iteratively copies entity groups to new nodes in a multi-step process. ElasTras' largest practical downside is that it assumes completely static entity groups, which is unrealistic assumption and therefore prohibitive for many real-world applications [Cor+12].

6.3   Multi-Shard Transactions

As reviewed in the previous chapter, Spanner [Cor+12], MDCC [Kra+13], Cock-roachDB [Coc], and F1 [Shu+13] implement transactions on top of eager geo-replication by trading correctness and fault tolerance against increased latency, whereas Walter [Sov+11] relaxes isolation to increase the efficiency of geo-replication.

FaRMville is a multi-shard transaction approach that was proposed by Drago-jevic et al. [Dra+15]. The design itself is based on DRAM memory and RDMA (Remote Direct Memory Access) for very low latency. RAM is made persistent through per-rack batteries for uninterrupted power supply. The transaction protocol uses optimistic transactions over distributed shard servers. To this end, the write set is locked by a coordinator executing the commit procedure. The versions of the read set are then validated for freshness and changes are persisted to a transaction log and each individual shard. Using the high-performance hardware setup, FaRMville achieves 4.5 million TPC-C *new order* transactions per second.[2]

TAPIR (Transactional Application Protocol for Inconsistent Replication) [Zha+15b] is based on the observation that replication and transaction protocols typically do the same work twice when enforcing a strict temporal order. The authors propose a consensus-based replication protocol that does not enforce ordering unless explicitly necessary. TAPIR only uses a single consistent operation: the prepare message of the 2PC protocol. All other operations are potentially inconsistent. TAPIR achieves strict serializability using optimistic multi-version timestamp ordering based on loosely synchronized clocks, where the validation happens on read and write sets at commit time. The authors show that commit latency can be reduced by 50% compared to consistent replication protocols. TAPIR assigns transaction timestamps in clients, but assumes a low clock drift for low abort rates. This makes the approach prohibitive for web-based use cases where browsers and mobile devices can exhibit arbitrary clock drift [Aki15, Aki16].

Baqend [Ges19] bears some similarity to FaRMville, but follows a very different design goal: while FaRMville optimizes intra-data center latency for transactions executed from application servers, Baqend is designed for remote web clients exe-cuting the transactions to support the Backend-as-as-Service model. The motivating idea is similar, though, as Baqend minimizes abort rates through caching and FaRMville minimizes them by use of low-latency storage hardware within a data center.

---

[2]The achieved transaction throughput is above the highest-ranking TPC-C result at that time, but below the performance of the coordination-free approach by Bailis et al. [Bai+14a].

6.4   Client-Coordinated Transactions

Percolator [PD10], Omid [GÃ+14], Baqend [Ges19], and the Cherry Garcia library [DFR15a] are approaches for extending NoSQL databases with ACID transactions using client coordination. While Omid and Percolator only address BigTable-style systems, Cherry Garcia and Baqend support heterogeneous data stores.

Google published the design of its real-time web crawler and search index Percolator [PD10]. Percolator is implemented as an external protocol on top of BigTable. It uses several metadata columns to implement a locking protocol with snapshot isolation guarantees. A client-coordinated 2PC enables multi-key transactions using a timestamp service for transaction ordering. Percolator's protocol is designed for high write throughput instead of low latency reads in order to accommodate massive incremental updates to the search index: latency is reported to be in the order of minutes. The client coordination, multi-round-trip commits and writes, and the lack of a deadlock detection protocol make it unsuitable for access across high-latency WANs.

Omid [GÃ+14] provides snapshot isolation for transactions with a lock-free middleware for multi-version concurrency control on top of a slightly modified HBase. It relies on a central *Transaction Status Oracle* (SO) (similar to the earlier ReTSO work [JRY11]) for assigning begin and commit timestamps to transactions and to perform a snapshot isolation validation at commit time. Omid is designed for application servers, where status information of the SO can be replicated into the servers to avoid most of the round-trips. For a highly distributed web scenario, however, relying on a single centralized SO limits scalability and incurs expensive wide-area round-trips for distant application servers.

In his PhD thesis, Dey proposes the Cherry Garcia library [Dey15] for transactions across heterogeneous cloud data stores. The library requires the data store to support strong consistency, multi-versioning, and compare-and-swap updates (e.g., as in Microsoft Azure Storage [Cal+11]). Similar to Percolator [PD10] and ReTSO [JRY11], the transaction protocol identifies read sets based on transaction begin timestamps and write sets based on transaction commit timestamps, with the metadata maintained in the respective data stores [DFR15a]. For the generation of sequentially ordered transaction timestamps, Cherry Garcia either requires a TrueTime-like API [Cor+12] with error bounds or a centralized timestamp oracle [GÃ+14]. In the two-phase transaction commit of Cherry Garcia, the client checks for any write-write and read-write conflicts and makes uncommitted data visible to other transactions. Cherry Garcia is not well-suited for low-latency, as a read potentially requires multiple round-trips to determine the latest valid version suitable for a read, thus increasing the probability of transaction aborts during validation.

Neither Percolator, Omid, Cherry Garcia, nor Baqend modify the underlying database system. However, the first three of these approaches assume that the client coordinating the transaction is a server in a three-tier application. Unlike Baqend, they are not suited for web and mobile clients participating in transactions, since the latency overhead would be prohibitive for starting transactions, reading and writing, as well as coordinating the commit. Baqend's DCAT approach for distributed transactions addresses this problem by caching reads, buffering writes, and only contacting the server for commits. Also, DCAT does not burden the primary database system with maintenance of transactional metadata, but instead employs a fast transaction validation and commits using a coordination service.

RAMP (Read Atomic Multi-Partition) by Bailis et al. [Bai+14c] also realizes client-coordinated transactions, but only offers a weak isolation level (*read atomic*) in order to be always available, even under network partitions. A *coordination-free* execution ensures that a transaction cannot be blocked by other transactions and will commit, if the system partition of each accessed object can be reached [Bai15]. While they are highly scalable, minimize server communication, and are guaranteed to commit, though, RAMP transactions do not prevent a number of anomalies that are often assumed by developers (e.g., lost updates [Bai+14c, p. 9]).

6.5   Middleware-Coordinated Transactions

An alternative to embedding transaction processing in the database system or the involved clients is to provide a transactional middleware that accepts transactions from applications and executes them over non-transactional database systems.

CloudTPS [WPC12] is a transaction middleware for web applications. It supports cross-shard transactions using a two-level architecture. In order to avoid a bottleneck through a single coordinator, CloudTPS employs Local Transaction Managers (LTMs) that manage mutually disjoint partitions of the underlying database. Isolation is implemented through timestamp ordering [WV02]. Each LTM executes a sub-transaction of the global transaction and ensures that local commits are properly ordered. A 2PC executed by a designated LTM over all other participating LTMs ensures atomicity of the global commit. Transactions are executed non-interactively in the middleware and have to be predefined at each LTM as a Java function. All keys accessed in a transaction have to be declared at transaction begin, so that the responsible LTMs are known in advance. As timestamp ordering is susceptible to conflicts, transactions in CloudTPS have to be short-lived and only access a limited set of keys (excluding range and predicate queries). Instead of persisting each write to the underlying storage system, LTMs hold the data independently, distributed through consistent hashing and replicated across multiple LTMs. Periodically, data is persisted to the storage system.

Xi et al. [Xie+15] proposed a scheme to effectively combine pessimistic and optimistic concurrency control algorithms. Their system Callas groups transactions by performance characteristics and applies the most appropriate concurrency control mechanism to each. This is enabled by a two-tiered protocol that applies locking across groups and arbitrary schemes within a group of similar characteristics.

Deuteronomy [Lev+15] follows the idea of separating data storage (data component, DC) and transaction management (transaction component, TC) and relies on heterogeneous database systems. The authors demonstrate that building on a high-performance key-value store, a throughput of over 6M operations per second can be achieved on scale-up hardware with an appropriate TC. Scalability, however, is limited to the threads of the underlying NUMA (Non-Uniform Memory Access) machines. Therefore, Deuteronomy is not ideally suited for scale-out architectures.

Hekaton [Dia+13], the storage engine of Microsoft SQL Server [Gra97], is another example for the wide-spread use of optimistic transactions in the industry. The authors introduce a new multi-version, optimistic concurrency control scheme for serializability that is optimized for OLTP workloads in main memory. Besides the validation of the read set, Hekaton also validates commit dependencies introduced by concurrent operations during the validation phase. While this optimization increases concurrency and hence throughput, it also introduces cascading aborts.

6.6 Deterministic Transactions

H-Store [Kal+08] and its commercial successor VoltDB [SW13] are horizontally scalable main-memory RDBMSs. Sometimes, this new class of scale-out relational databases is referred to as *NewSQL* [Gro+13]. Other examples of the NewSQL movement are Clustrix [Clu], a MySQL-compatible, scalable RDBMS, and NuoDB [Nuo], an RDBMS built on top of a distributed key-value store.

VoltDB is based on eager master-slave replication and shards data via application-defined columns (similar to MongoDB). Transactions are defined at deployment time as stored procedures written in Java or SQL. Each shard has a Single Partition Initiator (SPI) that works off a transaction queue for that partition in serial order. As data is held in memory, this lack of concurrency is considered an optimization to avoid locking overhead [Har+08]. Single-shard transactions are directly forwarded to SPIs and do not require additional concurrency control as the execution is serial. Read-only transactions can directly read from any replica without concurrency control (called *one-shot*). Multi-shard transactions are sequenced through a Multi Partition Initiator (MPI) that creates a consensus among SPIs for an interleaved transaction ordering. During execution, cross-shard communication is required to distribute intermediate results. Written data is atomically committed through 2PC. VoltDB scales well for workloads with many single-shard transactions. For multi-shard transactions serialized through the MPI, however, the consensus overhead causes throughput to decrease with increasing cluster size.

Calvin [Tho+12] is a transaction and replication service for enhancing available database systems with ACID transactions. Transactions in Calvin have to be run fully server-side (written in C++ or Python) and must not introduce non-determinism, similar to H-Store and VoltDB [Kal+08, SW13]. This permits Calvin to schedule the order of transactions before their execution. Client-submitted transactions are appended to a shared replicated log that is similar to the Tango approach [Bal+13]. To achieve acceptable performance despite this centralized component, requests are batched, persisted to a storage backend (e.g., Cassandra), and the batch identifiers are replicated via Paxos. The scheduler relies on the log order to create a deadlock-free, deterministic ordering of transactions using two-phase locking. As each transaction's read and write sets have to be declared in advance, allocation of locks can be performed before the transaction begin (*preclaiming* [WV02]). Transactions execute locally on each shard by exchanging the read sets with other shards and only writing local records. While Calvin achieves high throughput in TPC-C benchmarks, its model is strictly limited to deterministic, non-interactive transactions on pre-defined read and write sets, which eliminates most forms of queries. Furthermore, there is an inherent trade-off between commit latency and throughput introduced by the batching interval of the shared log.

6.7   Summary: Consistency vs. Latency in Distributed Applications

In this chapter, we discussed different seminal systems for distributed transaction processing, some of which are transactional database systems and some of which enable transactional guarantees on top of non-transactional database systems. Table 6.1 summarizes the pivotal properties of the systems discussed in this chapter.

Many distributed data management systems employ optimistic concurrency control to minimize abort rates (e.g. Megastore, G-Store,and MDCC), while some use pessimistic protocols in favor of write-heavy workloads (e.g. Calvin) or a combination of both for flexibility (F1). A few systems contrastingly rely on deterministic transactions (e.g. H-Store/VoltDB and Calvin) or custom concurrency protocols (e.g. RAMP) to increase scalability and throughput at the expense of reduced flexibility or consistency guarantees. Entity group transactions are lightweight and build on well-known single-node concurrency control schemes, but they also limit both scalability and the possible scope of transactions. A number of systems therefore implement distributed multi-shard transactions which may also rely on local commit procedures, but often employ client-coordinated transactions (Cherry Garcia, RAMP) or variants of two-phase commit (e.g. Spanner, F1, Percolator, MDCC, TAPIR, CloudTPS, Walter).

Table 6.1 Related transactional systems and their concurrency control protocols (*OCC*: optimistic concurrency control, *PCC*: pessimistic concurrency control, *TO*: timestamp ordering, *MVCC*: multi-version concurrency control), achieved isolation level (*SR*: serializability, *SI*: snapshot isolation, *RC*: read committed), transaction granularity, and commit protocol

System	Concurrency control	Isolation	Granularity	Commit protocol
Megastore [Bak+11]	OCC	SR	Entity group	Local
G-store [DAEA10]	OCC	SR	Entity group	Local
ElasTras [DAEA13]	OCC	SR	Entity group	Local
Cloud SQL server [Ber+11]	PCC	SR	Entity group	Local
Spanner [Cor+12]	PCC	SR/SI	Multi-shard	2PC
F1 [Shu+13]	PCC or OCC	SR/SI	Multi-shard	2PC
Percolator [PD10]	OCC	SI	Multi-shard	2PC
MDCC [Kra+13]	OCC	RC	Multi-shard	2PC-like
TAPIR [Zha+15b]	TO	SR	Multi-shard	2PC-like
CloudTPS [WPC12]	TO	SR	Multi-shard	2PC
Cherry garcia [DFR15a]	OCC	SI	Multi-shard	Client-coord.
Omid [GÃ+14]	MVCC	SI	Multi-shard	Local
FaRMville [Dra+15]	OCC	SR	Multi-shard	Local
RAMP [Bai+14c]	Custom	Read-atomic	Multi-shard	Client-coord.
Walter [Sov+11]	PCC	Parallel SI	Multi-shard	2PC
H-Store/VoltDB [Kal+08]	Deterministic CC	SR	Multi-shard	Local
Calvin [Tho+12]	Deterministic CC	SR	Multi-shard	Local
Orestes/Baqend with DCAT [Ges19]	OCC	SR	Multi-shard	Custom

References

[ADE12] Divyakant Agrawal, Sudipto Das, and Amr El Abbadi. *Data Management in the Cloud: Challenges and Opportunities*. Synthesis Lectures on Data Management. Morgan & Claypool Publishers, 2012. https://doi.org/10.2200/S00456ED1V01Y201211DTM032.

[Ady99] Atul Adya. "Weak consistency: a generalized theory and optimistic implementations for distributed transactions". PhD thesis. Massachusetts Institute of Technology, 1999. URL: http://www.csd.uoc.gr/~hy460/pdf/adya99weak.pdf (visited on 01/03/2015).

[Agu+07] Marcos K. Aguilera et al. "Sinfonia: a new paradigm for building scalable distributed systems". In: *ACM SIGOPS Operating Systems Review*. Vol. 41. ACM, 2007, pp. 159–174. URL: http://dl.acm.org/citation.cfm?id=1294278 (visited on 01/03/2015).

[Aki15] Tyler Akidau. "The world beyond batch: Streaming 101". In: *O'Reilly Media* (Aug. 2015). Accessed on 08/21/2017. URL: https://www.oreilly.com/ideas/the-world-beyond-batch-streaming-101.

[Aki16] Tyler Akidau. "The world beyond batch: Streaming 102". In: *O'Reilly Media* (Jan. 2016). Accessed on 08/21/2017. URL: https://www.oreilly.com/ideas/the-world-beyond-batch-streaming-102.

[ALO00] Atul Adya, Barbara Liskov, and Patrick E. O'Neil. "Generalized Isolation Level Definitions". In: *Proceedings of the 16th International Conference on Data Engineering, San Diego, California, USA, February 28 - March 3, 2000*. Ed. by David B. Lomet and Gerhard Weikum. IEEE Computer Society, 2000, pp. 67–78. https://doi.org/10.1109/ICDE.2000.839388.

[Bai+13c] Peter Bailis et al. "Highly Available Transactions: Virtues and Limitations". In: *Proceedings of the VLDB Endowment* 7.3 (2013). 00001.

[Bai+14a] Peter Bailis et al. "Coordination avoidance in database systems". In: *Proceedings of the VLDB Endowment* 8.3 (2014), pp. 185–196. URL: http://www.vldb.org/pvldb/vol8/p185-bailis.pdf (visited on 01/03/2015).

[Bai+14c] Peter Bailis et al. "Scalable Atomic Visibility with RAMP Transactions". In: *ACM SIGMOD Conference*. 2014. URL: https://amplab.cs.berkeley.edu/wp-content/uploads/2014/04/ramp-sigmod2014.pdf (visited on 09/28/2014).

[Bai15] Peter Bailis. "Coordination Avoidance in Distributed Databases". PhD thesis. University of California, Berkeley, USA, 2015. URL: http://www.escholarship.org/uc/item/8k8359g2.

[Bak+11] J. Baker et al. "Megastore: Providing scalable, highly available storage for interactive services". In: *Proc. of CIDR*. Vol. 11. 2011, pp. 223–234.

[Bal+13] Mahesh Balakrishnan et al. "Tango: distributed data structures over a shared log". en. In: ACM Press, 2013, pp. 325–340. ISBN: 978-1-4503-2388-8. https://doi.org/10.1145/2517349.2522732. URL: http://dl.acm.org/citation.cfm?doid=2517349.2522732 (visited on 01/03/2015).

[Ber+11] Philip A. Bernstein et al. "Adapting Microsoft SQL server for cloud computing". In: *Data Engineering (ICDE), 2011 IEEE 27th International Conference on*. IEEE. IEEE, 2011, pp. 1255–1263. URL: http://ieeexplore.ieee.org/xpls/abs_all.jsp?arnumber=5767935 (visited on 05/05/2014).

[Ber99] Philip A. Bernstein. "Review - A Majority Consensus Approach to Concurrency Control for Multiple Copy Databases". In: *ACM SIGMOD Digital Review* 1 (1999). URL: http://db/journals/dr/Bernstein99.html.

[BJ87] Ken Birman and Thomas Joseph. *Exploiting virtual synchrony in distributed systems*. Vol. 21. 5. ACM, 1987. URL: http://dl.acm.org/citation.cfm?id=37515 (visited on 01/03/2015).

[BN09] Philip A. Bernstein and Eric Newcomer. *Principles of Transaction Processing*. Morgan Kaufmann, 2009. ISBN: 1-55860-415-4.

[Cal+11] Brad Calder et al. "Windows Azure Storage: a highly available cloud storage service with strong consistency". In: *Proceedings of the Twenty-Third ACM Symposium on Operating Systems Principles*. ACM. ACM, 2011, pp. 143–157. URL: http://dl.acm.org/citation.cfm?id=2043571 (visited on 04/16/2014).

[Cas81] Marco A. Casanova. *The Concurrency Control Problem for Database Systems*. Vol. 116. Lecture Notes in Computer Science. Springer, 1981. ISBN: 3-540-10845-9. https://doi.org/10.1007/3-540-10845-9.

[Clu] *Clustrix: A New Approach to Scale-Out RDBMS*. http://www.clustrix.com/wp-content/uploads/2017/01/Whitepaper-ANewApproachtoScaleOutRDBMS.pdf. (Accessed on 05/20/2017). 2017. URL: http://www.clustrix.com/wp-content/uploads/2017/01/Whitepaper-ANewApproachtoScaleOutRDBMS.pdf (visited on 02/18/2017).

[Coc] *CockroachDB - the scalable, survivable, strongly-consistent SQL database*. https://github.com/cockroachdb/cockroach. (Accessed on 05/20/2017). 2017. URL: https://github.com/cockroachdb/cockroach (visited on 02/17/2017).

[Cor+12] James C. Corbett et al. "Spanner: Google's Globally-Distributed Database". In: *10th USENIX Symposium on Operating Systems Design and Implementation, OSDI 2012, Hollywood, CA, USA, October 8–10, 2012*. Ed. by Chandu Thekkath and Amin Vahdat. USENIX Association, 2012, pp. 261–264. URL: https://www.usenix.org/conference/osdi12/technical-sessions/presentation/corbett.

[Cor+13] James C. Corbett et al. "Spanner: Google's Globally Distributed Database". In: *ACM Trans. Comput. Syst.* 31.3 (2013), 8:1–8:22. https://doi.org/10.1145/2491245.

[CRF08] Michael J. Cahill, Uwe Röhm, and Alan D. Fekete. "Serializable Isolation for Snapshot Databases". In: *Proceedings of the 2008 ACM SIGMOD International Conference on Management of Data*. SIGMOD '08. Vancouver, Canada: ACM, 2008, pp. 729–738. ISBN: 978-1-60558-102-6. https://doi.org/10.1145/1376616.1376690. URL: http://doi.acm.org/10.1145/1376616.1376690.

[DAEA10] Sudipto Das, Divyakant Agrawal, and Amr El Abbadi. "G-store: a scalable data store for transactional multi key access in the cloud". In: *Proceedings of the 1st ACM symposium on Cloud computing*. ACM. 2010, pp. 163–174.

[DAEA13] Sudipto Das, Divyakant Agrawal, and Amr El Abbadi. "ElasTraS: An elastic, scalable, and self-managing transactional database for the cloud". en. In: *ACM Transactions on Database Systems* 38.1 (Apr. 2013), pp. 1–45. ISSN: 03625915. https://doi.org/10. 1145/2445583.2445588. URL: http://dl.acm.org/citation.cfm?doid=2445583.2445588 (visited on 11/25/2016).

[Das+11] Sudipto Das et al. "Albatross: lightweight elasticity in shared storage databases for the cloud using live data migration". In: *Proceedings of the VLDB Endowment* 4.8 (2011), pp. 494–505. URL: http://dl.acm.org/citation.cfm?id=2002977 (visited on 07/16/2014).

[Dey15] Akon Samir Dey. "Cherry Garcia: Transactions across Heterogeneous Data Stores". In: (2015).

[DFR15a] A. Dey, A. Fekete, and U. Röhm. "Scalable distributed transactions across heterogeneous stores". In: *2015 IEEE 31st International Conference on Data Engineering*. 2015, pp. 125–136. https://doi.org/10.1109/ICDE.2015.7113278.

[Dia+13] Cristian Diaconu et al. "Hekaton: SQL server's memory-optimized OLTP engine". In: *Proceedings of the 2013 international conference on Management of data*. ACM, 2013, pp. 1243–1254. URL: http://dl.acm.org/citation.cfm?id=2463710 (visited on 01/03/2015).

[Dra+15] Aleksandar DragojeviÄ et al. "No compromises: distributed transactions with consistency, availability, and performance". en. In: *Proceedings of the 25th Symposium on Operating Systems Principles*. ACM. ACM Press, 2015, pp. 54–70. ISBN: 978-1-4503-3834-9. https://doi.org/10.1145/2815400.2815425. URL: http://dl.acm. org/citation.cfm?doid=2815400.2815425 (visited on 11/25/2016).

[Esw+76] Kapali P. Eswaran et al. "The Notions of Consistency and Predicate Locks in a Database System". In: *Commun. ACM* 19.11 (1976), pp. 624–633. https://doi.org/10. 1145/360363.360369.

[EWS13] Robert Escriva, Bernard Wong, and Emin GÄijn Sirer. "Warp: Multikey transactions for keyvalue stores". In: *United Networks, LLC, Tech. Rep* 5 (2013). URL: http://dl.frz.ir/FREE/papers-we-love/distributed_systems/warp-multi-key-transactions-for-key-value-stores.pdf (visited on 01/03/2015).

[Fek+05] Alan Fekete et al. "Making snapshot isolation serializable". In: *ACM Transactions on Database Systems (TODS)* 30.2 (2005), pp. 492–528. URL: http://dl.acm.org/citation. cfm?id=1071615 (visited on 01/03/2015).

[FRT92] Peter A. Franaszek, John T. Robinson, and Alexander Thomasian. "Concurrency Control for High Contention Environments". In: *ACM Trans. Database Syst.* 17.2 (1992), pp. 304–345. https://doi.org/10.1145/128903.128906.

[Ges19] Felix Gessert. "Low Latency for Cloud Data Management". PhD thesis. University of Hamburg, Germany, 2019. URL: http://ediss.sub.uni-hamburg.de/volltexte/2019/ 9541/.

[GL06] J. Gray and L. Lamport. "Consensus on transaction commit". In: *ACM Transactions on Database Systems (TODS)* 31.1 (2006), pp. 133–160. URL: http://dl.acm.org/ citation.cfm?id=1132867 (visited on 11/28/2016).

[Gra+76] Jim Gray et al. "Granularity of Locks and Degrees of Consistency in a Shared Data Base". In: *Modelling in Data Base Management Systems, Proceeding of the IFIP*

Working Conference on Modelling in Data Base Management Systems, Freudenstadt, Germany, January 5–8, 1976. Ed. by G. M. Nijssen. North-Holland, 1976, pp. 365–394.

[Gra+81] Jim Gray et al. "A Straw Man Analysis of the Probability of Waiting and Deadlock in a Database System". In: *Berkeley Workshop*. 1981, p. 125.

[Gra97] Jim Gray. "Microsoft SQL Server". In: 1997.

[Gro+13] Katarina Grolinger et al. "Data management in cloud environments: NoSQL and NewSQL data stores". en. In: *Journal of Cloud Computing: Advances, Systems and Applications* 2.1 (2013), p. 22. ISSN: 2192-113X. https://doi.org/10.1186/2192-113X-2-22. URL: http://www.journalofcloudcomputing.com/content/2/1/22 (visited on 01/03/2015).

[GÃ+14] Ferro Daniel GÃşmez et al. "Omid: Lock-free Transactional Support for Distributed Data Stores". In: *ICDE*. 2014.

[Har+08] S. Harizopoulos et al. "OLTP through the looking glass, and what we found there". In: *Proceedings of the 2008 ACM SIGMOD international conference on Management of data*. 2008, pp. 981–992. URL: http://dl.acm.org/citation.cfm?id=1376713 (visited on 07/05/2012).

[HR83] Theo Haerder and Andreas Reuter. "Principles of transaction-oriented database recovery". In: *ACM Comput. Surv.* 15.4 (Dec. 1983), pp. 287–317.

[Här84] Theo Härder. "Observations on optimistic concurrency control schemes". In: *Inf. Syst.* 9.2 (1984), pp. 111–120. https://doi.org/10.1016/0306-4379(84)90020-6.

[JRY11] Flavio Junqueira, Benjamin Reed, and Maysam Yabandeh. "Lock-free transactional support for large-scale storage systems". In: *IEEE/IFIP International Conference on Dependable Systems and Networks Workshops (DSN-W 2011), Hong Kong, China, June 27–30, 2011*. IEEE, 2011, pp. 176–181. https://doi.org/10.1109/DSNW.2011.5958809.

[Kal+08] R. Kallman et al. "H-store: a high-performance, distributed main memory transaction processing system". In: *Proceedings of the VLDB Endowment* 1.2 (2008), pp. 1496–1499.

[KR81] H. T. Kung and J. T. Robinson. "On optimistic methods for concurrency control". In: *ACM Transactions on Database Systems (TODS)* 6.2 (1981), pp. 213–226. URL: http://dl.acm.org/citation.cfm?id=319567 (visited on 11/19/2012).

[Kra+13] Tim Kraska et al. "MDCC: Multi-data center consistency". In: *EuroSys*. ACM, 2013, pp. 113–126. URL: http://dl.acm.org/citation.cfm?id=2465363 (visited on 04/15/2014).

[Lam98] Leslie Lamport. "The part-time parliament". In: *ACM Transactions on Computer Systems (TOCS)* 16.2 (1998), pp. 133–169.

[Lec09] Jens Lechtenbörger.A"Two-Phase Commit Protocol". English. In: *Encyclopedia of Database Systems*. Ed. by LING LIU and M.TAMER ÃZSU. Springer US, 2009, pp. 3209–3213. ISBN: 978-0-387-35544-3. https://doi.org/10.1007/978-0-387-39940-9_2. URL: http://dx.doi.org/10.1007/978-0-387-39940-9_2.

[Lev+15] Justin J. Levandoski et al. "High Performance Transactions in Deuteronomy". In: *CIDR 2015, Seventh Biennial Conference on Innovative Data Systems Research, Asilomar, CA, USA, January 4–7, 2015, Online Proceedings*. www.cidrdb.org, 2015. URL: http://www.cidrdb.org/cidr2015/Papers/CIDR15_Paper15.pdf.

[Lis+99] Barbara Liskov et al. "Providing Persistent Objects in Distributed Systems". In: *ECOOP'99 - Object-Oriented Programming, 13th European Conference, Lisbon, Portugal, June 14–18, 1999, Proceedings*. Ed. by Rachid Guerraoui. Vol. 1628. Lecture Notes in Computer Science. Springer, 1999, pp. 230–257. https://doi.org/10.1007/3-540-48743-3_11.

[LM10] Avinash Lakshman and Prashant Malik. "Cassandra: a decentralized structured storage system". In: *ACM SIGOPS Operating Systems Review* 44.2 (2010), pp. 35–40. URL: http://dl.acm.org/citation.cfm?id=1773922 (visited on 04/15/2014).

[Nuo] *NuoDB: Emergent Architecture.* http://go.nuodb.com/rs/nuodb/images/Greenbook_ Final.pdf. (Accessed on 04/30/2017). 2017. URL: http://go.nuodb.com/rs/nuodb/ images/Greenbook_Final.pdf (visited on 02/18/2017).

[OL88] Brian M. Oki and Barbara Liskov. "Viewstamped Replication: A General Primary Copy". In: *Proceedings of the Seventh Annual ACM Symposium on Principles of Distributed Computing, Toronto, Ontario, Canada, August 15–17, 1988.* Ed. by Danny Dolev. ACM, 1988, pp. 8–17. https://doi.org/10.1145/62546.62549.

[PD10] Daniel Peng and Frank Dabek. "Large-scale Incremental Processing Using Distributed Transactions and Notifications." In: *OSDI.* Vol. 10. 2010, pp. 1–15. URL: https://www.usenix.org/legacy/events/osdi10/tech/full_papers/Peng.pdf?origin= publication_detail (visited on 01/03/2015).

[PG12] Dan RK Ports and Kevin Grittner. "Serializable snapshot isolation in PostgreSQL". In: *Proceedings of the VLDB Endowment* 5.12 (2012), pp. 1850–1861. URL: http://dl. acm.org/citation.cfm?id=2367523 (visited on 01/03/2015).

[SF12] Pramod J. Sadalage and Martin Fowler. *NoSQL distilled: a brief guide to the emerging world of polyglot persistence.* Pearson Education, 2012.

[Shu+13] Jeff Shute et al. "F1: A distributed SQL database that scales". In: *Proceedings of the VLDB Endowment* 6.11 (2013). 00004, pp. 1068–1079.

[Sov+11] Yair Sovran et al. "Transactional storage for geo-replicated systems". In: *Proceedings of the Twenty-Third ACM Symposium on Operating Systems Principles.* ACM, 2011, pp. 385–400.

[SS83] Dale Skeen and Michael Stonebraker. "A Formal Model of Crash Recovery in a Distributed System". In: *IEEE Trans. Software Eng.* 9.3 (1983), pp. 219–228. https:// doi.org/10.1109/TSE.1983.236608.

[SSS15] S. Sippu and E. Soisalon-Soininen. *Transaction Processing: Management of the Logical Database and its Underlying Physical Structure.* Data-Centric Systems and Applications. Springer International Publishing, 2015. ISBN: 9783319122922. URL: https://books.google.de/books?id=TN1sBgAAQBAJ.

[Sto+07] M. Stonebraker et al. "The end of an architectural era:(it's time for a complete rewrite)". In: *Proceedings of the 33rd international conference on Very large data bases.* 2007, pp. 1150–1160. URL: http://dl.acm.org/citation.cfm?id=1325981 (visited on 07/05/2012).

[SW13] Michael Stonebraker and Ariel Weisberg. "The VoltDB Main Memory DBMS". In: *IEEE Data Eng. Bull.* 36.2 (2013), pp. 21–27. URL: http://sites.computer.org/debull/ A13june/VoltDB1.pdf.

[Tho+12] Alexander Thomson et al. "Calvin: fast distributed transactions for partitioned database systems". In: *Proceedings of the 2012 ACM SIGMOD International Conference on Management of Data.* ACM. 2012, pp. 1–12.

[Tho98] A. Thomasian. "Concurrency control: methods, performance, and analysis". In: *ACM Computing Surveys (CSUR)* 30.1 (1998). 00119, pp. 70–119. URL: http://dl.acm.org/ citation.cfm?id=274443 (visited on 10/18/2012).

[WPC12] Zhou Wei, Guillaume Pierre, and Chi-Hung Chi. "CloudTPS: Scalable transactions for Web applications in the cloud". In: *Services Computing, IEEE Transactions on* 5.4 (2012), pp. 525–539.

[WV02] G. Weikum and G. Vossen. *Transactional information systems.* Series in Data Management Systems. Morgan Kaufmann Pub, 2002. ISBN: 9781558605084. URL: http://books.google.de/books?hl=de&lr=&id=wV5Ran71zNoC&oi=fnd&pg=PP2& dq=transactional+information+systems&ots=PgJAaN7R5X&sig=Iya4r9DiFhmb_ wWgOI5QMuxm6zU (visited on 06/28/2012).

[Xie+15] Chao Xie et al. "High-performance ACID via modular concurrency control". In: *Proceedings of the 25th Symposium on Operating Systems Principles, SOSP 2015, Monterey, CA, USA, October 4–7, 2015.* Ed. by Ethan L. Miller and Steven Hand. ACM, 2015, pp. 279–294. https://doi.org/10.1145/2815400.2815430.

[Zha+15b] Irene Zhang et al. "Building consistent transactions with inconsistent replication". In: *Proceedings of the 25th Symposium on Operating Systems Principles, SOSP 2015, Monterey, CA, USA, October 4–7, 2015*. Ed. by Ethan L. Miller and Steven Hand. ACM, 2015, pp. 263–278. https://doi.org/10.1145/2815400.2815404.

[ÖV11] M.T. Özsu and P. Valduriez. *Principles of distributed database systems*. Springer, 2011.

Chapter 7
Polyglot Persistence in Data Management

As applications become more data-driven and highly distributed, providing low response times to increasingly many users becomes more challenging within the scope of a single database system. Not only the variety of use cases is increasing, but also the requirements are becoming more heterogeneous: horizontal scalability, schema flexibility, and high availability are primary concerns for modern applications. While RDBMSs cover many of the functional requirements (e.g., ACID transactions and expressive queries), they cannot cover scalability, performance, and fault tolerance in the same way that specialized data stores can. The explosive growth of available systems through the Big Data and NoSQL movement sparked the idea of employing particularly well-suited database systems for subproblems of the overall application.

The architectural style *polyglot persistence* describes the usage of specialized data stores for different requirements. The term was popularized by Fowler in 2011 and builds on the idea of polyglot programming [SF12]. The core idea is that abandoning a "one size fits all" architecture can increase development productivity, resp. time-to-market, as well as performance. Polyglot persistence applies to single applications as well as complete organizations.

Figure 7.1 shows an example of a polyglot persistence architecture for an e-commerce application, as often found in real-world applications [Kle17]. Data is distributed to different database systems according to their associated requirements. For example, financial transactions are processed through a relational database, to guarantee correctness. As product descriptions form a semi-structured aggregate, they are well-suited for storage in a distributed document store that can guarantee scalability of data volume and reads. The log-structured storage management in wide-column stores is optimal for maintaining high write throughput for application-generated event streams. Additionally, they provide interfaces to apply complex data analysis through Big Data platforms such as Hadoop and Spark [Whi15, Zah+10]. The example illustrates that in polyglot persistence architectures,

© Springer Nature Switzerland AG 2020
F. Gessert et al., *Fast and Scalable Cloud Data Management*,
https://doi.org/10.1007/978-3-030-43506-6_7

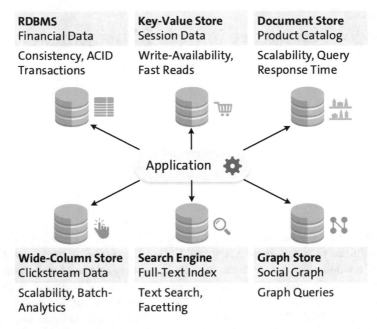

Fig. 7.1 Example of a polyglot persistence architecture with database systems for different requirements and types of data in an e-commerce scenario

there is an inherent trade-off between increased complexity of maintenance and development against improved, problem-tailored storage of application data.

In a nutshell, polyglot persistence adopts the idea of applying the best persistence technology for a given problem. In the following, we will present an overview of different strategies for implementing polyglot persistence and the challenges they entail.

7.1 Functional and Non-functional Requirements

The requirement for a fast *time-to-market* is supported by avoiding the impedance mismatch [Mai90, Amb12] between the application's data structures and the persistent data model. For example, if a web application using a JSON-based REST API can store native JSON documents in a document store, the development process is considerably simplified compared to systems where the application's data model has to be mapped to a database system's data model.

Performance can be maximized, if the persistence requirements allow for an efficient partitioning and replication of data combined with suitable index structures and storage management. If the application can tolerate relaxed guarantees for consistency or transactional isolation, database systems can leverage this to optimize throughput and latency.

Typical *functional* persistence requirements are:

- ACID transactions with different isolation levels
- Atomic, conditional, or set-oriented updates
- Query types: point lookups, scans, aggregations, selections, projections, joins, subqueries, Map-Reduce, graph queries, batch analyses, searches, real-time queries, dataflow graphs
- Partial or commutative update operations
- Data structures: graphs, lists, sets, maps, trees, documents, etc.
- Structured, semi-structured, or implicit schemas
- Semantic integrity constraints

Among the *non-functional requirements* are:

- Throughput for reads, writes, and queries
- Read and write latency
- High availability
- Scalability of data volume, reads, writes, and queries
- Consistency guarantees
- Durability
- Elastic scale-out and scale-in

The central challenge in polyglot persistence is determining whether a given database system satisfies a set of application-provided requirements and access patterns. While some performance metrics can be quantified with **benchmarks** such as YCSB, TPC, and others [Dey+14, Coo+10, Coo+10, Pat+11, BZS13, Ber+14, PF00, Wad+11, Fio+13, BT14, Ber15, Ber14], many non-functional requirements such as consistency and scalability are currently not covered through benchmarks or even diverge from the documented behavior [Win+15].

In a polyglot persistence architecture, the boundary of the database form the boundary of transactions, queries, and update operations. Thus, if data is persisted and modified in different databases, this entails consistency challenges. The application therefore has to explicitly control the synchronization of data across systems, e.g., through ETL batch jobs, or has to maintain consistency at the application level, e.g., through commutative data structures. Alternatively, data can be distributed in disjoint partitions which shifts the problem to cross-database queries, a well-studied topic in data integration [Len02]. In contrast to data integration problems, however, there is no autonomy of data sources. Instead, the application explicitly combines and modifies the databases for polyglot persistence [SF12].

Fig. 7.2 Polyglot persistence requirements for a product catalog in an e-commerce application

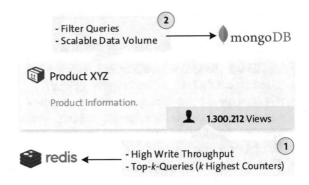

7.1.1 Implementation of Polyglot Persistence

To manage the increased complexity introduced by polyglot persistence, different architectures can be applied. We group them into the three architectural patterns *application-coordinated polyglot persistence*, *microservices*, and *polyglot database services*. As an example, consider the product catalog of the introductory e-commerce example (see Fig. 7.2). The product catalog should be able to answer simple filter queries (e.g., searching by keyword) as well as returning the top-k products according to access statistics. The functional requirement therefore is that the access statistics have to support a high write throughput (incrementing on each view) and top-k queries **(1)**. The product catalog has to offer filter queries and scalability of data volume **(2)**. These requirements can, for example, be fulfilled with the key-value store Redis and the document store MongoDB. With its sorted set data structure, Redis supports a mapping from counters to primary keys of products. Incrementing and performing top-k queries are efficiently supported with logarithmic time complexity in memory. MongoDB supports storing product information in nested documents and allows queries on the attributes of these documents. Using hash partitioning, the documents can efficiently be distributed over many nodes in a cluster to achieve scalability.

With **application-coordinated polyglot persistence** (see Fig. 7.3), the application server's data tier programmatically coordinates polyglot persistence. Typically, the mapping of data to databases follows the application's modularization. This pattern simplifies development, as each module is specialized for the use of one particular data store. Also, design decisions in data modeling as well as access patterns are encapsulated in a single module (*loose coupling*). The separation can also be relaxed: for the product catalog, it would not only be possible to model a counter and separate product data. Instead, a product could also be modeled as an entity containing a counter. The dependency between databases has to be considered both at development time and during operation. For example, if the format of the primary key changes, the new key structure has to be implemented for both systems in the code and in the database. Object-NoSQL mappers simplify the implementation

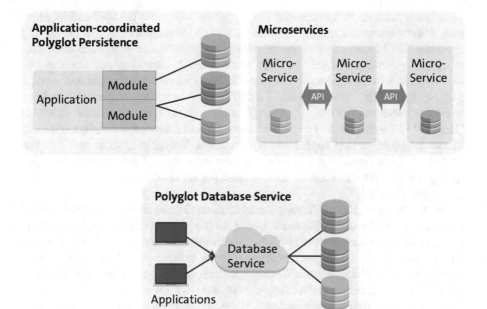

Fig. 7.3 Architectural patterns for the implementation of polyglot persistence: application-coordinated polyglot persistence, microservices, and polyglot database services

of application-coordinated polyglot persistence. However, currently, the functional scope of these mappers is very limited [Tor+17, Stö+15, Wol+13].

A practical example of application-coordinated polyglot persistence is Twitter's storage of user feeds [Kri13]. For fast read access, the newest tweets for each user are materialized in a Redis cluster. Upon publishing of a new tweet, the social graph is queried from a graph store and distributed among the Redis-based feeds for each relevant user (*Write Fanout*). As a persistent fallback for Redis, MySQL servers are managed and partitioned by the application tier.

To increase encapsulation of persistence decisions, **microservice** architectures are useful [New15] (see Sect. 2.1). Microservices allow narrowing the choice of a database system to one particular service and thus decouple the development and operations of services [DB13]. Technologically, IaaS/PaaS, containers, and cluster management frameworks provide sophisticated tooling for scaling and operating microservice architectures. In the example, the product catalog could be split into two microservices using MongoDB and Redis separately. The Redis-based service would provide an API for querying popular products and incrementing counters, whereas the MongoDB-based microservice would have a similar interface for retrieving product information. The user-facing business logic (e.g., the frontend in a two-tier architecture) simply has to invoke both microservices and combine the result.

In order to make polyglot persistence fully transparent for the application, **polyglot database services** need to abstract from implementation details of underlying systems. The key idea is to hide the allocation of data and queries to databases through a generic cloud service API. Some NoSQL databases and services use this approach, for example, to integrate full-text search with structured storage (e.g., in Riak [Ria] and Cassandra [LM10]), to store metadata consistently (e.g., in HBase [Hba] and BigTable [Cha+08]), or to cache objects (e.g., Facebook's TAO [Bro+13]). However, these approaches use a defined scheme for the allocation and cannot adapt to varying application requirements. Polyglot database services can also apply static rules for polyglot persistence: if the type of the data is known (for example a user object or a file), a rule-based selection of a storage system can be performed [SGR15].

In the example, the application could declare the throughput requirements of the counter and the scalability requirement for the product catalog. The task of the polyglot database service would then be to autonomously derive a suitable mapping for queries and data. The core challenge here is to base the selection of systems on quantifiable metrics of available databases and applying transparent rewriting of operations. A weaker form than fully-automated polyglot persistence are database services with **semi-automatic polyglot persistence**. In this model, the application can explicitly define which underlying system should be targeted, while reusing high-level features such as schema modeling, transactions, and business logic across systems through a unified API.

7.2 Multi-Tenancy and Virtualization in Cloud-Based Deployments

The Database-as-a-Service (DBaaS) model promises to shift the problem of configuration, scaling, provisioning, monitoring, backup, privacy, and access control to a service provider [Cur+11a]. Hacigumus et al. [HIM02] coined the term DBaaS and argued that it provided a new paradigm for organizations to alleviate the need for purchasing expensive hardware and software to build a scalable deployment. Lehner and Sattler [LS13] and Zhao et al. [Zha+14] provide a comprehensive overview of current research and challenges introduced by the DBaaS paradigm.

The DBaaS model emerged as a useful service category offered by PaaS and IaaS providers and is therefore mainly rooted in industry. Table 7.1 summarizes selected commercial systems and groups them by important properties such as data model, sharding strategy, and query capabilities. All systems except Cloudant are based on proprietary REST APIs and details about their internal architectures are not published (with the exception of Baqend which is the commercial variant of Orestes [Ges19]). Another observation is that fine-grained SLAs are not provided, due to the difficulty of satisfying tenant-specific requirements on a multi-tenant infrastructure.

Table 7.1 Selected industry DBaaS systems and their main properties: data model, category according to the CAP theorem, support for queries and indexing, replication model, sharding strategy, transaction support, and service level agreements

System	Data model	CAP	Queries/indexing	Replication	Sharding	Transactions	SLAs
Cloudant [Bie+15]	Document store	AP	Incremental MR views	Lazy, local and geo	Hashing	No	No
DynamoDB [Dyn]	Wide-column	CP	Local and Global index	Eager, local	Hashing	No	No
Azure tables [Cal+11]	Wide-column	CP	By key, scans	Eager, local	Hashing	No	99.9% Uptime
Google cloud datastore [Dat, Bak+11]	Wide-column	CP	Local and global index	Eager, geo	Entity groups	Per group	No
S3, Azure blobs, GCS [Amaa]	Blob-store	AP	No	Lazy, local and geo	Hashing	No	99.9% uptime (S3)
Baqend [Ges19]	Document	CP	Yes	Eager, local	Range	Yes	No

Most related work focuses on specific aspects of DBaaS models. Multi-tenancy and virtualization are closely related, as resource sharing between tenants requires some level of virtualization of underlying resources (the schema, database process, operating system, computing hardware, and storage systems). The trade-off between performance and isolation for multi-tenant systems has been studied extensively [Aul+11, Aul+08, Aul+09, KL11, SKM08, WB09, JA07].

7.2.1   Database Privacy and Encryption

Since a DBaaS is hosted by third party, security and privacy are particularly important. Several researchers have proposed solutions to prevent attackers and providers from analyzing data stored in a DBaaS system. A survey of the field is provided by Köhler et al. [KJH15]. The ideal solution for DBaaS privacy is fully homomorphic encryption, which enables arbitrary computations on encrypted data stored in the database. Though Gentry [Gen09] proposed a scheme in 2009, the performance overhead is still prohibitive for use in real-world application.

The naive approach to ensure data confidentiality is to perform queries only in the client, so that data can be fully encrypted. This approach is used in ZeroDB [EW16]. The obvious limitation is that the client and network quickly become the bottleneck: in ZeroDB, the query logic is executed in the client and each descent in the B-tree requires one round-trip, leading to very high latency. MIT's CryptDB project [Pop+11, Pop14] is based on a layered encryption scheme, where different encryption levels enable different query operators, e.g., homomorphic encryption for sum-based aggregation and deterministic encryption for equality predicates. CryptDB assumes a database proxy out of the threat scope that is responsible for rewriting queries with the appropriate keys before forwarding them to the database holding the encrypted data. The MySQL-based prototype exhibited a processing overhead of 26% compared to native access, but latency was increased by an order of magnitude. The problem of CryptDB is that the vulnerability is only moved into the proxy that is co-located with application servers and therefore typically cloud-hosted, too. Nonetheless, first commercial DBMSs have implemented explicitly declared encryption levels for queries on encrypted data, e.g., Microsoft SQL Server supporting random and deterministic encryption [Alw].

The problem of vulnerable proxies in CryptDB was addressed in a follow-up system called Mylar [Kar+16, PZ13, Pop+14]. Mylar implements multi-key keyword search on encrypted data with a middleware operating only on encrypted data without access to keys. The browser is responsible for encrypting and decrypting data based on user keys. Data is stored and encrypted using the key of the user owning the record. The core idea of the encrypted keyword search is that clients generate an encrypted token for search that works on any record irrespective of the key it was encrypted with. When a user grants access to another user, a delta value is constructed in a way that allows the server to transform tokens without leaking data. The downside of Mylar is that it only enables keyword search. Performance is further limited, as the server has to scan every record for a token comparison, only per-record duplicates of keywords can be indexed. Nonetheless, Mylar is an important step towards secure sharing of information between application users and it is also notable for providing security against attacks of both middleware and database.

Relational Cloud is a visionary architecture for a secure, scalable, and multi-tenant DBaaS by Curino et al. [Cur+11a]. It proposes to use private database virtualization for multi-tenancy and CryptDB for privacy. Access to the database is handled through a JDBC driver which directs requests to load-balancing frontend servers that partition data across backend servers to store the actual data in CryptDB. The partitioning engine Schism [Cur+10] is based on workload graphs: whenever two tuples are accessed within a transaction, the weight of their edge is increased. By finding a partitioning of tuples with a minimal cut, cross-node transactions are minimized. The partitioning rules are compacted and generalized by training a decision tree that is used in frontend servers for routing. The consolidation engine Kairos [Cur+11b] monitors workloads and outputs a mapping from virtual machines to physical nodes in order to optimize combined resource requirements of multiple tenants.

7.2.2 Service Level Agreements

Various approaches have been proposed for SLAs in cloud services and DBaaS systems [Cun+07, Zha+14, ABC14, Bas12, Xio+11, Ter+13, LBMAL14, Pad+07, Sak14]. Traditionally, this topic has been tackled in the context of workload management for mainframe systems, to optimize simple performance metrics like query response time [Cas+07, LS13]. Many approaches rely on the underlying virtualization environment to enforce SLAs by means of live migration, e.g., Zephyr [Elm+11], Albatross [Das+11], Dolly [Cec+11], and Slacker [Bar+12]. Baset [Bas12] reviews SLAs of commercial cloud providers like AWS, Azure, and Rackspace and concludes that performance-based SLAs are not guaranteed by any provider. Furthermore, the burden of providing evidence of SLA violations rests on the customer.

Xiong et al. have proposed ActiveSLA [Xio+11] as an admission control framework for DBaaS systems. By predicting the probability of a query completing before its deadline, a cost-based decision on allowing or rejecting the query can be made using the SLA. Chi et al. [CMH11] have proposed a similar approach that uses an SLA-based scheduler *iCBS* to minimize expected total costs. Sakr et al. [SL12] presented the CloudDB AutoAdmin framework that monitors SLAs of cloud-hosted databases and triggers application-defined rules upon violations to help developers build on SLAs. Armbrust et al. [Arm+11] proposed the SQL extension PIQL (Performance Insightful Query Language) that predicts SLA compliance using a query planner which is aware of developer-provided hints. Instead of choosing the fastest plan, the optimizer only outputs plans where the number of operations is known in advance. Lang et al. [Lan+12] formulate the SLA problem for DBaaS systems as an optimization task of mapping client workloads to available hardware resources. In particular, they provide a way for DBaaS providers to choose the class of hardware that best suits the performance SLOs of their tenants. The Polyglot Persistence Mediator (PPM) in Orestes [SGR15] is a DBaaS approach to combine service level agreements with schema design for database-driven applications. Instead of focusing on a specific performance SLA as common in most related work, the approach lets application developers express each functional and non-functional data management requirement based as schema annotations.

Problems closely related to SLAs are resource and storage allocation [Mad+15, Sou+09], pricing models [LS13, p. 145], and workload characterization [GKA09, Gul+12]. Since we focus on the perspective of application architects, though, we consider low-level hardware and virtual machine allocation schemes to be out of scope for this book.

7.3   Auto-Scaling and Elasticity

For providing elasticity, DBaaS systems have to automatically scale in and out to accommodate the current and future mix of tenant workloads. The ability to forecast workloads enables the most efficient forms of auto-scaling, as the service does not have to react to overload situations and SLA violations, but can instead proactively adjust its capacities. Kim et al. [Kim+16] and Lorido-Botran et al. [LBMAL14] provide an overview of commonly employed workload predictors and auto-scaling techniques from the literature. Related work on auto-scaling can be grouped into approaches for threshold-based rules (e.g., [Has+12, Han+12, KF11, MBS11, Gha+11, CS13]), reinforcement learning (e.g., [Dut+10, BHD13, Tes+06, BRX13, XRB12]), queuing theory (e.g., [Urg+08, VPR07, ZCS07]), time series analysis and prediction (e.g., [CDM11, GGW10, She+11, Fan+12, Isl+12, PN09]), control theory (e.g., [Pad+09, Xu+07, Bod+09, ATE12, PH09]), and database live-migration (e.g., [Elm+11, Das+11, Cec+11, Bar+12, DAEA13]). While auto-scaling does not replace capacity planning, it significantly increases flexibility as the cloud infrastructure can be adapted at runtime.

Complex, proactive models are usually stronger for sudden surges in demand, but most of the algorithms proposed in the literature strongly depend on a certain workload type. Marcus and Papaemmanouil [MP17] argue that scalability and query planning decisions for cloud data management should not depend on humans or simple rules but instead harness machine learning techniques, in particular reinforcement learning. An example of a system that follows this idea is Quaestor [Ges+17] which applies deep reinforcement learning to find suitable caching TTLs [Sch+16].

7.4   Database Benchmarking

Different benchmarks have been proposed to evaluate latency, throughput, consistency, and other non-functional properties of distributed and cloud databases [Dey+14, Coo+10, Coo+10, Pat+11, BZS13, Ber+14, BT11, BK13, BT14, Ber15, Ber14].

The *Yahoo Cloud Serving Benchmark* (YCSB) [Coo+10] was published in 2010 and is the de-facto standard for benchmarking NoSQL systems. YCSB is designed to measure throughput and latency for CRUD and scan operations performed against different data stores [Fri+14, Win+15]. The main shortcoming is the missing distribution of workload generation to prevent clients from becoming the actual bottleneck. The second problem is that YCSB's thread-per-request model incurs high overhead and increases latency [FWR17].

While YCSB's generic workloads make it easily applicable to any data store, its lack of application-specific workloads render the results hard to interpret. Particularly in contrast to the widely used TPC benchmarks [PF00] for RDBMSs, YCSB neither covers queries nor transactions. *BG* [BG13] was proposed as an alternative to YCSB that models interactions in a social network. BG not only collects performance indicators, but also measures the conformance to application-specific SLAs and consistency. The *Under Pressure Benchmark* (UPB) [Fio+13] is based on YCSB and quantifies the availability of replicated data stores by comparing the performance during normal operation with the performance during node failures.

7.4.1   Consistency Benchmarking

As consistency is one of the central properties that many cloud data management systems trade against other non-functional properties for performance reasons, various benchmarks have been proposed to quantify eventual consistency and staleness. Wada et al. [Wad+11] proposed a methodology to measure the staleness of reads for cloud databases based on a single reader and writer. As reader and writer rely on simple timestamps for consistency checks, the strategy is highly dependent on clock synchronization and unsuitable for geo-replicated systems. Bermbach et al. [BT11, BT14] extended the approach by supporting multiple, distributed readers frequently polling the data store. This uncovered a pattern for the staleness windows of Amazon S3. However, the scheme still assumes clock synchronization and therefore might lead to questionable results [BZS13].

Golab and Rahman et al. [GLS11, Rah+12] argue that a consistency benchmark should not introduce a workload that stresses the system artificially, but should rather extend existing workloads to also capture staleness information. The authors propose an extension of YCSB that tracks timestamps and uses them to compute an empirical Δ for the Δ-atomicity of the underlying data store by finding the maximum time between two operations that yielded a stale result.

YCSB++ [Pat+11] circumvents the problem of clock synchronization by relying on a centralized Zookeeper instance for coordination of readers and writers to measure consistency. As a consequence, YCSB++ can only provide a lower bound for the inconsistency window. NoSQLMark [Win+15] is a database benchmarking framework that provides both lower and upper bounds for measurements to make results more meaningful. In addition, its implementation is validated using the tool SickStore as a safeguard against implementation or other errors.

Bailis et al. proposed the *Probabilistically Bounded Staleness* (PBS) [Bai+12, Bai+14b] prediction model to estimate the staleness of Dynamo-style systems based on messaging latencies between nodes. PBS relies on a Monte Carlo simulation sampling from latency distributions to calculate the probability of a stale read for a given time after a write $((\Delta, t)-$atomicity). The YCSB wrapper for Monte Carlo simulations (YMCA) [Ges19, Section 4.3.1] is an adaption of this approach for YCSB workloads and arbitrary topologies of database nodes and caches. The YMCA allows studying staleness introduced not only by replication, but also by invalidation-based and expiration-based caching. Furthermore, the YMCA simulation frees the analysis from the trade-off between errors introduced by clock drift and imprecision introduced by coordination delay, as exact simulation times can be used.

Any database system can potentially be provided in the form of a DBaaS. However, low-latency access, elastic scalability, polyglot persistence, cross-database transactions, and efficient multi-tenancy play important roles for scalable web applications and have only partly been addressed by related work so far.

7.5   REST APIs, Multi-Model Databases and Backend-as-a-Service

Most cloud services, including DBaaS and Backend-as-a-Service (BaaS) systems, use REST APIs to ensure interoperability and accessibility from heterogeneous environments. Originally proposed as an architectural style by Fielding [Fie00], REST now commonly refers to HTTP-based interfaces. HTTP [Fie+99] emerged as the standard for distributing information on the Internet. Originally, it was employed for static data, but now serves sophisticated use cases from web and mobile application to Internet of Things (IoT) applications. The growing adoption of HTTP/2 [IET15] solving the connection multiplexing problem of HTTP/1.1 facilitates this movement. For web applications, REST and HTTP have largely replaced RPC-based approaches (e.g., XML RPC or Java RMI [Dow98]), wire protocols (e.g., PostgreSQL protocol [Pos]), and web services (specifically, SOAP and WS-* standards family [Alo+04]).

Google's GData [Gda] and Microsoft's OData (Open Data Protocol) [Oda] are two approaches for standardized REST/HTTP CRUD APIs that are used by some of their respective cloud services. Many commercial DBaaS systems offer custom

REST APIs tailored for one particular database (e.g., DynamoDB, Cloudant). A first theoretic attempt for a unified DBaaS REST API has been made by Haselman et al. [HTV10] for RDBMSs. Dey [Dey15] proposed REST+T as a REST API for transactions. In REST+T, each object is modeled as a state machine modified through HTTP methods.

7.5.1   Backend-as-a-Service

According to Roberts [Rob16], *serverless* architectures are applications that depend on cloud services for server-side logic and persistence. The two major categories of serverless services are Function-as-a-Service (FaaS) and Backend-as-a-Service (BaaS). Both approaches are rooted in commercial cloud platforms rather than research efforts.

FaaS refers to stateless, event-triggered business logic executed on a 3rd-party platform [Rob16]. Industry offerings are AWS Lambda, Microsoft Azure Functions, and Google Cloud Functions. While FaaS offers a very simple and scalable programming model, its applicability is limited by the lack of persistent state. The major difference between FaaS and Platform-as-a-Service lies in the ability of FaaS to seamlessly scale on a per-request basis, as no application server infrastructure (e.g., Rails, Django, Java EE) is required. The term "BaaS" refers to services that enable the development of rich client applications through database access, authentication and authorization mechanisms, as well as SDKs for websites and mobile apps. BaaS therefore is a natural extension of DBaaS towards scenarios of direct client access Apps without intermediate application servers.

Many commercial BaaS platforms are available (e.g., Firebase, Kinvey, and Azure Mobile Services, Baqend). Most of these platforms are based on proprietary software and unpublished architectures which hinders a comparison. However, different open-source BaaS platforms have been developed. They typically consist of an API server (e.g., Node.js or Java) for BaaS functionality and user-submitted code and a NoSQL database system for persistence (e.g., MongoDB, Cassandra or CouchDB).

Meteor [HS16] is a development framework and server for running real-time web applications. It is based on MongoDB and directly exposes the MongoDB query language to JavaScript clients for both ad-hoc and real-time queries. Node.js-based application servers run custom code and standard APIs, e.g., for user login. Scalability is limited, as each application server subscribes to the MongoDB replication log (*oplog tailing*),[1] in order to match subscribed queries to updates. Each server therefore has to maintain the aggregate throughput of a potentially

---

[1]Historically, there is another approach called poll-and-diff that relies on periodic query execution for discovery of result changes. However, poll-and-diff does not scale with the number of real-time query subscribers.

sharded MongoDB cluster which is often infeasible in practice. As the replication log furthermore only contains partial information on updates, the application servers need to perform additional database queries to check for a match.

Deployd [Dep], Hoodie [Hoo], and Parse Server [Par] are based on Node.js, too. Deployd [Dep] is a simple API server for common app functionalites and a simple, MongoDB-based CRUD persistence API. It is focused on simplicity and is neither horizontally scalable nor multi-tenant. Hoodie [Hoo] is a BaaS that combines CouchDB and a client-side CouchDB clone called PouchDB for offline-capable apps with synchronization. Through CouchDB change feeds, clients can subscribe to simple CRUD events with limited querying capabilities. Hoodie is focused on offline-first applications and offers no support for data and request scalability.

Parse Server [Par] is an open-source implementation of the Parse platform that was acquired by Facebook in 2013 and later discontinued [Lac16]. It has extensive mobile SDKs that go beyond wrapping the REST API and also provide widgets and tooling for building the frontend. Parse Server is based on Node.js and MongoDB and supports file storage, a JSON CRUD API, user management, access control, and real-time queries that are functionally similar to those provided by Meteor, but without support for ordering [Wan16]. The real-time query architecture relies on broadcasting every update to every server that holds WebSocket connections to clients through a single Redis instance. This does not allow the system to scale upon increasing update workloads beyond single-server capacity. Parse Server does not expose many data management abstractions such as indexes, partial updates, concurrency control, and schemas, making it unsuitable for performance-critical and advanced applications. In particular, the latency of HTTP requests is not reduced through caching. However, in order to prevent the browser from performing two round-trips due to cross-origin pre-flight requests, REST semantics are violated and every interaction is wrapped in an HTTP POST and GET request [Gri13].

BaasBox [Bas] and Apache Usergrid [Use] are open-source Java-based BaaS platforms. BaasBox [Bas] is a simple single-server platform based on the multi-model database OrientDB [Tes13]. Its main capabilities are CRUD-based persistence and a simple social media API for app development. Apache Usergrid [Use] is a scalable BaaS built on Cassandra and geared towards mobile applications. Through a REST API and SDKs, it supports typical features such as user management, authorization, JSON and file storage, as well as custom business logic expressed in Java. Multi-tenancy is achieved through a shared database model by running private API servers for each tenant, while consolidating rows in a single Cassandra cluster. Query support is limited due to Cassandra's architecture and there are no consistency guarantees nor multi-key transactions.

Baqend[2] is the commercial variant of Orestes [Ges19] and is designed to support large-scale, low-latency web applications through web caching. While Baqend's caching acceleration works out-of-the-box for all applications and websites built on the platform, it can also be applied to arbitrary legacy websites through the

---

[2]Baqend: https://www.baqend.com.

performance plugin Speed Kit [WGW+20]. Baqend further provides execution of custom code through user-defined Node modules and thereby offers FaaS features in its BaaS model. Similar to Meteor, Baqend provides push-based real-time queries on top of MongoDB. However, Baqend's architecture decouples data storage from stateless application logic to solve the scalability issue that Meteor is subject to. At the time of writing, Baqend's real-time query mechanism is the only[3] one scalable with respect to both update throughput and query concurrency. Baqend is also the only BaaS to expose ACID transactions and explicit fine-grained control over consistency levels.

7.5.2   Polyglot Persistence

The term polyglot persistence was introduced by Leberknight [Leb08] and later popularized by Fowler [SF12]. Most web-scale architectures are heavily based on polyglot persistence both within application components as well as across different applications. Twitter uses Redis [San17] for storing tweets, a custom eventually consistent wide-column store named Manhattan [Sch16] for user and analytics data, Memcache [Fit04] for caching, a custom graph store called FlockDB as well as MySQL, HDFS, and an object store [Has17]. Google, Facebook, and Amazon are also recognized for their broad spectrum of employed database systems. While there is no shortage of polyglot persistence architectures in practice, little research has gone into addressing the problem of how to design, implement, and maintain polyglot persistence architectures.

Object-relational (OR) and object-document (OD) mappers are important classes of tools that limit vendor lock-in and minimize impedance mismatch [Mai90, Amb12]. By abstracting from implementation details of database systems, they facilitate polyglot persistence. Popular mappers are Hibernate, DataNucleus, Kundera, EclipseLink, OpenJPA, Entity Framework, Active Record, Spring Data, Core Data, Doctrine, Django, and Morphia [Ire+09, Tor+17, DeM09]. Torres et al. [Tor+17] provide a comprehensive overview of mappers and propose a catalog of criteria to evaluate their capabilities (e.g., metadata extraction, foreign key support and inheritance). Störl et al. [Stö+15] reviewed mappers specifically targeted to NoSQL databases. The authors observed that, while basic CRUD functionality works well across all analyzed mappers, query expressiveness vastly differs. This is a consequence of providing high-level query languages in the mapper, that potentially cannot be mapped to the limited querying capabilities of the underlying database system and therefore has to be emulated client-side. Also, the authors observed that the overhead introduced by some mappers is significant, in particular for updates and deletes. Wolf et al. [Wol+13] describe the steps required to adapt traditional OR-mappers such as Hibernate to key-value stores. Their effort makes

---

[3]For an in-depth discussion of the state of the art in real-time databases, we refer to [WRG19].

it obvious that there is a significant feature gap between state-of-the-art mapper abstractions and capabilities found in low-level data stores.

Multi-model databases address polyglot persistence of data models and seek to provide them in a single data store. This imposes heterogeneous requirements on a single database system and hence implies tremendous engineering challenges. ArangoDB [Ara] and OrientDB [Tes13] are two examples of systems that provide main APIs for storing and querying documents, but also support graph traversal and key-value storage. While these systems simplify operations by integrating polyglot capabilities into single systems, there are more sophisticated solutions available for each of the supported polyglot models. Several RDBMSs also incorporate non-relational data models such as XML and JSON [Cro06] as a data type with SQL extensions to modify and query its contents. The major limitation of multi-model approaches is that the data model is only one of many requirements that necessitate polyglot persistence (e.g., scalability and latency). Many requirements are directly tied to replication, sharding, and query processing architectures and therefore are very difficult to consolidate in a single system.

7.6 Summary

Modern (web) applications are complex as they need to address an increasing number of functional and non-functional requirements. Finding, deploying, and operating the right system—or set of systems—for a given application scenario is therefore becoming an ever greater challenge. Ideally, application developers would be able to express requirements as SLAs in a declarative way and then let a polyglot database service determine the optimal mapping to actual systems in transparent fashion. But while there already are first approaches to adapt the choice of a database system to the actual requirements and workloads of the application, the challenge of automating polyglot persistence is mostly unsolved as of today.

References

[ABC14] Ioannis Arapakis, Xiao Bai, and B. Barla Cambazoglu. "Impact of Response Latency on User Behavior in Web Search". In: *Proceedings of the 37th International ACM SIGIR Conference on Research & Development in Information Retrieval*. SIGIR '14. Gold Coast, Queensland, Australia: ACM, 2014, pp. 103–112. ISBN: 978-1-4503-2257-7. https://doi.org/10.1145/2600428.2609627. URL: http://doi.acm.org/10.1145/2600428.2609627.

[Alo+04] Gustavo Alonso et al. "Web services". In: *Web Services*. Springer, 2004, pp. 123–149.

[Alw] *Always Encrypted (Database Engine)*. https://msdn.microsoft.com/en-us/library/mt163865.aspx. (Accessed on 05/20/2017). 2017. URL: https://msdn.microsoft.com/en-us/library/mt163865.aspx.

[Amaa] *Amazon Simple Storage Service (S3)*. //aws.amazon.com/documentation/s3/. (Accessed on 07/28/2017). 2017. URL: //aws.amazon.com/documentation/s3/ (visited on 02/18/2017).

[Amb12] Scott Ambler. *Agile database techniques: Effective strategies for the agile software developer*. John Wiley & Sons, 2012.

[Ara] *ArangoDB*. https://www.arangodb.com/documentation/. (Accessed on 05/20/2017). 2017. URL: https://www.arangodb.com/documentation/ (visited on 02/18/2017).

[Arm+11] Michael Armbrust et al. "PIQL: Success-Tolerant Query Processing in the Cloud". In: *PVLDB* 5.3 (2011), pp. 181–192. URL: http://www.vldb.org/pvldb/vol5/p181_michaelarmbrust_vldb2012.pdf.

[ATE12] Ahmed Ali-Eldin, Johan Tordsson, and Erik Elmroth. "An adaptive hybrid elasticity controller for cloud infrastructures". In: *2012 IEEE Network Operations and Management Symposium, NOMS 2012, Maui, HI, USA, April 16–20, 2012*. Ed. by Filip De Turck, Luciano Paschoal Gaspary, and Deep Medhi. IEEE, 2012, pp. 204–212. https://doi.org/10.1109/NOMS.2012.6211900.

[Aul+08] S. Aulbach et al. "Multi-tenant databases for software as a service: schema-mapping techniques". In: *Proceedings of the 2008 ACM SIGMOD international conference on Management of data*. 2008, pp. 1195–1206. URL: http://dl.acm.org/citation.cfm?id=1376736 (visited on 11/15/2012).

[Aul+09] Stefan Aulbach et al. "A comparison of flexible schemas for software as a service". In: *Proceedings of the ACM SIGMOD International Conference on Management of Data, SIGMOD 2009, Providence, Rhode Island, USA, June 29 - July 2, 2009*. Ed. by Ugur Çetintemel et al. ACM, 2009, pp. 881–888. https://doi.org/10.1145/1559845.1559941.

[Aul+11] Stefan Aulbach et al. "Extensibility and Data Sharing in evolving multitenant databases". In: *Proceedings of the 27th International Conference on Data Engineering, ICDE 2011, April 11–16, 2011, Hannover Germany*. Ed. by Serge Abiteboul et al. IEEE Computer Society, 2011, pp. 99–110. https://doi.org/10.1109/ICDE.2011.5767872.

[Bai+12] Peter Bailis et al. *Probabilistically bounded staleness for practical partial quorums*. Tech. rep. 8. 2012, pp. 776–787. URL: http://dl.acm.org/citation.cfm?id=2212359 (visited on 07/16/2014).

[Bai+14b] Peter Bailis et al. "Quantifying eventual consistency with PBS". en. In: *The VLDB Journal* 23.2 (Apr. 2014), pp. 279–302. ISSN: 1066-8888, 0949-877X. https://doi.org/10.1007/s00778-013-0330-1. URL: http://link.springer.com/10.1007/s00778-013-0330-1 (visited on 01/03/2015).

[Bak+11] J. Baker et al. "Megastore: Providing scalable, highly available storage for interactive services". In: *Proc. of CIDR*. Vol. 11. 2011, pp. 223–234.

[Bar+12] Sean Barker et al. "Cut me some slack: Latency-aware live migration for databases". In: *Proceedings of the 15th international conference on extending database technology*. ACM, 2012, pp. 432–443. URL: http://dl.acm.org/citation.cfm?id=2247647 (visited on 07/16/2014).

[Bas] *The BaasBox server*. https://github.com/baasbox/baasbox. (Accessed on 05/20/2017). 2017. URL: https://github.com/baasbox/baasbox (visited on 02/19/2017).

[Bas12] Salman A. Baset. "Cloud SLAs: present and future". In: *ACM SIGOPS Operating Systems Review* 46.2 (2012), pp. 57–66. URL: http://dl.acm.org/citation.cfm?id=2331586 (visited on 01/03/2015).

[Ber+14] David Bermbach et al. "Towards an Extensible Middleware for Database Benchmarking". In: *Performance Characterization and Benchmarking. Traditional to Big Data - 6th TPC Technology Conference, TPCTC 2014, Hangzhou, China, September 1–5, 2014. Revised Selected Papers*. Ed. by Raghunath Nambiar and Meikel Poess. Vol. 8904. Lecture Notes in Computer Science. Springer, 2014, pp. 82–96. https://doi.org/10.1007/978-3-319-15350-6_6.

[Ber14] David Bermbach. *Benchmarking Eventually Consistent Distributed Storage Systems.* eng. Karlsruhe, Baden: KIT Scientific Publishing, 2014. ISBN: 978-3-7315-0186-2 3-7315-0186-4 978-3-7315-0186-2.

[Ber15] David Bermbach. "An Introduction to Cloud Benchmarking". In: *2015 IEEE International Conference on Cloud Engineering, IC2E 2015, Tempe, AZ, USA, March 9–13, 2015.* IEEE Computer Society, 2015, p. 3. https://doi.org/10.1109/IC2E.2015.65.

[BG13] Sumita Barahmand and Shahram Ghandeharizadeh. "BG: A Benchmark to Evaluate Interactive Social Networking Actions". In: *CIDR 2013, Sixth Biennial Conference on Innovative Data Systems Research, Asilomar, CA, USA, January 6–9, 2013, Online Proceedings.* www.cidrdb.org, 2013. URL: http://www.cidrdb.org/cidr2013/Papers/ CIDR13_Paper93.pdf.

[BHD13] Enda Barrett, Enda Howley, and Jim Duggan. "Applying reinforcement learning towards automating resource allocation and application scalability in the cloud". In: *Concurrency and Computation: Practice and Experience* 25.12 (2013), pp. 1656–1674. https://doi.org/10.1002/cpe.2864.

[Bie+15] Christopher D Bienko et al. *IBM Cloudant: Database as a Service Advanced Topics.* IBM Redbooks, 2015.

[BK13] David Bermbach and Jörn Kuhlenkamp. "Consistency in Distributed Storage Systems - An Overview of Models, Metrics and Measurement Approaches". In: *Networked Systems - First International Conference, NETYS 2013, Marrakech, Morocco, May 2–4, 2013, Revised Selected Papers.* Ed. by Vincent Gramoli and Rachid Guerraoui. Vol. 7853. Lecture Notes in Computer Science. Springer, 2013, pp. 175–189. https:// doi.org/10.1007/978-3-642-40148-0_13.

[Bod+09] Peter Bodík et al. "Statistical Machine Learning Makes Automatic Control Practical for Internet Datacenters". In: *Proceedings of the 2009 Conference on Hot Topics in Cloud Computing.* HotCloud'09. San Diego, California: USENIX Association, 2009. URL: http://dl.acm.org/citation.cfm?id=1855533.1855545.

[Bro+13] Nathan Bronson et al. "TAO: Facebook's Distributed Data Store for the Social Graph." In: *USENIX Annual Technical Conference.* 2013, pp. 49–60. URL: http://dl.frz.ir/ FREE/papers-we-love/datastores/tao-facebook-distributed-datastore.pdf (visited on 09/28/2014).

[BRX13] Xiangping Bu, Jia Rao, and Cheng-Zhong Xu. "Coordinated Self-Configuration of Virtual Machines and Appliances Using a Model-Free Learning Approach". In: *IEEE Trans. Parallel Distrib. Syst.* 24.4 (2013), pp. 681–690. https://doi.org/10.1109/TPDS. 2012.174.

[BT11] David Bermbach and Stefan Tai. "Eventual consistency: How soon is eventual? An evaluation of Amazon S3's consistency behavior". In: *Proceedings of the 6th Workshop on Middleware for Service Oriented Computing, MW4SOC 2011, Lisbon, Portugal, December 12–16, 2011.* Ed. by Karl M. Göschka, Schahram Dustdar, and Vladimir Tosic. ACM, 2011, p. 1. https://doi.org/10.1145/2093185.2093186.

[BT14] David Bermbach and Stefan Tai. "Benchmarking Eventual Consistency: Lessons Learned from Long-Term Experimental Studies". In: *2014 IEEE International Conference on Cloud Engineering, Boston, MA, USA, March 11–14, 2014.* IEEE Computer Society, 2014, pp. 47–56. https://doi.org/10.1109/IC2E.2014.37.

[BZS13] David Bermbach, Liang Zhao, and Sherif Sakr. "Towards Comprehensive Measurement of Consistency Guarantees for Cloud-Hosted Data Storage Services". In: *Performance Characterization and Benchmarking - 5th TPC Technology Conference, TPCTC 2013, Trento, Italy, August 26, 2013, Revised Selected Papers.* Ed. by Raghunath Nambiar and Meikel Poess. Vol. 8391. Lecture Notes in Computer Science. Springer, 2013, pp. 32–47. https://doi.org/10.1007/978-3-319-04936-6_3.

[Cal+11] Brad Calder et al. "Windows Azure Storage: a highly available cloud storage service with strong consistency". In: *Proceedings of the Twenty-Third ACM Symposium on Operating Systems Principles.* ACM. ACM, 2011, pp. 143–157. URL: http://dl.acm. org/citation.cfm?id=2043571 (visited on 04/16/2014).

[Cas+07] Pierre Cassier et al. *System Programmer's Guide To–Workload Manager*. IBM, 2007.

[CDM11] Eddy Caron, Frédéric Desprez, and Adrian Muresan. "Pattern Matching Based Forecast of Non-periodic Repetitive Behavior for Cloud Clients". In: *J. Grid Comput.* 9.1 (2011), pp. 49–64. https://doi.org/10.1007/s10723-010-9178-4.

[Cec+11] Emmanuel Cecchet et al. "Dolly: virtualization-driven database provisioning for the cloud". In: *ACM SIGPLAN Notices*. Vol. 46. ACM, 2011, pp. 51–62. URL: http://dl. acm.org/citation.cfm?id=1952691 (visited on 07/16/2014).

[Cha+08] Fay Chang et al. "Bigtable: A distributed storage system for structured data". In: *ACM Transactions on Computer Systems (TOCS)* 26.2 (2008), p. 4.

[CMH11] Yun Chi, Hyun Jin Moon, and Hakan Hacigümüs. "iCBS: Incremental Costbased Scheduling under Piecewise Linear SLAs". In: *PVLDB* 4.9 (2011), pp. 563–574. URL: http://www.vldb.org/pvldb/vol4/p563-chi.pdf.

[Coo+10] Brian F. Cooper et al. "Benchmarking cloud serving systems with YCSB". In: *Proceedings of the 1st ACM symposium on Cloud computing*. ACM, 2010, pp. 143– 154. URL: http://dl.acm.org/citation.cfm?id=1807152 (visited on 11/26/2016).

[Cro06] Douglas Crockford. "JSON: Javascript object notation". In: *URL* http://www.json.org (2006).

[CS13] Emiliano Casalicchio and Luca Silvestri. "Autonomic management of cloud-based systems: the service provider perspective". In: *Computer and Information Sciences III*. Springer, 2013, pp. 39–47.

[Cun+07] Ítalo S. Cunha et al. "Self-Adaptive Capacity Management for MultiTier Virtualized Environments". In: *Integrated Network Management, IM 2007. 10th IFIP/IEEE International Symposium on Integrated Network Management, Munich, Germany, 21– 25 May 2007*. IEEE, 2007, pp. 129–138. https://doi.org/10.1109/INM.2007.374777.

[Cur+10] Carlo Curino et al. "Schism: a workload-driven approach to database replication and partitioning". In: *Proceedings of the VLDB Endowment* 3.1-2 (2010), pp. 48–57. URL: http://dl.acm.org/citation.cfm?id=1920853 (visited on 01/03/2015).

[Cur+11a] Carlo Curino et al. "Relational Cloud: A Database-as-a-Service for the Cloud". In: *Proc. of CIDR*. 2011. URL: http://dspace.mit.edu/handle/1721.1/62241 (visited on 04/15/2014).

[Cur+11b] Carlo Curino et al. "Workload-aware database monitoring and consolidation". In: *Proceedings of the ACM SIGMOD International Conference on Management of Data, SIGMOD 2011, Athens, Greece, June 12–16, 2011*. Ed. by Timos K. Sellis et al. ACM, 2011, pp. 313–324. https://doi.org/10.1145/1989323.1989357.

[DAEA13] Sudipto Das, Divyakant Agrawal, and Amr El Abbadi. "ElasTraS: An elastic, scalable, and self-managing transactional database for the cloud". en. In: *ACM Transactions on Database Systems* 38.1 (Apr. 2013), pp. 1–45. ISSN: 03625915. https://doi.org/10. 1145/2445583.2445588. URL: http://dl.acm.org/citation.cfm?doid=2445583.2445588 (visited on 11/25/2016).

[Das+11] Sudipto Das et al. "Albatross: lightweight elasticity in shared storage databases for the cloud using live data migration". In: *Proceedings of the VLDB Endowment* 4.8 (2011), pp. 494–505. URL: http://dl.acm.org/citation.cfm?id=2002977 (visited on 07/16/2014).

[Dat] *Google Cloud Datastore*. https://cloud.google.com/datastore/docs/concepts/overview. (Accessed on 05/20/2017). 2017. URL: https://cloud.google.com/datastore/docs/ concepts/overview (visited on 02/18/2017).

[DB13] Regine Dörbecker and Tilo Böhmann. "The Concept and Effects of Service Modularity - A Literature Review". In: *46th Hawaii International Conference on System Sciences, HICSS 2013, Wailea, HI, USA, January 7–10, 2013*. IEEE Computer Society, 2013, pp. 1357–1366. https://doi.org/10.1109/HICSS.2013.22.

[DeM09] Linda DeMichiel. "JSR 317: Java Persistence 2.0". In: *Java Community Process, Tech. Rep* (2009).

[Dep]   *Deployd: a toolkit for building realtime APIs* https://github.com/deployd/deployd. (Accessed on 05/20/2017). 2017. URL: https://github.com/deployd/deployd (visited on 02/19/2017).

[Dey+14] Anamika Dey et al. "YCSB+T: Benchmarking web-scale transactional databases". In: *Data Engineering Workshops (ICDEW), 2014 IEEE 30th International Conference on*. IEEE. 2014, pp. 223–230.

[Dey15] Akon Samir Dey. "Cherry Garcia: Transactions across Heterogeneous Data Stores". In: (2015).

[Dow98] Troy Bryan Downing. *Java RMI: remote method invocation*. IDG Books Worldwide, Inc., 1998.

[Dut+10] Xavier Dutreilh et al. "From Data Center Resource Allocation to Control Theory and Back". In: *IEEE International Conference on Cloud Computing, CLOUD 2010, Miami, FL, USA, 5–10 July, 2010*. IEEE Computer Society, 2010, pp. 410–417. https:// doi.org/10.1109/CLOUD.2010.55.

[Dyn]   *DynamoDB*. http://docs.aws.amazon.com/amazondynamodb/latest/developerguide/ Introduction.html. (Accessed on 05/20/2017). 2017. URL: http://docs.aws. amazon.com/amazondynamodb/latest/developerguide/Introduction.html   (visited on 01/13/2017).

[Elm+11] Aaron J. Elmore et al. "Zephyr: live migration in shared nothing databases for elastic cloud platforms". In: *Proceedings of the 2011 ACM SIGMOD International Conference on Management of data*. ACM, 2011, pp. 301–312. URL: http://dl.acm. org/citation.cfm?id=1989356 (visited on 07/16/2014).

[EW16] Michael Egorov and MacLane Wilkison. "ZeroDB white paper". In: *arXiv preprint arXiv:1602.07168* (2016).

[Fan+12] Wei Fang et al. "RPPS: A Novel Resource Prediction and Provisioning Scheme in Cloud Data Center". In: *2012 IEEE Ninth International Conference on Services Computing, Honolulu, HI, USA, June 24–29, 2012*. Ed. by Louise E. Moser, Manish Parashar, and Patrick C. K. Hung. IEEE Computer Society, 2012, pp. 609–616. https:// doi.org/10.1109/SCC.2012.47.

[Fie+99] R. Fielding et al. "RFC 2616: Hypertext Transfer ProtocolâHTTP/1.1, 1999". In: *URL http://www.rfc.net/rfc2616.html* (1999).

[Fie00] R. T Fielding. "Architectural styles and the design of network-based software architectures". PhD thesis. Citeseer, 2000.

[Fio+13] Alessandro Gustavo Fior et al. "Under Pressure Benchmark for DDBMS Availability". In: *JIDM* 4.3 (2013), pp. 266–278. URL: http://seer.lcc.ufmg.br/index.php/jidm/ article/view/249.

[Fit04] Brad Fitzpatrick. "Distributed caching with Memcached". In: *Linux journal* 2004.124 (2004), p. 5.

[Fri+14] Steffen Friedrich et al. "NoSQL OLTP Benchmarking: A Survey". In: *44. Jahrestagung der Gesellschaft fÃijr Informatik, Informatik 2014, Big Data KomplexitÃd't meistern, 22.–26. September 2014 in Stuttgart, Deutschland*. Ed. by Erhard PlÃüdereder et al. Vol. 232. LNI. GI, 2014, pp. 693–704. ISBN: 978-3-88579-626-8.

[FWR17] Steffen Friedrich, Wolfram Wingerath, and Norbert Ritter. "Coordinated Omission in NoSQL Database Benchmarking". In: *Datenbanksysteme für Business, Technologie und Web (BTW 2017), 17. Fachtagung des GI-Fachbereichs, Datenbanken und Informationssysteme" (DBIS), 6.–10. März 2017, Stuttgart, Germany, Workshopband*. Ed. by Bernhard Mitschang et al. Vol. P-266. LNI. GI, 2017, pp. 215–225.

[Gda]   *Google Data APIs*. https://developers.google.com/gdata/. (Accessed on 05/26/2017). 2017. URL: https://developers.google.com/gdata/ (visited on 02/17/2017).

[Gen09] Craig Gentry. "A fully homomorphic encryption scheme". PhD thesis. Stanford University, 2009.

[Ges+17] Felix Gessert et al. "Quaestor: Query Web Caching for Database-as-a-Service Providers". In: *Proceedings of the VLDB Endowment* (2017).

[Ges19] Felix Gessert. "Low Latency for Cloud Data Management". PhD thesis. University of Hamburg, Germany, 2019. URL: http://ediss.sub.uni-hamburg.de/volltexte/2019/9541/.

[GGW10] Zhenhuan Gong, Xiaohui Gu, and John Wilkes. "PRESS: PRedictive Elastic ReSource Scaling for cloud systems". In: *Proceedings of the 6th International Conference on Network and Service Management, CNSM 2010, Niagara Falls, Canada, October 25–29, 2010*. IEEE, 2010, pp. 9–16. https://doi.org/10.1109/CNSM.2010.5691343.

[Gha+11] Hamoun Ghanbari et al. "Exploring alternative approaches to implement an elasticity policy". In: *Cloud Computing (CLOUD), 2011 IEEE International Conference on*. IEEE. 2011, pp. 716–723.

[GKA09] Ajay Gulati, Chethan Kumar, and Irfan Ahmad. "Storage workload characterization and consolidation in virtualized environments". In: *Workshop on Virtualization Performance: Analysis, Characterization, and Tools (VPACT)*. Citeseer. 2009.

[GLS11] Wojciech Golab, Xiaozhou Li, and Mehul A. Shah. "Analyzing consistency properties for fun and profit". In: *ACM PODC*. ACM, 2011, pp. 197–206. URL: http://dl.acm.org/citation.cfm?id=1993834 (visited on 09/28/2014).

[Gri13] Ilya Grigorik. *High performance browser networking*. English. [S.l.]: O'Reilly Media, 2013. ISBN: 1-4493-4476-3 978-1-4493-4476-4. URL: https://books.google.de/books?id=tf-AAAAQBAJ.

[Gul+12] Ajay Gulati et al. "Workload dependent IO scheduling for fairness and efficiency in shared storage systems". In: *19th International Conference on High Performance Computing, HiPC 2012, Pune, India, December 18–22, 2012*. IEEE Computer Society, 2012, pp. 1–10. https://doi.org/10.1109/HiPC.2012.6507480.

[Han+12] Rui Han et al. "Lightweight Resource Scaling for Cloud Applications". In: *12th IEEE/ACM International Symposium on Cluster, Cloud and Grid Computing, CCGrid 2012, Ottawa, Canada, May 13–16, 2012*. IEEE Computer Society, 2012, pp. 644–651. https://doi.org/10.1109/CCGrid.2012.52.

[Has+12] Masum Z. Hasan et al. "Integrated and autonomic cloud resource scaling". In: *2012 IEEE Network Operations and Management Symposium, NOMS 2012, Maui, HI, USA, April 16–20, 2012*. Ed. by Filip De Turck, Luciano Paschoal Gaspary, and Deep Medhi. IEEE, 2012, pp. 1327–1334. https://doi.org/10.1109/NOMS.2012.6212070.

[Has17] Mazdak Hashemi. *The Infrastructure Behind Twitter: Scale*. https://blog.twitter.com/2017/the-infrastructure-behind-twitter-scale. (Accessed on 05/25/2017). 2017. URL: https://blog.twitter.com/2017/the-infrastructure-behind-twitter-scale (visited on 02/18/2017).

[Hba] *HBase*. http://hbase.apache.org/. (Accessed on 05/25/2017). 2017. URL: http://hbase.apache.org/ (visited on 07/16/2014).

[HIM02] H. Hacigumus, B. Iyer, and S. Mehrotra. "Providing database as a service". In: *Data Engineering, 2002. Proceedings. 18th International Conference on*. 2002, pp. 29–38. URL: http://ieeexplore.ieee.org/xpls/abs_all.jsp?arnumber=994695 (visited on 10/16/2012).

[Hoo] *GitHub - hoodiehq/hoodie: A backend for Offline First applications*. https://github.com/hoodiehq/hoodie. (Accessed on 05/25/2017). 2017. URL: https://github.com/hoodiehq/hoodie (visited on 02/17/2017).

[HS16] Stephan Hochhaus and Manuel Schoebel. *Meteor in action*. Manning Publ., 2016.

[HTV10] T. Haselmann, G. Thies, and G. Vossen. "Looking into a REST-Based Universal API for Database-as-a-Service Systems". In: *CEC*. 2010, pp. 17–24. URL: http://ieeexplore.ieee.org/xpls/abs_all.jsp?arnumber=5708388 (visited on 10/15/2012).

[Ire+09] Christopher Ireland et al. "A Classification of Object-Relational Impedance Mismatch". In: IEEE, 2009, pp. 36–43. ISBN: 978-1-4244-3467-1. https://doi.org/10.1109/DBKDA.2009.11. URL: http://ieeexplore.ieee.org/lpdocs/epic03/wrapper.htm?arnumber=5071809 (visited on 01/03/2015).

[Isl+12] Sadeka Islam et al. "Empirical prediction models for adaptive resource provisioning in the cloud". In: *Future Generation Comp. Syst.* 28.1 (2012), pp. 155–162. https:// doi.org/10.1016/j.future.2011.05.027.

[JA07] Dean Jacobs and Stefan Aulbach. "Ruminations on Multi-Tenant Databases". In: *Datenbanksysteme in Business, Technologie und Web (BTW 2007), 12. Fachtagung des GI-Fachbereichs "Datenbanken und Informationssysteme" (DBIS), Proceedings, 7.–9. März 2007, Aachen, Germany.* Ed. by Alfons Kemper et al. Vol. 103. LNI. GI, 2007, pp. 514–521. URL: http://subs.emis.de/LNI/Proceedings/Proceedings103/ article1419.html.

[Kar+16] Nikolaos Karapanos et al. "Verena: End-to-End Integrity Protection for Web Applications". In: *IEEE Symposium on Security and Privacy, SP 2016, San Jose, CA, USA, May 22–26, 2016.* IEEE Computer Society, 2016, pp. 895–913. https://doi.org/10. 1109/SP.2016.58.

[KF11] Pawel Koperek and Wlodzimierz Funika. "Dynamic Business Metrics-driven Resource Provisioning in Cloud Environments". In: *Parallel Processing and Applied Mathematics - 9th International Conference, PPAM 2011, Torun, Poland, September 11–14, 2011. Revised Selected Papers, Part II.* Ed. by Roman Wyrzykowski et al. Vol. 7204. Lecture Notes in Computer Science. Springer, 2011, pp. 171–180. https:// doi.org/10.1007/978-3-642-31500-8_18.

[Kim+16] In Kee Kim et al. "Empirical Evaluation of Workload Forecasting Techniques for Predictive Cloud Resource Scaling". In: *9th IEEE International Conference on Cloud Computing, CLOUD 2016, San Francisco, CA, USA, June 27 - July 2, 2016.* IEEE Computer Society 2016, pp. 1–10. https://doi.org/10.1109/CLOUD.2016.0011.

[KJH15] Jens Köhler, Konrad Jünemann, and Hannes Hartenstein. "Confidential database-as-a-service approaches: taxonomy and survey". In: *Journal of Cloud Computing* 4.1 (2015), p. 1. ISSN: 2192-113X. https://doi.org/10.1186/s13677-014-0025-1.

[KL11] Tim Kiefer and Wolfgang Lehner. "Private Table Database Virtualization for DBaaS". In: *IEEE 4th International Conference on Utility and Cloud Computing, UCC 2011, Melbourne, Australia, December 5–8, 2011.* IEEE Computer Society, 2011, pp. 328–329. https://doi.org/10.1109/UCC.2011.52.

[Kle17] Martin Kleppmann. *Designing Data-Intensive Applications.* English. 1 edition. O'Reilly Media, Jan. 2017. ISBN: 978-1-4493-7332-0.

[Kri13] Raffi Krikorian. *Timelines at Scale.* http://infoq.com/presentations/Twitter-Timeline-Scalability. (Accessed on 04/30/2017). 2013. URL: http://infoq.com/presentations/ Twitter-Timeline-Scalability.

[Lac16] Kevin Lacker. "Moving On". In: *Parse Blog* (Jan. 2016). Accessed on 12/09/2017. URL: http://blog.parseplatform.org/announcements/moving-on/.

[Lan+12] Willis Lang et al. "Towards Multi-tenant Performance SLOs". In: *IEEE 28th International Conference on Data Engineering (ICDE 2012), Washington, DC, USA (Arlington, Virginia), 1–5 April, 2012.* Ed. by Anastasios Kementsietsidis and Marcos Antonio Vaz Salles. IEEE Computer Society, 2012, pp. 702–713.https://doi.org/10. 1109/ICDE.2012.101.

[LBMAL14] Tania Lorido-Botran, Jose Miguel-Alonso, and JoseA. Lozano. "A Review of Autoscaling Techniques for Elastic Applications in Cloud Environments". English. In: *Journal of Grid Computing* 12.4 (2014), pp. 559–592. ISSN: 1570–7873. https://doi. org/10.1007/s10723-014-9314-7.

[Leb08] Scott Leberknight. *Polyglot Persistence.* http://www.sleberknight.com/blog/sleberkn/ entry/polyglot_persistence. (Accessed on 04/30/2017). 2008. URL: http://www. sleberknight.com/blog/sleberkn/entry/polyglot_persistence.

[Len02] Maurizio Lenzerini. "Data Integration: A Theoretical Perspective". In: *Proceedings of the Twenty-first ACM SIGACT-SIGMOD-SIGART Symposium on Principles of Database Systems, June 3–5, Madison, Wisconsin, USA.* Ed. by Lucian Popa, Serge Abiteboul, and Phokion G. Kolaitis. ACM, 2002, pp. 233–246. https://doi.org/10. 1145/543613.543644.

[LM10] Avinash Lakshman and Prashant Malik. "Cassandra: a decentralized structured storage system". In: *ACM SIGOPS Operating Systems Review* 44.2 (2010), pp. 35–40. URL: http://dl.acm.org/citation.cfm?id=1773922 (visited on 04/15/2014).

[LS13] Wolfgang Lehner and Kai-Uwe Sattler. *Web-Scale Data Management for the Cloud.* Englisch. Auflage: 2013. New York: Springer, Apr 2013. ISBN: 978-1-4614-6855-4.

[Mad+15] Gabor Madl et al. "Account clustering in multi-tenant storage management environments". In: *2015 IEEE International Conference on Big Data, Big Data 2015, Santa Clara, CA, USA, October 29 - November 1, 2015.* IEEE, 2015, pp. 1698–1707. https://doi.org/10.1109/BigData.2015.7363941.

[Mai90] David Maier. "Representing database programs as objects". In: *Advances in database programming languages.* ACM. 1990, pp. 377–386.

[MBS11] Michael Maurer, Ivona Brandic, and Rizos Sakellariou. "Enacting SLAs in clouds using rules". In: *European Conference on Parallel Processing.* Springer. 2011, pp. 455–466.

[MP17] Ryan Marcus and Olga Papaemmanouil. "Releasing Cloud Databases from the Chains of Performance Prediction Models". In: *CIDR.* 2017.

[New15] Sam Newman. *Building microservices - designing fine-grained systems, 1st Edition.* O'Reilly, 2015. ISBN: 9781491950357. URL: http://www.worldcat.org/oclc/904463848.

[Oda] *OData - open data protocol.* http://www.odata.org/. (Accessed on 06/05/2017). 2017. URL: http://www.odata.org/ (visited on 02/17/2017).

[Pad+07] Pradeep Padala et al. "Adaptive control of virtualized resources in utility computing environments". In: *Proceedings of the 2007 EuroSys Conference, Lisbon, Portugal, March 21–23, 2007.* Ed. by Paulo Ferreira, Thomas R. Gross, and Luís Veiga. ACM, 2007, pp. 289–302. https://doi.org/10.1145/1272996.1273026.

[Pad+09] Pradeep Padala et al. "Automated control of multiple virtualized resources". In: *Proceedings of the 4th ACM European conference on Computer systems.* ACM, 2009, pp. 13–26. URL: http://dl.acm.org/citation.cfm?id=1519068 (visited on 07/16/2014).

[Par] *Parse Server.* http://parseplatform.github.io/docs/parse-server/guide/. (Accessed on 07/28/2017). 2017. URL: http://parseplatform.github.io/docs/parse-server/guide/ (visited on 02/19/2017).

[Pat+11] Swapnil Patil et al. "YCSB++: benchmarking and performance debugging advanced features in scalable table stores". In: *ACM Symposium on Cloud Computing in conjunction with SOSP 2011, SOCC '11, Cascais, Portugal, October 26–28, 2011.* Ed. by Jeffrey S. Chase and Amr El Abbadi. ACM, 2011, p. 9. https://doi.org/10.1145/2038916.2038925.

[PF00] Meikel Pöss and Chris Floyd. "New TPC Benchmarks for Decision Support and Web Commerce". In: *SIGMOD Record* 29.4 (2000), pp. 64–71. https://doi.org/10.1145/369275.369291.

[PH09] Sang-Min Park and Marty Humphrey. "Self-Tuning Virtual Machines for Predictable eScience". In: *9th IEEE/ACM International Symposium on Cluster Computing and the Grid, CCGrid 2009, Shanghai, China, 18–21 May 2009.* Ed. by Franck Cappello, Cho-Li Wang, and Rajkumar Buyya. IEEE Computer Society, 2009, pp. 356–363. https://doi.org/10.1109/CCGRID.2009.84.

[PN09] Radu Prodan and Vlad Nae. "Prediction-based real-time resource provisioning for massively multiplayer online games". In: *Future Generation Comp. Syst.* 25.7 (2009), pp. 785–793. https://doi.org/10.1016/j.future.2008.11.002.

[Pop+11] R. A. Popa et al. "CryptDB: protecting confidentiality with encrypted query processing". In: *Proceedings of the Twenty-Third ACM Symposium on Operating Systems Principles.* 00095. 2011, pp. 85–100. URL: http://dl.acm.org/citation.cfm?id=2043566 (visited on 11/16/2012).

[Pop+14] Raluca Ada Popa et al. "Building Web Applications on Top of Encrypted Data Using Mylar". In: *Proceedings of the 11th USENIX Symposium on Networked Systems Design and Implementation, NSDI2014, Seattle, WA, USA, April 2–4, 2014*. Ed. by Ratul Mahajan and Ion Stoica. USENIX Association, 2014, pp. 157–172. URL: https://www.usenix.org/conference/nsdi14/technical-sessions/presentation/popa.

[Pop14] Raluca Ada Popa. "Building practical systems that compute on encrypted data". PhD thesis. Massachusetts Institute of Technology, 2014.

[Pos] *PostgreSQL: Documentation: 9.6: High Availability, Load Balancing, and Replication*. https://www.postgresql.org/docs/9.6/static/high-availability.html. (Accessed on 07/28/2017). 2017. URL: https://www.postgresql.org/docs/9.6/static/high-availability.html (visited on 02/04/2017).

[PZ13] Raluca A. Popa and Nickolai Zeldovich. "Multi-Key Searchable Encryption". In: *IACR Cryptology ePrint Archive* 2013 (2013), p. 508. URL: http://eprint.iacr.org/2013/508.

[Rah+12] Muntasir Raihan Rahman et al. "Toward a Principled Framework for Benchmarking Consistency". In: *CoRR* abs/1211.4290 (2012). URL: http://arxiv.org/abs/1211.4290.

[Ria] *Riak*. http://basho.com/products/. (Accessed on 05/25/2017). 2017. URL: http://basho.com/products/ (visited on 01/13/2017).

[Rob16] Mike Roberts. *Serverless Architectures*. https://martinfowler.com/articles/serverless.html. (Accessed on 07/28/2017). 2016. URL: https://martinfowler.com/articles/serverless.html (visited on 02/19/2017).

[Sak14] Sherif Sakr. "Cloud-hosted databases: technologies, challenges and opportunities". In: *Cluster Computing* 17.2 (2014), pp. 487–502. URL: http://link.springer.com/article/10.1007/s10586-013-0290-7 (visited on 07/16/2014).

[San17] Salvatore Sanfilippo. *Redis*. http://redis.io/. (Accessed on 07/16/2017). 2017. URL: http://redis.io/ (visited on 09/02/2015).

[Sch+16] Michael Schaarschmidt et al. "Learning Runtime Parameters in Computer Systems with Delayed Experience Injection". In: *Deep Reinforcement Learning Workshop, NIPS 2016*. 2016.

[Sch16] Peter Schuller. "Manhattan, our real-time, multi-tenant distributed database for Twitter scale". In: *Twitter Blog* (2016).

[SF12] Pramod J. Sadalage and Martin Fowler. *NoSQL distilled: a brief guide to the emerging world of polyglot persistence*. Pearson Education, 2012.

[SGR15] Michael Schaarschmidt, Felix Gessert, and Norbert Ritter. "Towards Automated Polyglot Persistence". In: *Datenbanksysteme fÃijr Business, Technologie und Web (BTW), 16. Fachtagung des GI-Fachbereichs "Datenbanken und Informationssysteme"*. 2015.

[She+11] Zhiming Shen et al. "CloudScale: elastic resource scaling for multitenant cloud systems". In: *ACM Symposium on Cloud Computing in conjunction with SOSP 2011, SOCC '11, Cascais, Portugal, October 26–28, 2011*. Ed. by Jeffrey S. Chase and Amr El Abbadi. ACM, 2011, p. 5. https://doi.org/10.1145/2038916.2038921.

[SKM08] Aameek Singh, Madhukar R. Korupolu, and Dushmanta Mohapatra. "Server-storage virtualization: integration and load balancing in data centers". In: *Proceedings of the ACM/IEEE Conference on High Performance Computing, SC 2008, November 15–21, 2008, Austin, Texas, USA*. IEEE/ACM, 2008, p. 53. https://doi.org/10.1145/1413370.1413424.

[SL12] Sherif Sakr and Anna Liu. "SLA-Based and Consumer-centric Dynamic Provisioning for Cloud Databases". In: *2012 IEEE Fifth International Conference on Cloud Computing, Honolulu, HI, USA, June 24–29, 2012*. Ed. by Rong Chang. IEEE Computer Society, 2012, pp. 360–367. https://doi.org/10.1109/CLOUD.2012.11.

[Sou+09] Gokul Soundararajan et al. "Dynamic Resource Allocation for Database Servers Running on Virtual Storage". In: *7th USENIX Conference on File and Storage Technologies, February 24–27, 2009, San Francisco, CA, USA. Proceedings*. Ed. by Margo I. Seltzer and Richard Wheeler. USENIX, 2009, pp. 71–84. URL: http://www.usenix.org/events/fast09/tech/full_papers/soundararajan/soundararajan.pdf.

[Stö+15] Uta Störl et al. "Schemaless NoSQL Data Stores Object-NoSQL Mappers to the Rescue?" In: *Datenbanksysteme für Business, Technologie und Web (BTW), 16. Fachtagung des GI-Fachbereichs "Datenbanken und Informationssysteme" (DBIS), 4.-6.3.2015 in Hamburg, Germany. Proceedings.* Ed. by Thomas Seidl et al. Vol. 241. LNI. GI, 2015, pp. 579–599. URL: http://subs.emis.de/LNI/Proceedings/Proceedings241/article13.html (visited on 03/10/2015).

[Ter+13] Douglas B. Terry et al. "Consistency-based service level agreements for cloud storage". In: *ACM SIGOPS 24th Symposium on Operating Systems Principles, SOSP '13, Farmington, PA, USA, November 3–6, 2013*. Ed. by Michael Kaminsky and Mike Dahlin. ACM, 2013, pp. 309–324. https://doi.org/10.1145/2517349.2522731.

[Tes+06] G. Tesauro et al. "A Hybrid Reinforcement Learning Approach to Autonomic Resource Allocation". In: *Proceedings of the 2006 IEEE International Conference on Autonomic Computing*. ICAC '06. Washington, DC, USA: IEEE Computer Society, 2006, pp. 65–73. ISBN: 1-4244-0175-5. https://doi.org/10.1109/ICAC.2006.1662383.

[Tes13] Claudio Tesoriero. *Getting Started with OrientDB*. Packt Publishing Ltd, 2013.

[Tor+17] Alexandre Torres et al. "Twenty years of object-relational mapping: A survey on patterns, solutions, and their implications on application design". In: *Information and Software Technology* 82 (2017), pp. 1–18.

[Urg+08] Bhuvan Urgaonkar et al. "Agile dynamic provisioning of multi-tier Internet applications". In: *TAAS* 3.1 (2008), 1:1–1:39. https://doi.org/10.1145/1342171.1342172.

[Use] *Apache Usergrid*. https://usergrid.apache.org/. (Accessed on 07/16/2017). 2017. URL: https://usergrid.apache.org/ (visited on 02/19/2017).

[VPR07] Daniel A. Villela, Prashant Pradhan, and Dan Rubenstein. "Provisioning servers in the application tier for e-commerce systems". In: *ACM Trans. Internet Techn.* 7.1 (2007), p. 7. https://doi.org/10.1145/1189740.1189747.

[Wad+11] Hiroshi Wada et al. "Data Consistency Properties and the Tradeoffs in Commercial Cloud Storage: the Consumers' Perspective". In: *CIDR 2011, Fifth Biennial Conference on Innovative Data Systems Research, Asilomar, CA, USA, January 9–12, 2011, Online Proceedings*. www.cidrdb.org, 2011, pp. 134–143. URL: http://www.cidrdb.org/cidr2011/Papers/CIDR11_Paper15.pdf.

[Wan16] Mengyan Wang. "Parse LiveQuery Protocol Specification". In: *GitHub: ParsePlatform/parse-server* (Mar. 2016). Accessed on 12/14/2017. URL: https://github.com/parse-community/parse-server/wiki/Parse-LiveQuery-Protocol-Specification.

[WB09] Craig D. Weissman and Steve Bobrowski. "The design of the force.com multitenant internet application development platform". In: *Proceedings of the ACM SIGMOD International Conference on Management of Data, SIGMOD 2009, Providence, Rhode Island, USA, June 29 - July 2, 2009*. Ed. by Ugur Çetintemel et al. ACM, 2009, pp. 889–896. https://doi.org/10.1145/1559845.1559942.

[WGW+20] Wolfram Wingerath, Felix Gessert, Erik Witt, et al. "Speed Kit: A Polyglot & GDPR-Compliant Approach For Caching Personalized Content". In: *36th IEEE International Conference on Data Engineering, ICDE 2020, Dallas, Texas, April 20–24, 2020*. 2020.

[Whi15] Tom White. *Hadoop - The Definitive Guide: Storage and Analysis at Internet Scale (4. ed., revised & updated)*. O'Reilly, 2015. ISBN: 978-1-491-90163-2. URL: http://www.oreilly.de/catalog/9781491901632/index.html.

[Win+15] Wolfram Wingerath et al. "Who Watches the Watchmen? On the Lack of Validation in NoSQL Benchmarking". In: *Datenbanksysteme fÄijr Business, Technologie und Web (BTW), 16. Fachtagung des GI-Fachbereichs "Datenbanken und Informationssysteme"*. 2015.

[Wol+13] Florian Wolf et al. "Hibernating in the Cloud-Implementation and Evaluation of Object-NoSQL-Mapping." In: *BTW*. Citeseer, 2013, pp. 327–341.

[WRG19] Wolfram Wingerath, Norbert Ritter, and Felix Gessert. *Real-Time & Stream Data Management: Push-Based Data in Research & Practice*. Ed. by Susan Evans. Springer

International Publishing, 2019. ISBN: 978-3-030-10554-9. https://doi.org/10.1007/978-3-030-10555-6.

[Xio+11] P. Xiong et al. "ActiveSLA: A profit-oriented admission control framework for database-as-a-service providers". In: *Proceedings of the 2nd ACM Symposium on Cloud Computing*. 00019. ACM, 2011, p. 15. URL: http://dl.acm.org/citation.cfm?id=2038931 (visited on 11/15/2012).

[XRB12] Cheng-Zhong Xu, Jia Rao, and Xiangping Bu. "URL: A unified reinforcement learning approach for autonomic cloud management". In: *J. Parallel Distrib. Comput.* 72.2 (2012), pp. 95–105. https://doi.org/10.1016/j.jpdc.2011.10.003.

[Xu+07] Jing Xu et al. "On the Use of Fuzzy Modeling in Virtualized Data Center Management". In: *Fourth International Conference on Autonomic Computing (ICAC'07), Jacksonville, Florida, USA, June 11–15, 2007*. IEEE Computer Society, 2007, p. 25. https://doi.org/10.1109/ICAC.2007.28.

[Zah+10] Matei Zaharia et al. "Spark: cluster computing with working sets". In: *Proceedings of the 2nd USENIX conference on Hot topics in cloud computing*. 2010, pp. 10–10. URL: http://static.usenix.org/legacy/events/hotcloud1/tech/full_papers/Zaharia.pdf (visited on 01/03/2015).

[ZCS07] Qi Zhang, Ludmila Cherkasova, and Evgenia Smirni. "A Regression-Based Analytic Model for Dynamic Resource Provisioning of Multi-Tier Applications". In: *Fourth International Conference on Autonomic Computing (ICAC'07), Jacksonville, Florida, USA, June 11–15, 2007*. IEEE Computer Society, 2007, p. 27. https://doi.org/10.1109/ICAC.2007.1.

[Zha+14] Liang Zhao et al. *Cloud Data Management*. Englisch. Auflage: 2014. Springer, 2014.

[IET15] IETF. "RFC 7540 - Hypertext Transfer Protocol Version 2 (HTTP/2)". In: (2015).

Chapter 8
The NoSQL Toolbox: The NoSQL Landscape in a Nutshell

In this chapter, we highlight the design space of distributed database systems, dividing it by the four dimensions sharding, replication, storage management, and query processing. The goal is to provide a comprehensive set of data management requirements that have to be considered for designing a flexible backend for globally distributed web applications. Therefore, we survey the implementation techniques of systems and discuss how they are related to different functional and non-functional properties (goals) of data management systems.

Every significantly successful database is designed for a particular class of applications, or to achieve a specific combination of desirable system properties. The simple reason why there are so many different database systems is that it is not possible for any system to achieve all desirable properties at once. Traditional relational databases such as PostgreSQL have been built to provide the full functional package: a very flexible data model, sophisticated querying capabilities including joins, global integrity constraints, and transactional guarantees. On the other end of the design spectrum, there are key-value stores like Dynamo that scale with data and request volume and offer high read and write throughput as well as low latency, but barely any functionality apart from simple lookups.

In order to illustrate which techniques are suitable to achieve specific system properties, we provide the **NoSQL Toolbox** (Fig. 8.1) that connects each technique to the functional and non-functional properties it enables (positive edges only). In the following, we will review each of the four major categories of techniques in scalable data management: sharding, replication, storage management, and query processing.

© Springer Nature Switzerland AG 2020
F. Gessert et al., *Fast and Scalable Cloud Data Management*,
https://doi.org/10.1007/978-3-030-43506-6_8

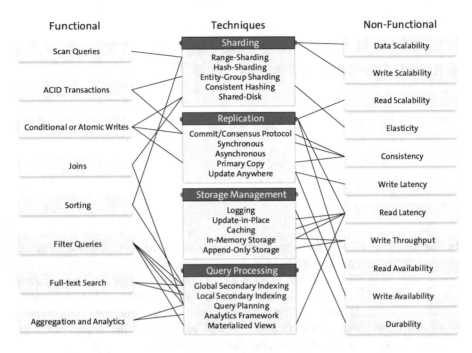

Fig. 8.1 The NoSQL Toolbox: It connects the techniques of NoSQL databases with the desired functional and non-functional system properties they support

8.1   Sharding

Several distributed relational database systems such as Oracle RAC or IBM DB2 pureScale rely on a **shared-disk architecture** where all database nodes access the same central data repository (e.g., a NAS or SAN). Thus, these systems provide consistent data at all times, but are also inherently difficult to scale. In contrast, the (NoSQL) database systems in the focus of this dissertation are built upon a **shared-nothing architecture**, meaning each system consists of many servers with private memory and private disks that are connected through a network. Thus, high scalability in throughput and data volume is achieved by **sharding** (partitioning) data across different nodes (**shards**) in the system.

There are three basic distribution techniques: range partitioning, hash partitioning, and entity-group sharding.

8.1.1   Range Partitioning

To make efficient scans possible, data can be partitioned into ordered and contiguous value ranges by **range-sharding**. However, this approach requires some coordination through a master that manages assignments. To ensure elasticity, the system has to be able to detect and resolve hotspots automatically by further splitting an overburdened shard.

Range sharding is supported by wide-column stores like BigTable, HBase or Hypertable [Wie15] and document stores, e.g., MongoDB, RethinkDB, Espresso [Qia+13] and DocumentDB [STR+15].

8.1.2 Hash Partitioning

Another way to partition data over several machines is **hash-sharding** where every data item is assigned to a shard server according to some hash value built from the primary key. This approach does not require a coordinator and also guarantees data to be evenly distributed across the shards, as long as the used hash function produces an even distribution. The obvious disadvantage, though, is that it only allows lookups and makes scans impossible. Hash sharding is used in key-value stores and is also available in some wide-column stores like Cassandra [LM10] or Azure Tables [Cal+11].

The shard server that is responsible for a record can be determined as $server_{id} = hash(id) \bmod servers$, for example. However, this hashing scheme requires all records to be reassigned every time a new server joins or leaves, because it changes with the number of shard servers ($servers$). Consequently, it is infeasible to use in elastic systems like Dynamo, Riak, or Cassandra, which allow additional resources to be added on-demand and again be removed when dispensable. For increased flexibility, elastic systems typically use **consistent hashing** [Kar+97] where records are not directly assigned to servers, but instead to logical partitions which are then distributed across all shard servers. Thus, only a fraction of data has to be reassigned upon changes in the system topology. For example, an elastic system can be downsized by offloading all logical partitions residing on a particular server to other servers and then shutting down the now idle machine. For details on how consistent hashing is used in NoSQL systems, please refer to DeCandia et al. [DeC+07].

8.1.3 Entity-Group Sharding

A data partitioning scheme with the goal of enabling single-partition transactions on co-located data is **entity-group sharding**. Partitions are called entity-groups and either explicitly declared by the application (e.g., in G-Store [DAEA10] and MegaStore [Bak+11]) or derived from transactions' access patterns (e.g., in Relational Cloud [Cur+11a] and Cloud SQL Server [Ber+11]). If a transaction accesses data that spans more than one group, data ownership can be transferred between entity-groups or the transaction manager has to fall back to more expensive multi-node transaction protocols.

8.2   Replication

In terms of CAP (cf. Sect. 4.3), conventional RDBMSs are often CA systems run in single-server mode: the entire system becomes unavailable on machine failure. System operators therefore secure data integrity and availability through expensive, but reliable high-end hardware. In contrast, NoSQL systems like Dynamo, BigTable, or Cassandra are designed for data and request volumes that cannot possibly be handled by one single machine, and therefore run on clusters consisting of potentially thousands of servers.[1] Since failures are inevitable and will occur frequently in any large-scale, distributed system, the software has to cope with them on a daily basis [Ham07]. In 2009, Dean [Dea09] stated that a typical new cluster at Google encounters thousands of hard drive failures, 1000 single-machine failures, 20 rack failures and several network partitions due to expected and unexpected circumstances in its first year alone. Many more recent cases of network partitions and outages in large cloud data centers have been reported [BK14]. Replication allows the system to maintain availability and durability in the face of such errors. But storing the same records on different machines (**replica servers**) in the cluster introduces the problem of synchronization between them and thus a trade-off between consistency on the one hand and latency and availability on the other.

Gray et al. [GHa+96] propose a two-tier classification of different replication strategies according to *when* updates are propagated to replicas and *where* updates are accepted. There are two possible choices on tier one ("when"): **eager** (*synchronous*) replication propagates incoming changes synchronously to all replicas before a commit can be returned to the client, whereas **lazy** (*asynchronous*) replication applies changes only at the receiving replica and passes them on asynchronously. The great advantage of *eager* replication is consistency among replicas, but it comes at the cost of higher write latency and impaired availability due to the need to wait for other replicas [GHa+96]. *Lazy* replication is faster, because it allows replicas to diverge. As a consequence, though, stale data might be served. On the second tier ("where"), again, two different approaches are possible: either a **master-slave** (*primary copy*) scheme is pursued where changes can only be accepted by one replica (the master) or, in a **update anywhere** (*multi-master*) approach, every replica can accept writes. In *master-slave* protocols, concurrency control is not more complex than in a distributed system without replicas, but the entire replica set becomes unavailable, as soon as the master fails. Multi-master protocols require complex mechanisms for prevention or detection and reconciliation of conflicting

---

[1]Low-end hardware is used, because it is substantially more cost-efficient than high-end hardware [HB09, Section 3.1].

changes. Techniques typically used for these purposes are versioning, vector clocks, gossiping, and read repair (e.g., in Dynamo [DeC+07]), and convergent or commutative data types [Sha+11] (e.g., in Riak).

All four combinations of the two-tier classification are possible. Distributed relational systems usually perform *eager master-slave* replication to maintain strong consistency. *Eager update anywhere* replication as for example featured in Google's Megastore [Bak+11] suffers from a heavy communication overhead generated by synchronization and can cause distributed deadlocks which are expensive to detect. NoSQL database systems typically rely on *lazy* replication, either in combination with the master-slave approach (CP systems, e.g., HBase and MongoDB) or the update anywhere approach (AP systems, e.g., Dynamo and Cassandra). Many NoSQL systems leave the choice between latency and consistency to the client, i.e., for every request, the client decides whether to wait for a response from any replica to achieve minimal latency or for a certainly consistent response (by a majority of the replicas or the master) to prevent stale data.

An aspect of replication that is not covered by the two-tier scheme is the distance between replicas. The obvious advantage of placing replicas near one another is low latency, but close proximity of replicas might also reduce the positive effects on availability; for example, if two replicas of the same data item are placed in the same rack, the data item is not available on rack failure in spite of replication. But more than the possibility of mere temporary unavailability, placing replicas nearby also bears the peril of losing all copies at once in a disaster scenario.

Geo-replication can protect the system against unavailability and data loss and potentially improves read latency for distributed access from clients. *Eager* geo-replication, as implemented in Google's Megastore [Bak+11], Spanner [Cor+13], MDCC [Kra+13], and Mencius [MJM08] allows for higher write latency to achieve linearizability or other strong consistency models. In contrast, *lazy* geo-replication as in Dynamo [DeC+07], PNUTS [Coo+08], Walter [Sov+11], COPS [Llo+11], Cassandra [LM10], and BigTable [Cha+08] relaxes consistency in favor of availability and latency. Charron-Bost et al. [CBPS10, Chapter 12] and Öszu and Valduriez [ÖV11, Chapter 13] provide a comprehensive discussion of database replication.

8.3   Storage Management

For best performance, database systems need to be optimized for the storage media they employ to serve and persist data. These are typically main memory (RAM), solid-state drives (SSDs), and spinning disk drives (HDDs) that can be used in any combination. Unlike RDBMSs in enterprise setups, distributed NoSQL databases avoid specialized shared-disk architectures in favor of shared-nothing clusters that are based on commodity servers (employing commodity storage media).

Storage devices are typically visualized as a "storage pyramid" (see Fig. 8.2) [Hel07]. The huge variety of cost and performance characteristics of RAM, SSD,

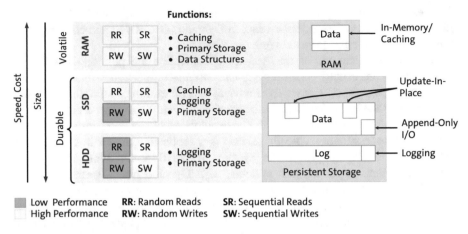

Fig. 8.2 The storage pyramid and its role in NoSQL systems

and HDD storage and the different strategies to leverage their strengths (storage management) is one reason for the diversity of NoSQL databases. Storage management has a spatial dimension (where to store data) and a temporal dimension (when to store data). Update-in-place and append-only I/O are two complementary spatial techniques of organizing data; in-memory prescribes RAM as the location of data, whereas logging is a temporal technique that decouples main memory and persistent storage and thus provides control over when data is actually persisted. Besides the major storage media, there is also a set of transparent caches (e.g., L1-L3 CPU caches and disk buffers, not shown in the figure), that are only implicitly leveraged through well-engineered database algorithms that promote data locality.

Stonebraker et al. [Sto+07] have found that in typical RDBMSs, only 6.8% of the execution time is spent on "useful work", while the rest is spent on:

- buffer management (34.6%), i.e., caching to mitigate slower disk access
- latching (14.2%), to protect shared data structures from race conditions caused by multi-threading
- locking (16.3%), to guarantee logical isolation of transactions
- logging (11.9%), to ensure durability in the face of failures
- hand-coded optimizations (16.2%)

This motivates that large performance improvements can be expected if RAM is used as primary storage (cf. **in-memory** databases [Zha+15a]). The downside are high storage costs and lack of durability—a small power outage can destroy the database state. This can be solved in two ways: the state can be replicated over n in-memory server nodes protecting against $n - 1$ single-node failures (e.g., HStore, VoltDB [Kal+08, SW13]) or by **logging** to durable storage (e.g., Redis or SAP Hana [Car13, Pla13]). Through logging, a random write access pattern can be transformed to a sequential one comprised of received operations and their associated properties (e.g., redo information). In most NoSQL systems, the commit rule for logging is respected, which demands every write operation that is confirmed as successful to be logged and the log to be flushed to persistent storage. In order to avoid the rotational latency of HDDs incurred by logging each operation individually, log flushes can be batched together (group commit) which slightly increases the latency of individual writes, but drastically improves overall throughput.

SSDs and more generally all storage devices based on NAND flash memory differ substantially from HDDs in various aspects: "(1) asymmetric speed of read and write operations, (2) no in-place overwrite—the whole block must be erased before overwriting any page in that block, and (3) limited program/erase cycles" [MKC+12]. Thus, a database system's storage management must not treat SSDs and HDDs as slightly slower, persistent RAM, since random writes to an SSD are roughly an order of magnitude slower than sequential writes. Random reads, on the other hand, can be performed without any performance penalties. There are some database systems (e.g., Oracle Exadata, Aerospike) that are explicitly engineered for these performance characteristics of SSDs. In HDDs, both random reads and writes are 10–100 times slower than sequential access. Logging hence suits the strengths of SSDs and HDDs which both offer a significantly higher throughput for sequential writes.

For in-memory databases, an **update-in-place** access pattern is ideal: it simplifies the implementation and random writes to RAM are essentially equally fast as sequential ones, with small differences being hidden by pipelining and the CPU-cache hierarchy. However, RDBMSs and many NoSQL systems employ an update-in-place update pattern for persistent storage, too. To mitigate the slow random access to persistent storage, main memory is usually used as a cache and complemented by logging to guarantee durability. In RDBMSs, this is achieved through a complex buffer pool which not only employs cache-replace algorithms appropriate for typical SQL-based access patterns, but also ensures ACID semantics. NoSQL databases have simpler buffer pools that profit from simpler queries and the lack of ACID transactions. The alternative to the buffer pool model is to leave caching to the OS through virtual memory (e.g., employed in MongoDB's MMAP storage engine). This simplifies the database architecture, but has the downside of giving less control over which data items or pages reside in memory and when they get evicted. Also read-ahead (speculative reads) and write-behind (write buffering) transparently performed by the operating system lack sophistication as they are based on file system logics instead of database queries.

Append-only storage (also referred to as log-structuring) tries to maximize throughput by writing sequentially. Although log-structured file systems have a long research history, append-only I/O has only recently been popularized for databases by BigTable's use of Log-Structured Merge (LSM) trees [Cha+08] consisting of an in-memory cache, a persistent log, and immutable, periodically written storage files. LSM trees and variants like Sorted Array Merge Trees (SAMT) and Cache-Oblivious Look-ahead Arrays (COLA) have been applied in many NoSQL systems (e.g., Cassandra, CouchDB, LevelDB, Bitcask, RethinkDB, WiredTiger, RocksDB, InfluxDB, TokuDB) [Kle17]. Designing a database to achieve maximum write performance by always writing to a log is rather simple, the difficulty lies in providing fast random and sequential reads. This requires an appropriate index structure that is either actively maintained as a copy-on-write (COW) data structure (e.g., CouchDB's COW B-trees) or only periodically persisted as an immutable data structure (e.g., in BigTable-style systems). An issue of all log-structured storage approaches is costly garbage collection (compaction) to reclaim space of updated or deleted items.

In virtualized environments like Infrastructure-as-a-Service clouds, many of the discussed characteristics of the underlying storage layer are hidden. In the future, the availability of storage class memory combining speed of main memory with persistence will also require novel approaches for storage management [Nan+16].

8.4   Query Processing

The querying capabilities of a NoSQL database mainly follow from its distribution model, consistency guarantees, and data model. **Primary key lookup**, i.e., retrieving data items by a unique ID, is supported by every NoSQL system, since it is compatible to range- as well as hash-partitioning. **Filter queries** return all items (or projections) that meet a predicate specified over the properties of data items from a single table. In their simplest form, they can be performed as *filtered full-table scans*. For hash-partitioned databases, this implies a *scatter-gather* pattern where each partition performs the predicated scan and results are merged. For range-partitioned systems, any conditions on the range attribute can be exploited to select partitions.

To circumvent the inefficiencies of $O(n)$ scans, secondary indexes can be employed. These can either be **local secondary indexes** that are managed in each partition or **global secondary indexes** that index data over all partitions [Bak+11]. As the global index itself has to be distributed over partitions, consistent secondary index maintenance would necessitate slow and potentially unavailable commit protocols. Therefore, in practice, most systems only offer eventual consistency for these indexes (e.g., Megastore, Google AppEngine Datastore, DynamoDB) or do not support them at all (e.g., HBase, Azure Tables). When executing global queries over local secondary indexes, the query can only be targeted to a subset of partitions, if the query predicate and the partitioning rules intersect. Otherwise, results have to be assembled through scatter-gather. For example, a user table with range-partitioning over an age field can service queries that have an equality condition on age from one partition, whereas queries over names need to be evaluated at each partition. A special case of global secondary indexing is full-text search, where selected fields or complete data items are fed into either a database-internal inverted index (e.g., MongoDB) or to an external search platform such as ElasticSearch or Solr (Riak Search, DataStax Cassandra).

Query planning is the task of optimizing a query plan to minimize execution costs [Hel07]. For aggregations and joins, query planning is essential as these queries are very inefficient and hard to implement in application code. The wealth of

literature and results on relational query processing is largely disregarded in current
NoSQL systems for two reasons. First, the key-value and wide-column model are
centered around CRUD and scan operations on primary keys which leave little
room for query optimization. Second, most work on distributed query processing
focuses on OLAP (online analytical processing) workloads that favor throughput
over latency whereas single-node query optimization is not easily applicable for
partitioned and replicated databases [Kos00, ESW78, ÖV11]. However, it remains
an open research challenge to generalize the large body of applicable query
optimization techniques, especially in the context of document databases.[2]

In-database analytics can be performed either natively (e.g., in MongoDB,
Riak, CouchDB) or through external analytics platforms such as Hadoop, Spark
and Flink (e.g., in Cassandra and HBase). The prevalent native batch analytics
abstraction exposed by NoSQL systems is MapReduce[3] [DG04]. Due to I/O,
communication overhead, and limited execution plan optimization, these batch- and
micro-batch-oriented approaches have high response times. **Materialized views** are
an alternative with lower query response times. They are declared at design time
and continuously updated on change operations (e.g., in CouchDB and Cassandra).
However, similar to global secondary indexing, view consistency is usually relaxed
in favor of fast, highly available writes, when the system is distributed [Lab+09].
As only few database systems come with built-in support for ingesting and
querying unbounded streams of data, **near-real-time analytics** pipelines commonly
implement either the **Lambda Architecture** [MW15] or the **Kappa Architecture**
[Kre14]: the former complements a batch processing framework like Hadoop
MapReduce with a stream processor such as Storm [Boy+14] and the latter
exclusively relies on stream processing and forgoes batch processing altogether.

8.5 Summary: System Studies

To conclude this chapter, we provide a qualitative comparison of some of a selection
of the most prominent key-value, document, and wide-column stores. We present
the results in strongly condensed comparisons and refer to the documentation of the
individual systems and our tutorials [GR15, GR16, GWR17, WGR+18, WGR19]
for in-detail information. The proposed **NoSQL Toolbox** (see Fig. 8.1, p. 176)
is a means of abstraction that can be used to classify database systems along
three dimensions: functional requirements, non-functional requirements, and the
techniques used to implement them. We argue that this classification characterizes

---

[2]Currently only RethinkDB can perform general θ-joins. MongoDB's aggregation framework has
support for left-outer equi-joins in its aggregation framework and CouchDB allows joins for pre-
declared MapReduce views.

[3]An alternative to MapReduce are generalized **data processing pipelines**, where the database tries
to optimize the flow of data and locality of computation based on a more declarative query language
(e.g., MongoDB's aggregation framework [Mon]).

	Funct. Req.								Non-Funct. Req.										
	Scan Queries	ACID Transactions	Conditional Writes	Joins	Sorting	Filter Queries	Full-Text Search	Analytics	Data Scalability	Write Scalability	Read Scalability	Elasticity	Consistency	Write Latency	Read Latency	Write Throughput	Read Availability	Write Availability	Durability
MongoDB	x		x		x	x	x	x	x	x	x		x	x	x	x	x		x
Redis	x	x	x								x		x	x	x	x	x		
HBase	x		x		x			x	x	x	x	x	x			x			
Riak						x	x	x	x	x	x	x		x	x	x	x	x	
Cassandra	x		x		x			x	x	x	x	x		x			x	x	x
MySQL	x	x	x	x	x	x	x	x			x		x						

	Techniques																			
	Range-Sharding	Hash-Sharding	Entity-Group Sharding	Consistent Hashing	Shared-Disk	Transaction Protocol	Sync. Replication	Async. Replication	Primary Copy	Update Anywhere	Logging	Update-in-Place	Caching	In-Memory Storage	Append-Only Storage	Global Indexing	Local Indexing	Query Planning	Analytics Framework	Materialized Views
MongoDB	x	x						x	x		x	x	x				x	x	x	
Redis								x	x		x	x		x						
HBase	x						x		x		x		x		x					
Riak		x	x					x		x	x	x	x			x	x		x	
Cassandra		x	x					x		x	x		x			x	x	x		x
MySQL					x	x		x	x		x	x	x				x	x		

Fig. 8.3 A direct comparison of functional requirements, non-functional requirements and techniques among MongoDB, Redis, HBase, Riak, Cassandra, and MySQL according to the proposed NoSQL Toolbox

many database systems well and thus can be used to meaningfully contrast different database systems: Figure 8.3 shows a direct comparison of MongoDB, Redis, HBase, Riak, Cassandra, and MySQL in their respective default configurations. A more verbose comparison of central system properties is presented in Table 8.1 (see p. 185).

The methodology used to identify the specific system properties consists of an in-depth analysis of publicly available documentation and literature on the systems [Mon, CD13, Car13, San17, Hba, Ria, CH16, LM10, Mys]. Furthermore, some

Table 8.1 A qualitative comparison of MongoDB, HBase, Cassandra, Riak, and Redis

Dimension	MongoDB	HBase	Cassandra	Riak	Redis
Model	Document	Wide-column	Wide-column	Key-value	Key-value
CAP	CP	CP	AP	AP	CP
Scan performance	High (with appropriate shard key)	High (only on row key)	High (using compound index)	N/A	High (depends on data structure)
Disk latency per get by row key	~Several disk seeks	~Several disk seeks	~Several disk seeks	~One disk seek	In-memory
Write performance	High (append-only I/O)	High (append-only I/O)	High (append-only I/O)	High (append-only I/O)	Very high, in-memory
Network latency	Configurable: nearest slave, master (*read preference*)	Designated region server	Configurable: R replicas contacted	Configurable: R replicas contacted	Designated master
Durability	Configurable: none, WAL, replicated (*write concern*)	WAL, row-level versioning	WAL, W replicas written	Configurable: writes, durable writes, W replicas written	Configurable: none, periodic logging, WAL
Replication	Master-slave, synchronicity configurable	File-system-level (HDFS)	Consistent hashing	Consistent hashing	Asynchronous master-slave
Sharding	Hash- or range-based on attribute (s)	Range-based (row key)	Consistent hashing	Consistent hashing	Only in Redis Cluster: hashing
Consistency	linearizable (master writes with quorum reads) or eventual (else)	Linearizable	Eventual, optional linearizable updates (*lightweight transactions*)	Eventual, client-side conflict resolution	Master reads: linearizable, slave reads: eventual
Atomicity	Single document	Single row, or explicit locking	Single column (multi-column updates may cause dirty writes)	Single key/value pair	Optimistic multi-key transactions, atomic Lua scripts

(continued)

Table 8.1 (continued)

Dimension	MongoDB	HBase	Cassandra	Riak	Redis
Conditional updates	Yes (mastered)	Yes (mastered)	Yes (Paxos-coordinated)	No	Yes (mastered)
Interface	Binary TCP	Thrift	Thrift or TCP/CQL	REST or TCP/Protobuf	TCP/Plain-Text
Special data types	Objects, arrays, sets, counters, files	Counters	Counters	CRDTs for counters, flags, registers, maps	Sets, hashes, counters, sorted sets, lists, HyperLogLogs, bit vectors
Queries	Query by example (filter, sort, project), range queries, MapReduce, aggregation, limited joins	Get by row key, scans over row key ranges, project CFs/columns	Get by Partition Key and filter/sort over cluster key, FT-search	Get by ID or local secondary index, materialized views, MapReduce, FT-search	Data Structure Operations
Secondary Indexing	Hash, B-Tree, geospatial indexes	None	Local sorted index, global secondary hash index, search index (Solr)	Local secondary indexes, search index (Solr)	Not explicit
License	GPL 3.0	Apache 2	Apache 2	Apache 2	BSD

properties had to be evaluated by researching the open-source code bases, personal communication with the developers, as well as a meta-analysis of reports and benchmarks by practitioners.

The comparison elucidates how SQL and NoSQL databases are designed to fulfill very different needs: RDBMSs provide a broad set of functionalities whereas NoSQL databases excel on the non-functional side through scalability, availability, low latency, and high throughput. However, there are also large differences among the NoSQL databases. Riak and Cassandra, for example, can be configured to fulfill many non-functional requirements, but are only eventually consistent and do not feature many functional capabilities apart from data analytics and, in case of Cassandra, conditional updates. MongoDB and HBase, on the other hand, offer stronger consistency and more sophisticated functional capabilities such as scan queries and—only in MongoDB—filter queries, but do not maintain read and write availability during partitions and tend to display higher read latencies. As the only non-partitioned system in this comparison apart from MySQL, Redis shows a special set of trade-offs centered around the ability to maintain extremely high throughput at low latency using in-memory data structures and asynchronous master-slave replication.

This diversity illustrates that for enabling low latency cloud data management, no single database technology can cover all use cases. Therefore, latency reductions have to operate across different database systems and requirements.

References

[Bak+11] J. Baker et al. "Megastore: Providing scalable, highly available storage for interactive services". In: *Proc. of CIDR*. Vol. 11. 2011, pp. 223–234.

[Ber+11] Philip A. Bernstein et al. "Adapting Microsoft SQL server for cloud computing". In: *Data Engineering (ICDE), 2011 IEEE 27th International Conference on*. IEEE. IEEE, 2011, pp. 1255–1263. URL: http://ieeexplore.ieee.org/xpls/abs_all.jsp?arnumber=5767935 (visited on 05/05/2014).

[BK14] Peter Bailis and Kyle Kingsbury. "The network is reliable". In: *Queue* 12.7 (2014), p. 20. URL: http://dl.acm.org/citation.cfm?id=2655736 (visited on 01/03/2015).

[Boy+14] Oscar Boykin et al. "Summingbird: A Framework for Integrating Batch and Online MapReduce Computations". In: *VLDB* 7.13 (2014).

[Cal+11] Brad Calder et al. "Windows Azure Storage: a highly available cloud storage service with strong consistency". In: *Proceedings of the Twenty-Third ACM Symposium on Operating Systems Principles*. ACM. ACM, 2011, pp. 143–157. URL: http://dl.acm.org/citation.cfm?id=2043571 (visited on 04/16/2014).

[Car13] Josiah L. Carlson. *Redis in Action*. Greenwich, CT, USA: Manning Publications Co., 2013. ISBN: 1617290858, 9781617290855.

[CBPS10] Bernadette Charron-Bost, Fernando Pedone, and André Schiper, eds. *Replication: Theory and Practice*. Vol. 5959. Lecture Notes in Computer Science. Springer, 2010.

[CD13] Kristina Chodorow and Michael Dirolf. *MongoDB - The Definitive Guide*. O'Reilly, 2013. ISBN: 978-1-449-38156-1. URL: http://www.oreilly.de/catalog/9781449381561/index.html.

[CH16]   Jeff Carpenter and Eben Hewitt. *Cassandra: The Definitive Guide*. "O'Reilly Media, Inc.", 2016.

[Cha+08]   Fay Chang et al. "Bigtable: A distributed storage system for structured data". In: *ACM Transactions on Computer Systems (TOCS)* 26.2 (2008), p. 4.

[Coo+08]   B. F. Cooper et al. "PNUTS: Yahoo!'s hosted data serving platform". In: *PVLDB* 1.2 (2008), pp. 1277–1288. URL: http://dl.acm.org/citation.cfm?id=1454167 (visited on 09/12/2012).

[Cor+13]   James C. Corbett et al. "Spanner: Google's Globally Distributed Database". In: *ACM Trans. Comput. Syst.* 31.3 (2013), 8:1–8:22. DOI: 10.1145/2491245.

[Cur+11a] Carlo Curino et al. "Relational Cloud: A Database-as-a-Service for the Cloud". In: *Proc. of CIDR*. 2011. URL: http://dspace.mit.edu/handle/1721.1/62241 (visited on 04/15/2014).

[DAEA10]   Sudipto Das, Divyakant Agrawal, and Amr El Abbadi. "G-store: a scalable data store for transactional multi key access in the cloud". In: *Proceedings of the 1st ACM symposium on Cloud computing*. ACM. 2010, pp. 163–174.

[Dea09]   Jeff Dean. *Designs, lessons and advice from building large distributed systems*. Keynote talk at LADIS 2009. 2009.

[DeC+07]   G. DeCandia et al. "Dynamo: amazon's highly available key-value store". In: *ACM SOSP*. Vol. 14. 17. ACM. 2007, pp. 205–220. URL: http://dl.acm.org/citation.cfm?id=1294281 (visited on 09/12/2012).

[DG04]   Jeffrey Dean and Sanjay Ghemawat. "MapReduce: Simplified Data Processing on Large Clusters". In: *Proceedings of the 6th Conference on Symposium on Operating Systems Design & Implementation - Volume 6*. OSDI'04. San Francisco, CA: USENIX Association, 2004, pp. 10–10. URL: http://dl.acm.org/citation.cfm?id=1251254.1251264.

[ESW78]   Robert S. Epstein, Michael Stonebraker, and Eugene Wong. "Distributed Query Processing in a Relational Data Base System". In: *Proceedings of the 1978 ACM SIGMOD International Conference on Management of Data, Austin, Texas, USA, May 31 - June 2, 1978*. Ed. by Eugene I. Lowenthal and Nell B. Dale. ACM, 1978, pp. 169–180. DOI: 10.1145/509252.509292.

[GHa+96]   Jim Gray, Pat Hell and, et al. "The dangers of replication and a solution". In: *SIGMOD Rec.* 25.2 (June 1996), pp. 173–182.

[GR15]   Felix Gessert and Norbert Ritter. "Skalierbare NoSQL- und Cloud- Datenbanken in Forschung und Praxis". In: *Datenbanksysteme für Business, Technologie und Web (BTW 2015) - Workshopband, 2.-3. März 2015, Hamburg, Germany*. 2015, pp. 271–274.

[GR16]   Felix Gessert and Norbert Ritter. "Scalable Data Management: NoSQL Data Stores in Research and Practice". In: *32nd IEEE International Conference on Data Engineering, ICDE 2016*. 2016.

[GWR17]   Felix Gessert, Wolfram Wingerath, and Norbert Ritter. "Scalable Data Management: An In-Depth Tutorial on NoSQL Data Stores". In: *BTW (Workshops)*. Vol. P-266. LNI. GI, 2017, pp. 399–402.

[Ham07]   James Hamilton. "On designing and deploying internet-scale services". In: *21st LISA*. USENIX Association, 2007.

[HB09]   Urs Hoelzle and Luiz Andre Barroso. *The Datacenter As a Computer: An Introduction to the Design of Warehouse-Scale Machines*. Morgan and Claypool Publishers, 2009.

[Hba]   *HBase*. http://hbase.apache.org/. (Accessed on 05/25/2017). 2017. URL: http://hbase.apache.org/ (visited on 07/16/2014).

[Hel07]   Joesph Hellerstein. "Architecture of a Database System". In: *Foundations and Trends in Databases* 1.2 (Nov. 2007), pp. 141–259. ISSN: 1931-7883, 1931-7891. DOI: 10.1561/1900000002. URL: http://www.nowpublishers.com/product.aspx?product=DBS&doi=1900000002 (visited on 01/03/2015).

[Kal+08] R. Kallman et al. "H-store: a high-performance, distributed main memory transaction processing system". In: *Proceedings of the VLDB Endowment* 1.2 (2008), pp. 1496–1499.

[Kar+97] David R. Karger et al. "Consistent hashing and random trees: distributed caching protocols for relieving hot spots on the World Wide Web". In: *ACM Symposium on Theory of Computing*. 1997, pp. 654–663. DOI: 10.1145/258533.258660.

[Kle17]   Martin Kleppmann. *Designing Data-Intensive Applications*. English. 1 edition. O'Reilly Media, Jan. 2017. ISBN: 978-1-4493-7332-0.

[Kos00]   Donald Kossmann. "The State of the art in distributed query processing". In: *ACM Comput. Surv.* 32.4 (2000), pp. 422–469. DOI: 10.1145/371578.371598.

[Kra+13] Tim Kraska et al. "MDCC: Multi-data center consistency". In: *EuroSys*. ACM, 2013, pp. 113–126. URL: http://dl.acm.org/citation.cfm?id=2465363 (visited on 04/15/2014).

[Kre14]   Jay Kreps. *Questioning the Lambda Architecture*. https://www.oreilly.com/ideas/questioning-the-lambda-architecture. (Accessed on 09/23/2018). 2014.

[Lab+09] Alexandros Labrinidis et al. "Caching and Materialization for Web Databases". In: *Foundations and Trends in Databases* 2.3 (2009), pp. 169–266. DOI: 10.1561/1900000005.

[Llo+11] Wyatt Lloyd et al. "Don't settle for eventual: scalable causal consistency for wide-area storage with COPS". In: *Proceedings of the Twenty-Third ACM Symposium on Operating Systems Principles*. ACM, 2011, pp. 401–416. URL: http://dl.acm.org/citation.cfm?id=2043593 (visited on 01/03/2015).

[LM10]   Avinash Lakshman and Prashant Malik. "Cassandra: a decentralized structured storage system". In: *ACM SIGOPS Operating Systems Review* 44.2 (2010), pp. 35–40. URL: http://dl.acm.org/citation.cfm?id=1773922 (visited on 04/15/2014).

[MJM08]   Yanhua Mao, Flavio Paiva Junqueira, and Keith Marzullo. "Mencius: Building Efficient Replicated State Machine for WANs". In: *8th USENIX Symposium on Operating Systems Design and Implementation, OSDI 2008, December 8–10, 2008, San Diego, California, USA, Proceedings*. Ed. by Richard Draves and Robbert van Renesse. USENIX Association, 2008, pp. 369–384. URL: http://www.usenix.org/events/osdi08/tech/full_papers/mao/mao.pdf.

[MKC+12] Changwoo Min, Kangnyeon Kim, Hyunjin Cho, et al. "SFS: random write considered harmful in solid state drives". In: *FAST*. 2012.

[Mon]   *MongoDB*. https://www.mongodb.com/. (Accessed on 06/18/2017). 2017.

[MW15]   Nathan Marz and James Warren. *Big Data: Principles and Best Practices of Scalable Realtime Data Systems*. Manning Publications Co., 2015.

[Mys]   *MySQL Documentation*. https://dev.mysql.com/doc/. (Accessed on 09/15/2017). 2017.

[Nan+16] Mihir Nanavati et al. "Non-volatile storage". In: *Commun. ACM* 59.1 (2016), pp. 56–63. DOI: 10.1145/2814342.

[Pla13]   Hasso Plattner. *A course in in-memory data management*. Springer, 2013.

[Qia+13] Lin Qiao et al. "On brewing fresh espresso: LinkedIn's distributed data serving platform". In: *Proceedings of the 2013 international conference on Management of data*. ACM, 2013, pp. 1135–1146. URL: http://dl.acm.org/citation.cfm?id=2465298 (visited on 09/28/2014).

[Ria]   *Riak*. http://basho.com/products/. (Accessed on 05/25/2017). 2017. URL: http://basho.com/products/ (visited on 01/13/2017).

[San17]   Salvatore Sanfilippo. *Redis*. http://redis.io/. (Accessed on 07/16/2017). 2017. URL: http://redis.io/ (visited on 09/02/2015).

[Sha+11] M. Shapiro et al. "A comprehensive study of convergent and commutative replicated data types". In: (2011). URL: http://hal.upmc.fr/inria-00555588/ (visited on 11/23/2012).

[Sov+11]   Yair Sovran et al. "Transactional storage for geo-replicated systems". In: *Proceedings of the Twenty-Third ACM Symposium on Operating Systems Principles*. ACM, 2011, pp. 385–400.

[Sto+07]   M. Stonebraker et al. "The end of an architectural era:(it's time for a complete rewrite)". In: *Proceedings of the 33rd international conference on Very large data bases*. 2007, pp. 1150–1160. URL: http://dl.acm.org/citation.cfm?id=1325981 (visited on 07/05/2012).

[STR+15]   Dharma Shukla, Shireesh Thota, Karthik Raman, et al. "Schemaagnostic indexing with Azure DocumentDB". In: *PVLDB* 8.12 (2015).

[SW13]   Michael Stonebraker and Ariel Weisberg. "The VoltDB Main Memory DBMS". In: *IEEE Data Eng. Bull.* 36.2 (2013), pp. 21–27. URL: http://sites.computer.org/debull/A13june/VoltDB1.pdf.

[WGR+18]   Wolfram Wingerath, Felix Gessert, Norbert Ritter, et al. "Real-Time Data Management for Big Data". In: *Proceedings of the 21th International Conference on Extending Database Technology, EDBT 2018, Vienna, Austria, March 26–29, 2018*. OpenProceedings.org, 2018.

[WGR19]   Wolfram Wingerath, Felix Gessert, and Norbert Ritter. "NoSQL & Real-Time Data Management in Research & Practice". In: *Datenbanksysteme für Business, Technologie und Web (BTW 2019), 18. Fachtagung des GI-Fachbereichs "Datenbanken und Informationssysteme" (DBIS), 4.-8. März 2019, Rostock, Germany, Workshopband*. 2019, pp. 267–270. URL: https://dl.gi.de/20.500.12116/21595.

[Wie15]   Lena Wiese. *Advanced data management: for SQL, NoSQL, cloud and distributed databases*. Berlin; Boston: De Gruyter, Oldenbourg, 2015. ISBN: 978-3-11-044140-6.

[Zha+15a] Hao Zhang et al. "In-Memory Big Data Management and Processing: A Survey". In: *IEEE Transactions on Knowledge and Data Engineering* 27.7 (July 2015), pp. 1920–1948. ISSN: 1041-4347. DOI: 10.1109/TKDE.2015.2427795. URL: http://ieeexplore.ieee.org/document/7097722/ (visited on 11/25/2016).

[ÖV11]   M.T. Özsu and P. Valduriez. *Principles of distributed database systems*. Springer, 2011.

Chapter 9
Summary and Future Trends

In this book, we highlighted core performance challenges across the web application stack: Performance depends on frontend rendering, networking and caching infrastructures, as well as data storage and business logic in the backend.

First, we discussed the requirements of web applications that include high availability, elastic scalability, quick page loads, engaging user experience, and a fast time-to-market. We showed that these requirements are difficult to achieve in cloud-based two- and three-tier architectures and that latency poses a pivotal challenge in heterogeneous cloud environments. Since the conflict between latency and correctness becomes clearly evident in NoSQL database systems and their various levels of relaxed consistency guarantees, we discussed in detail how the combination of data storage systems in polyglot persistence architectures complicates data management. We further explored how latency becomes critical problem in the context of distributed transactions as it is directly related to abort rates and thus can be the limiting factor for transaction throughput in distributed settings. Seeing that database systems cannot be efficiently employed in web applications as they lack Database- and Backend-as-a-Service (DBaaS/BaaS) interfaces for direct access from other cloud services or client devices, we covered today's DBaaS and BaaS systems in the later chapters. We then turned to the underlying database systems themselves and classified the different technological means for addressing varying functional and non-functional requirements in order to facilitate an informed choice regarding the right technology for a given set of requirements. In conclusion to this book, we will finally provide a concise discussion of how to find the right database system for a given application scenario.

© Springer Nature Switzerland AG 2020
F. Gessert et al., *Fast and Scalable Cloud Data Management*,
https://doi.org/10.1007/978-3-030-43506-6_9

9.1 From Abstract Requirements to Concrete Systems

Choosing a database system always means to choose one set of desirable properties over another. To break down the complexity of this choice, we present a binary decision tree in Fig. 9.1 that maps trade-off decisions to example applications and potentially suitable database systems. The leaf nodes cover applications ranging from simple caching (left) to Big Data analytics (right). Naturally, this view on the problem space is not complete, but it vaguely points towards a solution for a particular data management problem.

The first split in the tree is along the access pattern of applications: they either rely on fast lookups only (left half) or require more complex querying capabilities (right half). The fast lookup applications can be distinguished further by the data volume they process: if the main memory of one single machine can hold all the data, a single-node system like Redis or Memcache probably is the best choice, depending on whether functionality (Redis) or simplicity (Memcache) is favored. If the data volume is or might grow beyond RAM capacity or is even unbounded, a multi-node system that scales horizontally might be more appropriate. The most important decision in this case is whether to favor availability (AP) or consistency (CP) as described by the CAP theorem. Systems like Cassandra and Riak can deliver an always-on experience, while systems like HBase, MongoDB, and DynamoDB deliver strong consistency.

The right half of the tree covers applications requiring more complex queries than simple lookups. Here, too, we first distinguish the systems by the data volume they have to handle according to whether single-node systems are feasible (HDD-size) or

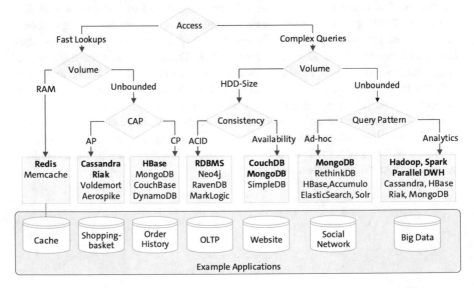

Fig. 9.1 A decision tree for mapping requirements to (NoSQL) database system candidates

distribution is required (unbounded volume). For common OLTP (online transaction processing) workloads on moderately large data volumes, traditional RDBMSs or graph databases like Neo4J are optimal, because they offer ACID semantics. If, however, availability is essential, distributed systems like MongoDB, CouchDB or DocumentDB, are preferable.

If data volume exceeds the limits of a single machine, the choice depends on the prevalent query pattern: when complex queries have to be optimized for latency, as for example in social networking applications, MongoDB is very attractive, because it facilitates expressive ad-hoc queries. HBase and Cassandra are also useful in such a scenario, but excel at throughput-optimized Big Data analytics, when combined with Hadoop.

In summary, we are convinced that the proposed top-down model is an effective decision support to filter the vast amount of NoSQL database systems based on central requirements. The **NoSQL Toolbox** furthermore provides a mapping from functional and non-functional requirements to common implementation techniques in order to categorize the constantly evolving NoSQL space. In the following, we will conceive a DBaaS/BaaS middleware architecture that is designed to cover an as large subset of the decision tree as possible within a coherent REST/HTTP API.

9.2 Future Prospects

Today, the landscape of cloud data management is still undergoing massive changes and the coming years will decide over central paradigm shifts.

One of the pivotal questions is whether the trend towards a fragmented and highly specialized ecosystem of database systems continues (polyglot persistence) or whether middlewares will become capable of abstracting away database systems (polystores). Potentially even a new generation of one-size-fits-all databases could consolidate the recent advances in a single system: similar to programming languages and operating systems, the current heterogeneity of implementations might soon be replaced by the prevalence of a small number of core systems. As the trend towards novel machine learning techniques continues, these algorithms could quickly become first-class citizens in query languages and database interfaces. For cloud data management, it remains to be seen whether proprietary systems by large cloud vendors (e.g., Google's Spanner) have an inherent advantage in economies of scale that allows them to outperform even the best on-premise database systems.

This book aims to structure the great number of systems and approaches in modern cloud data management. However, standardization—e.g., of query languages for NoSQL data models—as well as comprehensive taxonomies—e.g., for SLAs or consistency models—need to be addressed in cloud data management research during the next years. We sincerely believe that these are the most exciting days to engage in cloud data management, as the progress in both research and commercial products may heavily influence computer science research as a whole for decades.

Printed in the United States
by Baker & Taylor Publisher Services